MW01075702

Harry Potter and Myth

Other Works by Valerie Estelle Frankel

Henry Potty and the Pet Rock: A Harry Potter Parody
Henry Potty and the Deathly Paper Shortage: A Harry Potter Parody
Buffy and the Heroine's Journey
From Girl to Goddess: The Heroine's Journey in Myth and Legend
Katniss the Cattail: The Unauthorized Guide to Name and Symbols in The Hunger Games
The Many Faces of Katniss Everdeen: The Heroine of The Hunger Games
Harry Potter, Still Recruiting: A Look at Harry Potter Fandom
Teaching with Harry Potter
An Unexpected Parody: The Spoof of The Hobbit Movie
Teaching with Harry Potter
Myths and Motifs in The Mortal Instruments
Winning the Game of Thrones: The Host of Characters & their Agendas
Winter is Coming: Symbols, Portents, and Hidden Meanings in A Game of Thrones
Bloodsuckers on the Bayou: The Myths, Symbols, and Tales Behind HBO's True Blood
The Girl's Guide to the Heroine's Journey
Choosing to be Insurgent or Allegiant: Symbols, Themes & Analysis of the Divergent Trilogy
Doctor Who and the Hero's Journey: The Doctor and Companions as Chosen Ones
Doctor Who: The What Where and How
Sherlock: Every Canon Reference You May Have Missed in BBC's Series 1-3
Symbols in Game of Thrones
How Game of Thrones Will End
Joss Whedon's Names
Pop Culture in the Whedonverse
Women in Game of Thrones: Power, Conformity, and Resistance
History, Homages and the Highlands: An Outlander Guide
The Catch-Up Guide to Doctor Who
Remember All Their Faces: A Deeper Look at Character, Gender and the Prison World of Orange Is The New Black
Everything I Learned in Life I Know from Joss Whedon
Empowered: The Symbolism, Feminism, and Superheroism of Wonder Woman
The Avengers Face their Dark Sides: Mastering the Myth-Making behind the Marvel Superheroes
The Symbolism and Sources of Outlander
The Comics of Joss Whedon: Critical Essays
Mythology in Game of Thrones
We're Home: Fandom, Fun, and Hidden Homages in Star Wars the Force Awakens
A Rey of Hope: Feminism, Symbolism and Hidden Gems in Star Wars: The Force Awakens
Chosen One: The Heroine's Journey of Katniss, Elsa, Tris, Bella, and Rey

Harry Potter and Myth

THE LEGENDS BEHIND CURSED CHILD, FANTASTIC BEASTS, AND ALL THE HERO'S JOURNEYS

VALERIE ESTELLE FRANKEL

ISBN-13: 978-1539131823
ISBN-10: 1539131823

VALERIE ESTELLE FRANKEL

Contents

"Harry's and Dorothy's Paths" was previously published in *Chosen One: The Heroine's Journey of Katniss, Elsa, Tris, Bella, and Rey* by Valerie Estelle Frankel

"Redefining Epic Heroes: Neville, Snape, and Draco" was presented at Portus 2008: A Harry Potter Symposium, Dallas, Texas, 2008.

"The Pantheon of Hogwarts Professors" was presented at Ascendio, The Harry Potter Conference, Orlando, FL, 2012.

"Reinventing Eve: Bible and Arthurian Myth Reborn in *Harry Potter* and *His Dark Materials*" was previously published in *New Myth* vol. 1: The Society for New Language Study, Midwestern State University, 2009.

"Harry Potter and the Rise of Nazism" was previously published in *Racialized Narratives in Children's Literature*, Washington State University, 2010.

PART I: HERO'S JOURNEY, HEROINE'S JOURNEY

HARRY'S AND DOROTHY'S PATHS

CHAPTER 1: HARRY'S AND DOROTHY'S PATHS

> Dorothy lived in the midst of the great Kansas prairies, with Uncle Henry, who was a farmer, and Aunt Em, who was the farmer's wife...When Dorothy stood in the doorway and looked around, she could see nothing but the great gray prairie on every side. Not a tree nor a house broke the broad sweep of flat country that reached to the edge of the sky in all directions. The sun had baked the plowed land into a gray mass, with little cracks running through it. Even the grass was not green, for the sun had burned the tops of the long blades until they were the same gray color to be seen everywhere.[1]

The first page of this beloved novel paints Dorothy Gale's childhood in a single depressing color. But Dorothy has Toto with his twinkling merry eyes to keep her from graying as well. And so she dreams of a better, livelier land somewhere over the rainbow. That's the nature of imagination—when we feel like colorful people trapped in a gray world, fantasy stretches forth in a vibrant rainbow that glows like Munchkinland in Technicolor.

Harry Potter too craves escape from his monochrome life. His dreary aunt and uncle care only for winning perfect lawn competitions and appearing as "normal" as possible. The mere mention of a flying motorbike nearly gives Uncle Vernon a stroke, for any imagination is forbidden. "Don't ask questions—that was the first rule for a quiet life with the Dursleys."[2]

Harry and Dorothy don't fit. They're different because of their creativity, hopes and wishes, because of the deeper perception that defines Rey, Katniss, Percy Jackson. When a pile of letters or a tornado arrives, the moment is scary, exciting, life-changing. Our hero feels poised on a new world of experience and understanding, echoing the changes inside as she or he grows into adolescence. Somewhere past the familiar threshold is a world of adventure and new opportunities. The child needs only to step over.

When Dorothy lands in Oz, she instantly provokes the Wicked Witch of the West by killing her sister. As the witch threatens her life, Oz's world of fantasy and beauty becomes too frightening, and Dorothy wants to go home. Refusing the call to adventure is common: "Hagrid, I think you must have made a mistake. I don't think I can be a wizard," Harry whispers.[3] "I can't possibly be the chosen one, the child of destiny," our hero protests. And yet, he is all the same. Over the course of his quest, Harry masters spells many adults only dream of and defeats Voldemort, the darkest wizard of them all. On her own quest, Dorothy rescues all of Oz from the wicked witch. Later in the series she becomes a princess of Oz, second only to the great ruler Ozma. Though such heroism may seem impossible to the extraordinary child struggling to fit in, world renown lies only a few hundred pages away.

At last, Dorothy starts down the Yellow Brick Road. It begins as a spiral, expanding outward in a symbol for the growing self. The spiral, like the snake, represented regeneration in ancient times, as the serpent could shed its skin and apparently live again. In the magic world, Dorothy must regenerate in the same way, casting off her old self like a discarded skin. She has already shed her status as helpless farmchild to become the "young lady who fell from a star," the Munchkins' liberator and future savior of Oz.

Harry Potter, too, grows in status upon entering the magic world. He spends his Muggle childhood friendless, stuck wearing baggy hand-me-downs resembling wrinkled elephant skin. But upon passing through the Leaky Cauldron, gateway from London to the magical world, everyone rushes to shake his hand. "Are you really Harry Potter?" new students ask on the Hogwarts Express.[4] They give the loudest cheer of all when he's chosen into Gryffindor House. For in the wizard world, Harry discovers he's famous, hailed as savior of the magic folk. In a few books he's teaching Defense against the Dark Arts to his fellow students and realizing he's the Chosen One.

This isn't surprising when one considers the nature of the magic world. "I had glasses all through my childhood and I was sick and tired of the person in the books who wore the glasses was always the brainy one and it really irritated me and I wanted to read about a hero wearing glasses," J.K. Rowling told readers in an interview.[5] We all dream of a place where we really belong, where we, the bookworms, geeks, and misfits, can be heroes, where no one tells us that fighting cartoon monsters or reading fantasy is a waste of time. A place where what we want and feel and dream really matters. And so we journey to Terebithia, Neverland, Fairie. These are the realm of the unconscious—the place of dreams and imagination where our most heartfelt terrors and wishes play out before us.

In the real world, one can battle through the unconscious in a nightmare, or withdraw from the world to meditate on a thorny problem. Of course, we'd rather tackle giant spiders than the roaring dragons of despair, the seeping swamps of loss. The inward journey teaches how to master the outer world—to fearlessly ask a girl out or stare down bullies. Thus our heroes literally journey into the unconscious realm of fairytales and magic, and return brimming with confidence.

Unlike our world, the fantasy world treats everyone justly: the good triumph and wicked are punished. Things we secretly believe are true there: animals reply when we speak to them and curses really work. Lighter things are true as well. As the Wizard of Oz informs the Scarecrow in the film: "Back where I come from we have universities, seats of great learning where men go to become great thinkers. And when they come out, they think deep thoughts—and with no more brains than you have. But they have one thing you haven't got! A diploma!"[6] Finally, an admission that schools and degrees don't guarantee genius! We grin because we knew it all along.

For students who have ever taken AP tests, it seems like truth in advertising that Hogwarts' NEWTS stand for Nastily Exhausting Wizarding Tests. And old-fashioned school songs and principal's remarks (often indistinguishable from nonsense) become nonsense in truth at Hogwarts. "Nitwit! Blubber! Oddment! Tweak!" Dumbledore proclaims for his start of term speech.[7] Here we smile, not just because it's silly, but because it sounds as meaningless as the long speeches other "geniuses" have made. Teachers who give us detention really work for the forces of evil, a magic book can carry us to a place of safety and wonder. Storms are caused by stormy moods, our deepest fears lurk in unexplored cupboards, a loving kiss can defend us from evil. Deep in our souls, we know these things, and in the magic world, they're true.

The connection between the outer world of farm chores and inner world of fantasy is heightened in *The Wizard of Oz* movie, as the same actors play roles in both worlds. This is a staple of fantasy, in which friends represent missing parts of the self. Dorothy's friends divide easily into aspects of her personality she must heal and unite: brains, love, and courage. But Harry's friends are only a little more subtle. The "Hogwarts Professor" John Granger names "Harry as spirit, Ron as body, and brainy Hermione, of course, as mind."[8] Harry takes charge in each book—he is the leader, the decision-maker. Ron is the emotional one who gets tongue-tied around girls, who impulsively shouts at Hermione, who's aghast when his sister starts dating. Hermione is the bookworm, rushing to research the latest monster or curse, drilling Harry in his own spellcasting and homework. Harry learns from both of them, growing through their different viewpoints and advice until the three strike out together to destroy Voldemort piece by piece in their final book.

Thus aided, the Chosen One journeys through the unconscious to battle through to adulthood and return, grown to man- or womanhood. Separation-initiation-return, says Joseph Campbell, author of the greatest works on the hero's journey. Granger notes: "In each book, Harry *separates* from his Muggle home on Privet Drive, is *initiated* and transformed in a series of magical trials and adventures, and *returns* to Muggledom at the end of the school year."[9] This initiation involves a mystery and crisis, and finally a battle with Voldemort deep beneath the school. Harry suffers a loss or death and must come to terms with this, and then return to Privet Drive wiser than he left. Dorothy, too, journeys in a cycle, as she leaves Kansas and returns once her quest is done.

Once in the world of magic and acceptance, the protagonist receives a quest. Generally a great villain tyrannizes the world, and the hero must conquer him to triumph. This echoes the son's struggle to overcome his father's dominance and create a new life for himself (most evident in the father-son conflicts of *King Arthur* or *Star Wars*). Though Rowling has stated the Harry and Lord Voldemort aren't literally related (what a creepy thought), they're symbolically linked throughout the story. As Ryan Weber observes in his essay, "Harry Potter's Quest: The Hero's Journey and the Shadow," the classic villain must have "a personal and psychologically irreversible connection with the hero":

> In the case of Voldemort and Harry, this is literally the case, for when Harry was attacked and scarred by Voldemort, the sorcerer permanently implanted a piece of himself within the mark. This forever binds the two, and causes Harry's scar to throb whenever Voldemort is near.

Voldemort, as Harry's creator, represents the tyrannical father that Harry must overcome to grow into independence.

The queen goddess in mythology was not a warrior but a creator, the earth itself worshipped as the Supreme Mother. Imitating her, the girl becomes a life-giver and protector, a goal which heroines risk everything to achieve. Dorothy saves Toto over and over, for he is her most childlike and sparkling self, her vulnerable side most in need of protection. Lyra of *The Golden Compass* quests for her best friend Roger; Bella Swan rescues her true love, daughter, and vampire clan; Coraline saves her parents. Katniss volunteers for the Hunger Games to save her sister, and Tris risks everything for her own parents and brother. These repeated rescues symbolize building a family and fighting to the death to defend it. By accomplishing her task, the heroine grows from child to mother-protector, ready to take her place as head of the household. Dorothy simply finds her way home to her worried aunt and uncle when she's grown into wholeness, incorporating wisdom, love, and courage into herself, along with the lessons of the humbug father and wicked mother. Only then can she see the path.

Talisman

Child heroes dominate the magical world through their spiritual gifts: Dorothy's incredible kindness as she rescues her three friends, Harry's dazzling courage and the abilities he took from Voldemort. Each child also receives a token, clearly split by gender.

Harry's magic talisman is a wand, representing enchanted swords throughout literature, from Excalibur to the Sword of Shannara. Though Harry doesn't learn the significance until book four, his wand shares a mysterious connection with Voldemort's, enabling him to escape certain death through the Priori Incantatem spell and a heroic burst of willpower. Later, Harry finds himself questing for the Elder Wand, most powerful weapon ever crafted, for only the greatest warrior can become king. In the final battle, however, Harry beats Voldemort with brilliance and faith instead of arms, trusting that the most powerful wand in history won't hurt him. "Does the wand in your hand know its last master was disarmed," Harry asks Voldemort. "Because if it does…I am the true master of the Elder Wand."[10] With this knowledge, Harry wins the duel with a single defensive spell.

While the hero always carries a magic sword (knife, lightsaber…), heroines almost never do. They get books and spyglasses, potions and amulets. This echoes a subtler form of questing, with cleverness, healing, and perception in place of combat. The magic slippers dominate Dorothy's adventures, providing the key to send her home. *The Wizard of Oz* is about a journey down the Yellow Brick Road, making shoes the all-important tool that Dorothy literally uses every step of the way. They get her in to see the Wizard and finally carry her back home once she's rescued her friends and all the Winkies.

In the book they're silver, the color of moon magic and feminine strength like Artemis's bow or Galadriel's ring. Silver's mirrorlike clarity suggests vision and deep knowledge, while the metal itself is moldable yet strong. The heroine's path mirrors this: blending flexibility and endurance, yielding to authority and yet outwitting it through mind, heart, and indescribable courage.

"Remember, never let those ruby slippers off your feet for a moment, or you will be at the mercy of the Wicked Witch of the West" warns Glinda, casting the shoes as Dorothy's protection.[11] In the film, Dorothy's slippers of sparkling ruby were chosen for their brightness in Technicolor. While red often represents power or even evil, here red suggests the lifeblood beating through Dorothy, contrasting her with the "dried-up" witch. The witch, all sallow in her green and black, obsesses over the slippers to the point of self-destruction, for they represent all she lacks. "When I gain those ruby slippers, my power will be the greatest in Oz!" she laughs.[12] Her sister, the Wicked Witch of the East, used the magic of the shoes to tyrannize the Munchkins until they celebrate her death with cheering and song. In *Wicked,* it was the shoes that fueled her self-importance and helped her snatch at power. Both witches find these are "shoes to die for." But as a universal icon, their power is far different.

Glittering crimson or shining silver, they add magic to an otherwise arduous trip, emphasizing the fairytale nature of Oz. Shoes symbolize life, joy, and fertility, tied to honeymooners' bumpers and coveted by Cinderella's princes or the Twelve Dancing Princesses as they fall in love. Dorothy is life and liveliness—the brightest person in Kansas and the savior of the Scarecrow, Tinman, and Lion—all characters seeking more humanity. By contrast, the Wicked Witch cowers in her tower, far from humankind. Water, the source of all life, is poison to her. Thus, the slippers offer power, but it is the power of the sparkle and growth she most lacks. In the end, they offer her own downfall and Dorothy's salvation, but it takes the entire book for Dorothy to understand their deepest magic.

Inner Strength

Dorothy Gale skips down the yellow brick road in a gingham dress, remaining "sweet" and "innocent" even while confronting monstrous kaliadas, surly trees, and a host of other vicious creatures. Her friends are male, but she does not hide behind the Scarecrow screaming, "Save me, I'm only a girl!" No one gives her a sword; she succeeds mostly through the traditionally "feminine" qualities of kindness and generosity of heart. Even in her bravest moments, she is protecting another from harm like a mother defending her young.

> Little Toto, now that he had an enemy to face, ran barking toward the Lion, and the great beast had opened his mouth to bite the dog, when Dorothy, fearing Toto would be killed, and heedless of danger, rushed forward and slapped the Lion upon his nose as hard as she could, while she cried out: "Don't you dare to bite Toto! You ought to be ashamed of yourself, a big beast like you, to bite a poor little dog!"[13]

True, King Arthur would not yell such a thing. But Dorothy tames the lion and makes him a valuable ally, when a burly warrior would have killed him. Dorothy is a young girl, and she succeeds on her quest by embracing that fact rather than denying it. Created at the turn of the century, when girls were supposed to be sweet and silent, Dorothy, like Anne of Green Gables, Jo March, and Caddie Woodlawn, shines as an active, vivacious heroine still popular today. Gretchen Ritter, though writing about politics, calls Dorothy "the all-American girl from the heartland, with a big heart, independence, and daring, a fine example of the sort of woman that the suffragettes had in mind when they promoted their cause."[14]

Harry Potter too relies on love rather than violence. Thinking of his guardian Sirius gives him the strength to battle the Dementors, to resist Voldemort's possession of him because Voldemort "could not bear to reside in a body so full of the force he detests," namely, love. As Dumbledore explains to Harry "It was your heart that saved you."[15] And at last, love allows him to lay down his life for his friends, sacrificing himself in the final book so that Voldemort will die. One of the last things Harry sees before his own march into death is Ginny comforting a frightened girl. "I want to go *home*. I don't want to fight anymore," she sobs.[16] It is for her and all those like her that he offers his sacrifice.

Encountering the Opposite

Halfway through his journey, the hero encounters the mystical feminine, who offers him the deep spiritual insight he needs to succeed. Harry Potter sees his mother, Lily, in mirrors, photographs, and memories locked in a swirling pensieve, and then finally summons her with the resurrection stone. "Stay with me," he tells her as he descends into the dark forest to die, and her presence banishes the Dementors, fear incarnate. Lily also defends him with her blood in each novel. "Love as powerful as your mother's for you leaves its own mark," Dumbledore explains. "To have been loved so deeply, even though the person who loved us is gone, gives us some protection forever."[17]

Thus the hero's maternal guardian protects him as she shows him how to tap the buried feminine within himself. Galadriel tests Frodo's heart with her magic mirror, and the Lady of the Lake gives Arthur a scabbard that will heal his wounds. She is life magic, the power of creation and emotion itself. As Campbell states, "The mystical marriage with the queen goddess of the world represents the hero's total mastery of life; for the woman is life, the hero its knower and master."[18] Meeting the mother is a moment of comforting magic, a time of healing before the dark trials ahead. Her light is one the hero can summon to shield him from the darkest peril. With it, he gains protection that will aid him in confronting his deadliest adversary—his father.

Harry is surrounded by mother figures: his "adoptive mother" Mrs. Weasley offers him love and compassion, knitting annual Christmas sweaters and welcoming him into her lively family. Hermione provides unwavering sisterly support. Just as significant, of course, is Harry's adolescent love for Ginny Weasley and her fierce blazing look, the image Harry takes with him into death. Harry has only a few weeks with Ginny, in which he's "happier than he could remember being for a very long time."[19] Though Ginny willingly stays behind, her faith in Harry carries him through his final quest, teaching him the perfect nature of selflessness and courage. When Harry embraces this feminine guidance, he deepens spiritually, until he can withstand Voldemort by sacrificing himself through the power of love.

The classic heroine, however, learns a far different lesson from encountering her father. Lyra of *The Golden Compass* discovers that her adored father is a murderer, as he kills her helpless friend Roger. Bella, as an immortal vampire, realizes how vulnerable and human her father is. Rey sees her mentor, Han, sacrificed, and Lucy sees the same with Aslan. Meg Murray crosses time and space to rescue her blinded and confused father, and they tesseract to a friendly planet. When Meg demands that he return to rescue her brother Charles Wallace, Meg's three witch mentors appear and tell Meg her father is not powerful enough. Meg gazes sadly at him. "I wanted you to do it all for me…I was scared, and I didn't want to have to do anything myself."[20] Still, she acknowledges she is the only one who can rescue Charles Wallace, so she returns to confront the monstrous IT.

Thus the heroine must learn (ironically enough) about the feminine power she already possesses from an encounter with the father figure. By realizing that his power over her has ended, the heroine finds independence and strength.

When Dorothy returns the witch's broomstick to the wizard, she has a similar realization. The first time she faces him, she quivers before the "Great and Powerful Oz." The second time, she has already defeated the wicked witch, a far more terrifying adversary. After that battle, the wizard is nothing and his refusal to see them sags with weakness.

> The Scarecrow at last asked the green girl to take another message to Oz, saying if he did not let them in to see him at once they would call the Winged Monkeys to help them, and find out whether he kept his promises or not. When the Wizard was given this message he was so frightened that he sent word for them to come to the Throne Room at four minutes after nine o'clock the next morning. He had once met the Winged Monkeys in the Land of the West, and he did not wish to meet them again.[21]

Confronting Oz, Dorothy and her friends find him a powerless fraud who has been deceiving them from the start. To Dorothy he appeared as a giant head; to the Scarecrow, a fairy; to the Tin Man, a great beast; and to the Cowardly Lion, a ball of flame. Like a politician, the wizard shows a different mask for each person he meets. But as he attempts to be all things to all people, he only emphasizes how small the human within truly is. After his dramatic displays, the shrunken man from Omaha has truly diminished. Emerging from behind his curtain, he begs the four adventurers for their help as he admits his own powerlessness. This lesson teaches Dorothy that the wizard cannot solve her quest for her. She must set out with her friends once more to seek Glinda and finish the journey she has begun.

Readers must remember that each fairytale character represents a part of the self. Just as the hero's mother is his own sensitivity and creative force, the heroine's father is the guardian, the intellect and system of rules meant to protect the self. Usually, in fairytales, the father fails to protect the daughter, or foolishly bargains her away (as in Beauty and the Beast style tales). He rarely understands the connection between the conscious and unconscious world: that things are not always as they appear. This lack of guidance reveals the young woman's innocence at the beginning of her journey. At the end, she returns as a goddess or teacher, great beyond the dreams of the once-authoritative father figure. This leap in power represents the growth in soul and knowledge that the heroine has achieved.

Inmost Cave

Just as every hero has done throughout myth immemorial, Harry and Dorothy both make their descent into the unknown as the greatest obstacle. They face death, alone and unaided, to confront their shadow selves and gain the power of death as well as life. If the magical world is the unconscious, the underworld is its deepest level, the place where the hero discovers his truest self.

Harry journeys under Hogwarts at the climaxes of the first three books, then into the graveyard, the Ministry's cellar, the Horcrux cave, and the Forbidden Forest. In *Deathly Hallows*, John Granger counts seven descents, from the "London underground" to Dobby's grave, to the vault under Gringotts. Why such a pattern of battling evil underground? The underworld offers death and darkness but with it the wisdom of mortality: to truly grow, Harry must pass a fearsome initiation. As Granger notes:

> Battling Quirrell, fanged by a basilisk, kissed by a dementor, tortured by the reborn Dark Lord, possessed by Voldemort in the Ministry, carried by the Inferi into the lake, and just flat-out killed by Voldemort in the finale, Harry dies a figurative death in every single book.[22]

Each of these symbolic deaths changes Harry, making him pay a steep price for growth on the hero's path. In the deserted graveyard where Voldemort reincarnates himself, Harry encounters his first real death (Cedric's) and can afterward see thestrals, indicating his growing understanding. Harry's final death, the deepest underworld of all, comes in book seven, where he journeys into the Forbidden Forest, Resurrection Stone at the ready, knowing Voldemort will kill him. "It did not occur to him now to try to escape, to outrun Voldemort. It was over, he knew it, and all that was left was the thing itself: dying."[23] Alone in the dark, and surrounded by enemies, Harry gives up his life for his friends. This is the true test of courage: laying down the wand and welcoming the sacrifice.

Winged monkeys carry Dorothy up to the witch's castle, not a descent but a climb. In many fairytales from Andersen's "The Little Mermaid" to "The Six Swans," the heroine's most dire struggle takes place high in the prince's castle, far from the mysterious protection of the forest or ocean. This, like the wicked witch's castle or the Death Star, is the world of order and tyranny, where the young heroine is truly helpless. Other heroines descend to the underworld: Lucy and Susan witness the White Witch murdering Aslan deep in the forest, while Lyra Belacqua crosses into the land of the dead. Katniss falls unconscious at the climax of all three of her own books.

In the Inmost Cave, Harry Potter battles his own evil shadow, his opposite in every way, yet bearing a symbolic connection to himself. One's shadow is all the qualities he or she has rejected: Harry is "a true Gryffindor," courageous above all, while Voldemort is the heir of conniving Salazar Slytherin. At the same time, Voldemort notices their connection: "Both half-bloods, orphans, raised by Muggles. Probably the only two Parselmouths to come to Hogwarts since the great Slytherin himself. We even *look* something alike...But after all, it was merely a lucky chance that saved you from me."[24] Though teenage Voldemort refers to Harry's escaping death, his statement is truer than he knows: Harry, an abused orphan from the Muggle world, could so easily have become Voldemort. The only thing stopping this, as Dumbledore points out, is Harry's choice.

Harry chooses love of friends over murder and power; when he battles Voldemort, he battles those choices he's rejected in his own life. This shadow is powerful beyond reasoning, a deadly match for the untrained hero. He is evil incarnate, monster as Harry is human, tall as Harry is short, dominant in power and knowledge as Harry is a student. While Harry loves enough to suffer deeply at Sirius's death (among others), Voldemort is love's antithesis. "You will hear many of his Death Eaters claiming they are in his confidences, that they alone are close to him, even understand him," Dumbledore says. "They are deluded. Lord Voldemort has never had a friend, nor do I believe that he has ever wanted one."[25] Rowling adds in an interview that Voldemort (unsurprisingly) never had a love interest: "He loved only power, and himself."[26] Upon invading Harry's mind, Voldemort cannot "bear to reside in a body so full of the force he detests."[27]

Voldemort symbolizes Harry's dark desires, his ambition without compassion, greed without limit, in contrast with Harry's simple wish for love and family, and his desire to save Hogwarts at all costs. Thus, Harry battles his own dark nature, repressed and unacknowledged. Jung writes: "The shadow personifies everything that the subject refuses to acknowledge about himself and yet is always thrusting itself upon him directly or indirectly—for instance, inferior traits of character and other incompatible tendencies."[28] In other words, the enemy is the part of ourselves we most dislike.

All this culminates with book five's prophecy: Harry and Voldemort's destinies are intertwined and "neither can live while the other survives."[29] Harry finds himself seeing through his enemy's eyes in the fifth book, marveling that he wants to strike Dumbledore as he dreams of Voldemort's dark desires. At last, Dumbledore explains that Voldemort's stealing Harry's blood results in his "having ensured this two-fold connection, having wrapped your destinies together more securely than ever two wizards were joined in history."[30] Thus, Harry and Voldemort are indeed two sides: light and dark, good and evil, yet with an intrinsic bond that may destroy them both. As Jung explains, "The shadow is a living part of the personality and therefore wants to live with it in some form. It cannot be argued out of existence or rationalized into harmlessness."[31] Harry cannot deny its existence, only face it and learn to accept the dark side within himself.

In book one, Harry faces, not only Voldemort and the defeat of his friends, but also the Mirror of Erised and his own repressed wishes. Weber explains:

> In the inmost cave lies the sorcerer's stone, which is the power to fuel Harry's shadow, and the magic mirror that reveals the strongest yearnings of Harry's heart. Naturally, it is here that the climax between Harry and his shadow must take place, and

since the shadow is the repressed qualities of Harry's own psyche, only his own positive attributes, his internal and inherited love, can be used to defeat it.[32]

Confronting Voldemort in the deepest darkness and viewing his greatest desires in the magic mirror forces Harry to confront all these feelings within himself, and thus gain self-knowledge and inner strength. This he does, emerging from the mirror chamber knowing he is truly a wizard fighting for goodness.

Dorothy faces her own shadow in the wicked witch's castle from which no one returns. Unlike sweet, loving Dorothy, the witch herself is like the queen of the underworld, never growing or changing, never drinking water or falling in love. All obey her mechanically, soullessly.

One must face death unarmed, unprotected. The winged monkeys of the book, chaos embodied, scatter and destroy the Tin Woodsman and Scarecrow, and cage the Lion. Still, it remains true that those who love us leave their protection on us forever. When the monkeys see the good witch's kiss on Dorothy's forehead, they deliver her unharmed to the wicked witch's castle rather than following orders and killing her "for she is protected by the Power of Good, and that is greater than the Power of Evil."[33] Bereft of cleverness and love, with courage chained up, Dorothy only manages to keep her innocence (Toto) and her goodness (the good witch's kiss). She also keeps the power of her shoes but doesn't know how to wield it.

In this scene, the two forces meet: good and evil as innocent child and merciless ruler. While Dorothy is frightened at confronting the story's villainess, the witch is far more terrified of Dorothy's powerful shoes: "She looked down at Dorothy's feet, and seeing the Silver Shoes, began to tremble with fear, for she knew what a powerful charm belonged to them."[34] If the shoes represent Dorothy's journey, then the witch is frightened because she has never journeyed herself, never gathered up brains, heart, and courage to become stronger. She is a hollow shell like the wizard, ruling through the illusion of power rather than through wisdom. If the shoes are fertility and life, the witch again cowers because she has none of those powers. She is so dried up she can't bleed, so sallow her face is green.

Now the Wicked Witch had a great longing to have for her own the Silver Shoes which the girl always wore. Her bees and her crows and her wolves were lying in heaps and drying up, and

23

she had used up all the power of the Golden Cap; but if she could only get hold of the Silver Shoes, they would give her more power than all the other things she had lost. She watched Dorothy carefully, to see if she ever took off her shoes, thinking she might steal them. But the child was so proud of her pretty shoes that she never took them off except at night and when she took her bath. The Witch was too much afraid of the dark to dare go in Dorothy's room at night to take the shoes, and her dread of water was greater than her fear of the dark, so she never came near when Dorothy was bathing. Indeed, the old Witch never touched water, nor ever let water touch her in any way.[35]

The book's Golden Cap that summons the flying monkeys suggests male authority—as a disembodied head shape it instantly echoes the Great and Powerful Oz. Whoever hides behind the pasteboard head or wears the cap gives orders and must instantly be obeyed. Gold is a masculine color, a day color, a sun color. This witch is like the wizard—authoritative on the surface with nothing beneath. Having burned though her masculine power sources of army and cap (for the three friends destroyed her hordes of bees and crows and wolves with their natural skills before the monkeys attacked), the witch longs for the feminine power, which is greater but which she cannot comprehend. She covers from the darkness and water, which are feminine realms, and she covets but cannot snatch the feminine silver slippers.

At first the Witch was tempted to run away from Dorothy; but she happened to look into the child's eyes and saw how simple the soul behind them was, and that the little girl did not know of the wonderful power the Silver Shoes gave her. So the Wicked Witch laughed to herself, and thought, "I can still make her my slave, for she does not know how to use her power."[36]

Dorothy has magic but not the strength or knowledge to wield it. She needs training from the most powerful, vicious woman in Oz: the wicked witch. For Dorothy, on the cusp of womanhood, has never ruled a farmhouse as Aunt Em has, has never ordered handymen about, or slaughtered animals at harvest time. To grow up, she'll need more than "sweetness," she'll need training in the harshness of the adult world. For this, she becomes the witch's servant.

"Dorothy followed her through many of the beautiful rooms in her castle until they came to the kitchen, where the Witch bade her clean the pots and kettles and sweep the floor and keep the fire fed with wood."[37] This is a common pattern through folklore, as Cinderella does her stepmother's chores and Psyche of Roman myth completes painful tasks for her mother-in-law, Venus. Alice in Wonderland serves the Red and White Queens, following their endless instructions. Ariel needs Ursula's charms to win her prince. And murderous Mrs. Coulter of *The Golden Compass* teaches her daughter Lyra valuable lessons on how to dress, wear makeup, and charm adults.

This is the heroine's crucible, burning away her happy childhood and forcing her through the pain of growing up. Dorothy's slavery continues until the wicked witch steals a slipper. This angers Dorothy—this vicious witch has no right to her own female power. Dorothy dashes feminine, life-giving water over her enemy, who melts away. Before a girl wielding the womanly power she's had all along, this lifeless mock-up of authority is powerless. In the movie, Dorothy is defending her friend, healing the Scarecrow who's on fire. While water brings life to the heroine's allies, it's death to the witch.

Dorothy's first act is to free the enslaved Winkies—since she's been a slave, she knows how miserable the Winkies must be. Her pain has taught her compassion, another lesson the witch never learned. The Winkies in turn pledge Dorothy a greater loyalty than they ever did to the witch, and help her save her friends. And so Dorothy has grown in the witch's castle from innocent victim to wise queen of the Winkies and flying monkeys alike, learning from her suffering until she can defeat the witch and replace her as a more worthy successor. From here, Dorothy puts on the golden cap of masculine authority and commands the monkeys to fly her to the Emerald City—no wonder the Wizard's terrified when she arrives!

Ascension

Having found the Philosopher's Stone, "Harry returns to his community, bringing renewal, wisdom, and treasures. The stone is destroyed, and his shadow, Voldemort, has temporarily dissipated."[38] Harry has faced his greatest desire: the Mirror of Erised and all it offers, along with his shadow-self. Now, he can return to Hogwarts and even to the Dursleys thanks to his enlightenment. Though he spends summers with them for seven books, Harry finally makes the magical world his home, becoming an Auror, marrying Ginny and having a magical family.

Likewise, Dorothy returns to Kansas. The next books like *Ozma of Oz* and *Dorothy and the Wizard in Oz*, see her journey from earth to the magical world and back. In book six, she finally makes Oz her permanent home and becomes one with the magic forever. Like Harry, Dorothy changes from battling through the magical land to ruling and guarding it. Both have truly mastered the realm of their own feelings.

The purpose of this journey, after all, is to achieve adulthood and balance. By defeating death and their own lingering dark sides, the hero and heroine reach the power and majesty of adulthood. As Dorothy learns about queenship and its semblance from the Wicked Witch of the West, she grows into someone strong enough to kick over the Wizard's pasteboard head and confront the fraud cowering behind it. Harry understands and rejects Voldemort's cruel path to power, choosing responsibility and sacrifice for himself as well.

Heroes and heroines may start on separate journeys, but they share the greatest steps that define their passage to adulthood. Both begin in the ordinary world, miserable and isolated. In the magical otherworld, they find friends and allies, but also terror, as their own dark shadows menace them. Defeating these terrible mothers and dark lords requires that the hero grow into his or her own power by descending into the underworld and reincarnating with hidden wisdom. This is the passage that defines who we are, regardless of gender.

---

[1] L. Frank Baum, *The Wonderful Wizard of Oz* (US: Signet Classics, 2006), 1.

[2] J. K Rowling, *Harry Potter and the Philosopher's Stone* (London: Bloomsbury Publishing Plc, 1997), 20.

[3] Ibid., 47.

[4] Ibid., 74.

[5] J.K. Rowling, Edinburgh "Cub Reporter" Press Conference, *ITV*, 16 July 2005. http://www.accio-quote.org/articles/2005/0705-edinburgh-ITVcubreporters.htm

[6] *The Wizard of Oz*, DVD, produced by King Vidor, Mervyn LeRoy, Richard Thorpe, and Victor Fleming (1939; US: MGM, 1999).

[7] Rowling, *Harry Potter and the Philosopher's Stone* 92.

[8] John Granger, *Harry Potter's Bookshelf: The Great Books behind the Hogwarts Adventures* (California, Berkeley Trade, 2009), 187.

[9] Ibid., 213-214.

[10] J. K Rowling, *Harry Potter and the Deathly Hallows*, (USA: Scholastic,

Inc, 2007), 743.

[11] *The Wizard of Oz*, DVD.

[12] *The Wizard of Oz*, DVD.

[13] Baum, *The Wonderful Wizard of Oz*, 43.

[14] Gretchen Ritter, *Goldbugs and Greenbacks: The Anti-Monopoly Tradition and the Politics of Finance in America* (NY: Cambridge University Press, 1997), 9.

[15] J. K. Rowling, *Harry Potter and the Order of the Phoenix.* (USA: Scholastic, Inc, 2003), 844.

[16] Rowling, *Deathly Hallows* 696.

[17] Rowling, *Philosopher's Stone* 216.

[18] Joseph Campbell, *The Hero With a Thousand Faces*, (New York: Princeton UP, 1973), 120.

[19] Rowling, *Half-Blood Prince*, 535.

[20] Madeline L' Engle, *A Wrinkle in Time* (USA: Random House, 2005), 187.

[21] Baum 130-131.

[22] Granger, *Harry Potter's Bookshelf*, 217.

[23] Rowling, *Deathly Hallows*, 692.

[24] Rowling, *Chamber*, 233.

[25] Rowling, *Half-Blood Prince*, 277.

[26] J.K. Rowling, interview by author, "Bloomsbury Live Chat with J.K. Rowling," July 30, 2007, Webchat, http://www.bloomsbury.com/jkrevent.

[27] Rowling, *Order of the Phoenix* 844.

[28] Carl Jung. *Archetypes and Collective Unconscious* in *Collected Works*, trans. R.F.C. Hull, vol. 9, pt. 1, 2nd ed. (Princeton: Princeton University Press, 1968), 285.

[29] Rowling, *Order of the Phoenix* 841.

[30] Rowling, *Deathly Hallows* 711.

[31] Ibid., 20.

[32] Ryan P. Weber, "Harry Potter's Quest: The Hero's Journey and the Shadow." *Headline Muse*. Issue #23: 2002. www.headlinemuse.com.

[33] Baum 107.

[34] Ibid., 108.

[35] Ibid., 110.

[36] Ibid., 108.

[37] Ibid., 108.

[38] Weber.

CHAPTER 2: REDEFINING EPIC HEROES: NEVILLE, SNAPE, AND DRACO

The best epics feature growth along the hero's path for far more than one character. *Lord of the Rings* follows Frodo, Aragorn, and even Gandalf on hero's journeys. As they grow from their original roles to become great leaders, minor characters likewise change, as Gimli and Legolas overcome prejudice to become fast friends, Sam grows from a simple gardener to Hobbiton's beloved mayor, and Merry and Pippin reach beyond bumbling youths to become knights of Rohan and Gondor.

The Harry Potter series clearly follows the title character through his invariably classic hero's journey. While other characters from Snape to Mrs. Weasley display great heroism and growth on their own quests, the series is Harry's story undisputedly, as he destroys four parts of Voldemort's soul (to each other characters' one) and casts the spell that destroys Voldemort forever. His role as Quidditch seeker mirrors this, as he regularly earns more points than the rest of the team combined. Yet others around Harry grow as well. The four stages of life, explored through the hero's journey, are child, hero, ruler, and sage. Or, to put it another way, Neville, Harry, Voldemort, and Dumbledore. Each person travels through these stages, absorbing their lessons to progress.

Harry must pass through every stage of life's journey: First he grows from an innocent child to an adolescent hero, poised on the threshold of adulthood and self-identification. To pass this stage, he battles his antithesis, the symbolic father or ruler of the household who blocks the hero's attempt to replace him. If the hero learns from this battle, he can ascend to adulthood and its challenges. Beyond this stage waits the realm of the grandfather/mentor, who guides new young heroes to challenge their fathers in a never-ending cycle.

Further on waits death and the untold power of the spirit world. Each stage offers a challenge that some characters pass and others never will. In fact, characters around Harry, from Draco to Snape, battle these stages just as Harry battles his great antagonist, Voldemort. These struggles reveal each of life's stages as characters do or don't summon their courage to face them.

Child

Both Neville and Dudley are comic figures in the early books, hopeless at simple tasks and apparently destined to remain so. Pixies lift Neville into the air, and Malfoy picks on him unmercifully. Every moment, he's crawling through the castle, searching for his toad, his remembrall, or some other misplaced item. He shivers with horror at the thought of Snape calling on him. Likewise, Dudley gains a pig's tail in the first book, and gobbles the twins' tongue ton toffee later, with disfiguring repercussions. He throws tantrums in the first book and can't manage to count his own birthday presents with any degree of skill. Dudley needs rescuing from Dementors in the fifth book and, despite his rising to be head of a gang, doesn't seem to have grown. Rowling says, "I think that when Dudley was attacked by the Dementors he saw himself, for the first time, as he really was. This was an extremely painful, but ultimately salutory lesson, and began the transformation in him."[1] Still the transformation involves his questioning why the family will go to safety while his cousin is left to die and his leaving Harry a single cup of tea – common decency, but not true altruism. Over the course of seven books, Dudley finally learns a modicum of compassion, with his weak "I don't think you're a waste of space."[2] Though Harry remarks it's a giant leap for Dudley, the wizards and witches are right to be unimpressed. Dudley, as shown when attacked by Dementors, cares mostly for his own skin. There's no evidence he's ever risked his life for another, or made more than the weakest of gestures. Thanks to his parents' spoiling him, he may remain a child forever.

Neville, however, grows enough courage and love by the end of book one to defy his few friends for the sake of everyone in Gryffindor. In five through seven, he joins the D.A., Harry's student protest against Umbridge's administration and finally leads his own student resistance. "It helps when people stand up to them, it gives everyone hope. I used to notice that when you did it, Harry."[3] Though he's following in Harry's footsteps, keeping the club's name,

Dumbledore's Army, and even the summoning coins, he's taking a heroic stand. He protects other students at the risk of his life, demonstrating fervent courage, but also love for others. At Harry's side, Neville becomes a hero, battling Death Eaters below the Ministry of Magic and in the corridors of Hogwarts.

In Neville's great defiant moment, he draws the Sword of Gryffindor and kills Nagini the Horcrux (technically fulfilling Harry's instructions rather than destroying the Longbottom family's enemy— Bellatrix). Once again, Neville is a hero but only as an assistant on Harry's quest to defeat Voldemort. While other characters, Snape, Molly, and others, display great heroism and growth on their own quests, the series is Harry's story undisputedly, as he destroys three parts of Revolting's soul (to each other characters' one) and casts the spell that destroys Voldemort forever. Quidditch is a microcosm of this phenomenon, in which one character generally earns more points than his entire rest of the team combined. Neville ends the story just as Harry ends almost every book: "surrounded by a knot of fervent admirers"[4] as he sits in the Hogwarts Dining Hall. Harry, by contrast, earns an ovation from the adult headmasters, signaling his mastery of adult skills: Neville has surpassed his fellow students and Harry has surpassed the greatest leaders of the wizarding world. Still, love for his friends has brought Neville from child to hero, while Dudley's empathy remains stunted.

Hero

Long before Harry matches wits with Voldemort, or even Snape, another rival threatens to destroy him. This is Draco Malfoy, avid dark arts student and apprentice death eater, just as Harry apprentices with the forces of good. Malfoy has definite magical talent: he repairs the magical cabinet and makes polyjuice potion in book six, and then masters fiendfyre in book seven. He was probably the person who put Madam Rosmerta under the Imperius Curse. At the same time, Malfoy cannot reach adulthood because he cannot take responsibility for his actions, or even make strong decisions. In these categories, Harry beats him every time.

He approaches Harry in the first book, not through admiration, but through a desire to unite strengths. "You'd be better served with a friend like me," he says, discounting affection in favor of strategic alliances. Ron's family lacks money and connections; therefore, Ron is a weak choice of friend. Harry is repelled by this attitude.

Instead of friends, Draco keeps followers, like the witless Crabbe and Goyle. Large and hulking, they are his bodyguards. He never treats them as equals, ordering them around and making them do his dirty work, standing lookout while he repairs the vanishing cabinet. Their clear leader, Draco looks down on the other boys as being ignorant and slow (which they clearly are). They rarely speak, instead functioning as sounding boards for Draco's schemes and diatribes against Harry and his companions. Ron and Hermione, by contrast, take the initiative and provide strong-willed, creative support over and over.

Though he takes Pansy Parkinson to the Yule Ball, we don't see Draco struggle with romance or friendship. Instead, she takes a servile role, choosing in book six to cuddle his head in her lap and "stroke the sleek blond hair off Malfoy's forehead, smirking as she did so, as though anyone would have loved to have been in her place."[5] Pansy seems triumphant and gloating rather than affectionate; again Malfoy's relationships display prestige and alliance rather than love. Harry, of course, falls in love with Cho Chang and Ginny Weasley, both talented seekers on the Quidditch field. Both heroines join the D.A. and truly care for him, as he does for them.

Harry's friends, mentors, and love interests all disagree with him from time to time, forcing Harry to learn from these conflicts. Draco, surrounded by tyrants and sycophants, loses these opportunities. This situation leaves Malfoy struggling to find his role. He sloppily poisons several of his classmates while attacking Dumbledore. "Forgive me, Draco, but they have been feeble attempts," Dumbledore comments. "So feeble, to be honest, that I wonder whether your heart has really been in it."[6] Clearly, it isn't. When asked to identify his classmates in the final book, he answers noncommittally, hesitating to condemn or save Harry and his friends. He ends the story with his family "huddled together as though unsure whether or not they were supposed to be there."[7] Unsure is the key word. Rowling adds:

> I pity Draco, just as I feel sorry for Dudley. Being raised by either the Malfoys or the Dursleys would be a very damaging experience, and Draco undergoes dreadful trials as a direct result of his family's misguided principles. However, the Malfoys do have a saving grace: they love each other. Draco is motivated quite as much by fear of something happening to his parents as to himself, while Narcissa risks everything when she

lies to Voldemort at the end of Deathly Hallows and tells him that Harry is dead, merely so that she can get to her son. [8]

Draco is at least somewhat spoiled, with constant shipments of candy and expensive racing brooms. While his mother fears hysterically for Draco's life, pleading for Snape's help in the sixth book, Draco makes few affectionate gestures toward his parents. "I can help you, Draco," Dumbledore offers. "I can send members of the Order to your mother tonight to hide her."[9] Draco hesitates and his wand trembles, possibly lowering. Once again, his lukewarm affections nudge him toward a half-hearted decision. Narcissa has asked Snape to look after Draco, which suggests both that Draco needs a babysitter and that no one at Hogwarts loves Draco enough to protect him without an Unbreakable Oath. Harry, of course, has Hagrid and Dumbledore (not to mention Sirius, Lupin, and, formerly, his parents) willing to die for him through bonds of affection.

His own ambition and malevolence block him from heroism, as he invites Death Eaters into Hogwarts to attack the innocent. Upon seeing Fenrir Greyback, Dumbledore comments, "I am a little shocked that Draco here invited you, of all people, into the school where his friends live"[10] Draco sullenly disavows responsibility. Harry, by contrast, blames himself for Sirius's death and others, until he finally dies in order to save the entire wizarding world from Voldemort's tyranny. He walks into death, beloved parents and friends by his side, full of desperate courage. Draco has no one he loves enough to die or kill for: even with his parents' life at stake he can't strike Dumbledore. While love propels Harry to defy Voldemort and duel Death Eaters, fear is not enough to prompt Draco to kill. Confronted with taking an innocent life, balanced against the absent Voldemort's threats, Draco can't do more than threaten his headmaster. Dumbledore correctly interprets his character by saying: "You are afraid to act until they [the Death Eaters] join you."[11] He weakly plots Dumbledore's death in the sixth book not in memory of loved ones or even through loyalty to Voldemort but simply through fear of Voldemort's reprisals. Harry, of course, offers his life willingly over and over for the chance to bring Voldemort down.

Draco lives for the appearance of power, bullying students and calling them mudbloods to make himself look superior. He revels in the Inquisitorial Squad and abuses his power as prefect. He becomes Slytherin Quidditch Seeker after his father made a generous donation of Nimbus 2001 brooms to the team. Later, he tries to trade on his father's reputation, rather than talent, to get into Slughorn's circle of protégés. Draco's father cautions that it's imprudent to appear Harry's enemy, since everyone in the wizarding world admires the boy: again the Malfoy obsession with ignoring feelings in favor of surfaces leaves Draco adrift. He mocks everyone nearly indiscriminately, making readers wonder if he has any cause at all. Harry, meanwhile, spends book five adamant that Voldemort has returned, even in the face of mockery, scorn, and (thanks to Umbridge) torture. His reputation means nothing compared to protecting those around him from Voldemort's misinformation.

While Harry loves his friends beyond words, Draco is truly his mother Narcissa's namesake: a narcissist. In the final scenes of book seven, Harry gives up his life and then risks it dueling Voldemort. Draco, once again, fails to take a clear side in the battle. Harry ends the series with the headmasters applauding him into adulthood, but Malfoy ends sitting with his parents, unwilling to leave their presence. The symbolism is clear.

Tyrant

Voldemort, along with other dark lords of the hero's journey, is a tyrant-king. He punishes uprisings with brutality, even going so far as to torture and kill his loyal followers. His values are equally tyrannical, valuing pure blood over the truth that any wizard can be powerful.

He represents the domineering father. Thus, the hero-son must defeat him in order to grow into a leader on his own. Meanwhile, Voldemort rules as leader of the Death Eaters and controller of the wizarding world once the ministry falls.

In the hero's journey, the son grows to replace his father as head of the household, represented by the villain's position of powerful ruler. Voldemort may not be Harry's literal father, but he is Harry's creator. The dark lord creates his own nemesis as he marks the boy as his equal.[12]

Of course, Voldemort is Harry's equal and opposite, wielding all the power and knowledge the boy lacks. Thus, Harry, born in July, conquers the dark lord born on the darkest night of the year. This contrast is heightened when Voldemort confronts him the graveyard of book four and forest of book seven. Both times, Voldemort is tall and looming, darkness accenting his unnatural power. Followers surround him, while Harry is alone. Yet Harry has power too, love and an unbroken soul. Voldemort, upon entering him, cannot abide Harry's presence thanks to his love for others. Voldemort has never cared for anyone, not even his most loyal Death Eaters. "You will hear many of his Death Eaters claiming they are in his confidences, that they alone are close to him, even understand him," Dumbledore says. "They are deluded. Lord Voldemort has never had a friend, nor do I believe that he has ever wanted one."[13] Rowling adds in her interview that Voldemort never had a love interest: "He loved only power, and himself."[14]

Both Snape and Voldemort grow up in Draco's world of uncertainty, without love to support them. As children, all three are rough and bullying. Dumbledore describes young Tom Riddle as "highly self-sufficient, secretive, and apparently friendless."[15] He creates the Death Eaters, "a mixture of the weak seeking protection, the ambitious seeking some shared glory, and the thuggish gravitating toward a leader who could show them more refined forms of cruelty."[16] Draco creates a similar entourage before joining the Death Eaters. Snape, though more of a loner, becomes a Death Eater as well. Rowling explains, "like many insecure, vulnerable people (like Wormtail) he craved membership of something big and powerful, something impressive."[17] Rowling added that teenage Lily might have loved Snape "if he had not loved Dark Magic so much, and been drawn to such loathsome people and acts."[18] Snape, as Lily points out is "well on the path to becoming a Death Eater." His skill in potions and Occlumency rivals Voldemort's own, and he craves (and then receives) the Dark Arts teaching position, which he addresses "like a lover." He actually shares many qualities with Voldemort: unhappy childhood, unnatural pallor, and loathing for Harry, the child hero who threatens all authority figures. Clearly, Snape is a lesser Voldemort, antagonizing Harry inside Hogwarts, and potentially growing to be a second Dark Lord.

Snape, as Voldemort's shadow, also mirrors Harry. Both grew up mistreated and unloved, forced to wear hideous hand-me-downs. Both were bullied at school, and both are half-blood. Both vow to defeat Lord Voldemort, in vengeance for those he's killed. At the same time, their other goals and desires are in opposition: Harry wants to grow up and defeat Voldemort and find love and peace. Snape will never have love, peace, childhood, or a happy family— they're all gone forever, thanks to Lily's death and his own empty adulthood. Just as Harry sacrifices himself for those living, Snape sacrifices himself for one dead—thus demonstrating his very strong link to death. Harry is tethered to life, so much so that he returns after Voldemort tries to kill him. Snape can't make that leap.

Snape's love for Lily transforms him, as in one instant he abandons his loyalties as Death Eater to beg Dumbledore for Lily's life. "What will you give," Dumbledore asks, sensing this one moment can throw Snape from his goals of evil and domination and set him on a new course. "Anything," Snape pledges.[19] With that, Dumbledore has bought Snape's loyalty forever, transforming him from a great villain to a mentor and protector for Harry.

Death Eaters value power and their own skins, eager to sacrifice innocents on their quest. Snape, however, has abandoned the father-tyrant model he once pursued. As sworn protector to Harry, Snape teaches Harry discipline and penance for his foolhardy actions. In this way, he gives Harry detention for his attack on Malfoy. He tutors Harry in Occlumency and offers all his memories to guide Harry down his darkest path: into self-sacrifice and certain death.

Snape, unlike Voldemort, falls truly in love, devoting himself to Lily from his oath of loyalty to his Patronus. Thus, he has the capacity to face his own mortality, trusting others like Lily's heir to preserve the wizarding world even when he's left it. Though he may deny it, his love for Lily has extended to Harry as he protests Dumbledore's apparent cold sacrifice of the boy. In turn this has helped him grow to love others. "How many have you watched die?" Dumbledore asks. "Lately only those whom I could not save." Snape replies bitterly.[20] Opening himself to Lily's love has indeed redeemed him. Rowling concludes, Snape is "a very flawed hero. An anti-hero, perhaps. He is not a particularly likeable man in many ways. He remains rather cruel, a bully, riddled with bitterness and insecurity – and yet he loved, and showed loyalty to that love."[21]

Voldemort, of course, fights only for himself, with no one to trust or protect. He cannot surrender his role as dark lord, even when Harry assures him he's already lost. Likewise, Voldemort cannot admit for a moment that his soul-fragments could be in danger or that there's any flaw in the all-powerful Elder Wand. This narrow-mindedness leads to his death. Harry, of course, is more flexible, willingly letting Ron, Hermione and Neville help him destroy Voldemort, and giving up his quest for the Hallows. Ironically, Harry actually is the one to have cheated death, by returning and mastering the Hallows. He has what Voldemort always wanted...and then at the end, he throws it away. The biggest test is letting go of the Hallows at the end, rather than clinging to their power.

This is the true test the father figure must face: releasing his grip on power and gracefully retiring to teach the next generation, as Dumbledore does. Beyond that waits death and enlightenment. Voldemort dies clinging to the Elder Wand, certain that it will protect him and denying the truth when Harry generously offers it. "Show some remorse," Harry urges, but Voldemort won't be swayed. The afterlife doesn't matter to him, since he's so adamant never to enter it, never to pay the price for adulthood: further movement along life's cycle. Voldemort clutches power in a white-knuckled grip, eagerly mutilating his soul to prevent the journey into old age and death. Ironically, this means he will spend eternity as a mutilated baby of a soul, having regressed rather than grown during his life.

Snape chose more wisely, Harry reveals in his duel with Voldemort: he allowed himself to love Lily. "He loved her," Harry tells Voldemort, "for nearly all of his life, from the time when they were children."[22] This knowledge is beyond Voldemort's comprehension. As Dumbledore does, Snape willingly relinquishes his life, passing from mentor to spirit without Voldemort's desperate defiance. When Snape sees Nagini caged, all he can focus on is completing Dumbledore's final instruction and passing his message to Harry. He stands before Voldemort, ignoring his own safety, to beg for permission to find Harry. With his dying breath, Snape bequeaths the message to Harry along with all his memories. Preparing Harry for his great sacrifice and saving the entire wizarding world far outweigh Snape's self-preservation. Love has redeemed Snape from the tyrannical dark father's path, and taught him to surrender to life's journey with grace.

Through love of Lily, Snape sacrifices himself for Harry, becoming, like Dumbledore, a spiritual protector. Rowling later assured her readers, "Harry would be instrumental in ensuring that Snape's portrait would appear there [in the headmaster's office] in due course."[23] Like Dumbledore, Snape will someday be preserved, guiding students as Dumbledore will. "Albus Severus," Harry tells his son. "You were named for two headmasters of Hogwarts. One of them was a Slytherin, and he was probably the bravest man I ever knew."[24] Even seventeen years after Snape's death, his memory is alive and counseling young wizards. This is Snape's legacy: eternally linked with Dumbledore as a spiritual protector. Voldemort has failed the final test and refused to show an instant of love or remorse. All he wanted was to keep his role as tyrant, and he has fallen below the weakest unborn soul as a result.

Sage

The elderly king rules his people with compassion. Still the wisest one knows his role is to usher in the next generation, and teach them the wisdom to ascend. As the hero rises, the mentor travels beyond, into the realm of death and memory. The wisest embrace this passing. Rowling says, "As Dumbledore explains, the real master of Death accepts that he must die, and that there are much worse things in the world of the living. It is not about striving for immortality, but about accepting mortality."[25] The sage king has two possible paths: stubborn refusal to accept change and death, or poised acceptance of the final journey.

Dumbledore, of course, is this mentor, ruler and patriarch of Hogwarts, and the only wizard so powerful Voldemort fears confronting him. However, other less noble kings cling to power and block the young hero from ascension. These shady mentors antagonize the hero on his journey, throwing up stumbling blocks and unwittingly aiding the enemy.

Fudge leads the Wizarding World until his worst fears confront him in the Department of Mysteries, forcing his dismissal at the end of *Order of the Phoenix*. He has always resented Dumbledore as a threat to his rule, and fears Voldemort's threat even more. "Deep down, Fudge knows Dumbledore's much more clever than he is, a much more powerful wizard...Accepting that Voldemort's back would mean trouble like the Ministry hasn't had to cope with for nearly fourteen years...Fudge just can't bring himself to face it," a member of the Order tells Harry.[26] When Dumbledore presses him to change his leadership, opening a dialogue with the giants, restraining the Dementors, and turning from peace to war, Fudge adamantly refuses. "He loves being Minister of Magic and he's convinced himself that he's the clever one and D's simply stirring up trouble"[27] Harry's friends add. Fudge clings to control so compulsively that he cannot change his policies, especially in the face of one with stronger knowledge and qualifications. He immediately imposes more control, appointing Umbridge as High Inquisitor and setting the Daily Prophet to discredit Harry and Dumbledore. "They want to turn you into someone nobody will believe," Hermione says. "Fudge is behind it, I'll bet anything."[28] Through his actions, he sets himself up as the inverse wise leader, blocking Harry from growth and uprooting any trust or support the public holds in Harry. His refusal to give way, of course, leads to his replacement, when Dumbledore incontrovertibly proves Voldemort's return.

Scrimgeour is better, bravely leading wizards to fight the Death Eaters. He, however, also abuses his position through the need for dominance. He uselessly imprisons Stan Shupike and insists on flimsy anti-Death Eater preparations, such as passwords and code phrases. Dumbledore and Harry agree that these protections are not very helpful. Scrimgeour, at last, accepts death and the loss of his position with admirable bravery, dying rather than betraying Harry's location.

Dumbledore learns power's price far earlier than the two ministers. Having followed Grindelwald's quest to conquer the world, he knows how power corrupts those who desire it. "I had proven, as a very young man, that power was my weakness and my temptation,"[29] he reveals, and so he turns down the invitation to be Minister of Magic. Thanks to this wisdom, he surrenders to the greater good, eagerly risking his life to find Horcruxes and teaching Harry everything he can. Dumbledore willingly steps down as headmaster over and over, bowing to the minster's order in book two and the need to protect Harry in book five. He accepts dismissal from the Wizengamot and losing his Order of Merlin, First Class, "as long as they don't take him off the Chocolate Frog cards."[30] In each case, he puts his own power aside in favor of the larger goal: defending the world from Voldemort.

He allows Draco to overpower him in the lightning struck tower, spending his only instant on immobilizing and protecting Harry. He surrenders his life with equal equanimity, since doing so will protect Snape and others. By following this path, he has not ended his journey: he guards Harry symbolically through his brother and painting, and literally at the misty King's Cross. As shown by the birth of Albus Severus Potter, Dumbledore will always be a part of Harry's life.

Other Journeys

Just as interesting as the heroes who ascend to the next life stage are those who never will. While Neville, Harry, Snape, Dumbledore, and others seize the book's lessons and learn from them, far more characters remain rooted at a single stage. Crabbe summons Fiendfyre, but learns nothing of responsibility or facing death: he burns down the Room of Requirement without a moment's hesitation over the consequences. Thus, still a confused adolescent, he causes his own destruction. Bellatrix glories in destroying life: like Voldemort, she will never step aside to let the next generation flourish. Likewise, Aberforth is a mentor, but he refuses to risk his life for others; thus, he cannot move beyond mentor into spirit. "He is still there, at the Hog's Head, playing with his goats," Rowling assures readers. [31]

Hagrid is in many ways a mentor, teaching Harry about the wizarding world and guiding him to Hogwarts. In other ways, he's a comrade, seeking help as often as he gives it, stuck in the child stage as he backs down from many challenges. He adopts a dragon but can't deal with him, he fills the forest with monstrous spiders and expresses surprise when they turn cannibalistic. He gets muddled while defending Buckbeak in court, so that Harry and his friends must finally rescue the hippogriff. Hagrid loses his wand and school to Tom Riddle's frame job, from which, we must assume, he can't defend himself. In the same book, he goes sadly and innocently to Azkaban. While questing with his great (literally!) love, Madame Maxime, she gets fed up with his latest adoption attempt and leaves, most likely after an argument. Hagrid only says, "She got a bit tired of him after a while, I must admit…so we split up on the journey home." [32] He dismisses her with a sigh and we never hear of Hagrid's great love again. Hagrid, confronted with Prefect Tom Riddle, Cornelius Fudge, Madame Maxime, and numerous pets, allows each challenge to pass, preferring to remain, unchanging, as an ungraduated student at Hogwarts. Lovable as he is, he never takes the single defiant step to push himself along his own journey.

Hermione and Ron only undergo faint echoes of heroism, as they're confined to their role as sidekicks. Neville faces Voldemort all alone, braving death to make a courageous last stand. He also organizes the other students into an underground resistance while alone at Hogwarts. Neither of Harry's best friends manages anything so independent or effective. Ron appears helpless in the lake of book four and with a broken leg in book three, both times needing rescue. His only standout moments appear as a Quidditch player *on Harry's team* and facing down the Horcrux locket. Harry graciously offers the latter moment to Ron as a reward for returning to his role as sidekick. While absent, Ron catches up on news and visits family but doesn't organize a mass revolution or find a Horcrux for Harry. In the locket, a shadow-Harry drives home that Ron will always come in second. At Harry's coaching and under his supervision, Ron finally manages to destroy the locket.

Hermione, likewise, is incredibly gifted, heroic, and even feminine, but not a strong heroine. Even with all her talents, she spends far too much time having boys rescue her. "Halfway through the first book, when Harry rescues her with Ron's assistance, the hierarchy of power is established. We learn that Hermione's bookish knowledge only goes so far. At the sight of a horrible troll, she 'sinks to the floor in fright ... her mouth open with terror.'"[33] She spends much of book two likewise incapacitated, entombed in stone like a victimized Snow White (a possible pun on her Shakespearean namesake, who masquerades as a shadow). Viktor rescues her from the lake in book four and the boys save her from torture in book seven. She only fakes breaking down in tears before Umbridge's interrogation, but the damage is done. As she appears screaming, fainting, and docily asleep in these moments, she can't shake off the image of Hollywood heroine needing rescue.

Indeed, the series lacks a single female as strong as Harry, Dumbledore, or Snape, all of whom have complicated pasts and inner struggles to master.

> McGonagall is Dumbledore's right hand and she defers to him in every respect. Whereas he has the wisdom to see beyond rules and the power to disregard them, McGonagall is bound by them and enforces them strictly. Although she makes a great effort to keep her feelings under control, in a situation of crisis she loses herself in emotions because she lacks Dumbledore's vision of the bigger picture. When Harry returns from the chamber of secrets, she clutches her chest, gasps and speaks weakly while the all-knowing Dumbledore beams.[34]

Ginny, Cho, Fleur, and Hermione are each superbly talented and recognized witches, but all get rescued by boys far too often. Fleur, though the finest champion of Beauxbatons, is rather a farce, needing Harry to rescue even her helpless little sister, and then rescue Fleur herself from the maze. In the second Triwizard task, all four heroes must rescue someone weaker than they: Fleur has her little sister, Harry has Ron, and Cho and Hermione float helplessly, awaiting their strong, manly boyfriends. McGonagall is incapacitated in book five, thanks to losing a duel against male wizards, and Sybill Trelawney is treated as a running joke, dismissed by fellow professors and only prophesying accurately when she isn't even aware of it. "She teaches divination, a subject that includes tea-leaf reading, palmistry, crystal gazing – all the intuitive arts commonly associated with female practitioners…Because most of her students and all of her colleagues dismiss her, the entire intuitive tradition of fortune-telling, a female domain, is discredited."[35]

The heroine's journey, though barely a whisper within Harry Potter's heroic currents, gets a few sparkling moments. Just as the hero faces down the tyrant, the heroine defeats the terrible mother, or child killer, in order to become a benevolent mother-protector, and then crone and spirit guide. Ginny grows from child to adolescent to mother and Lily from mother to spirit-guardian. As a doe, Lily's memory shows Harry the Sword of Gryffindor, and she walks with Harry as he goes toward his willing death.

Hermione, often criticized as a featureless repository of information, faces and absorbs lessons of the dark mother, the heroine's traditional antithesis. She actually disguises herself as Bellatrix, using her wand and entering her underworld-like vault. Before Hermione destroys the evil Horcrux (in the cup, a feminine symbol) and admits her love for Ron, she has to confront the most frightening side of adulthood and prove she's mastered it. Donning Bellatrix's appearance forces her to face her potential to be an evil mother and grow beyond the lesson.

Meanwhile, Molly Weasley, frumpy housewife, transcends her simple character to battle the dark mother and defeat her. Molly is the life-giver of the book, with seven children by birth and more by adoption, like Harry and Hermione. Her automatic antithesis is the child-killing, Lady Macbethlike Bellatrix, who tortures Hermione and orphans Neville. When Bellatrix threatens Molly's beloved Ginny, all Molly's protective instincts appear and Molly destroys her single-handedly. "You will never touch our children again," she screams, dispatching Bellatrix in a moment fans adored.[36] Thus many heroines grow, defeating killers and finding adulthood. Still, the heroes have more growth and depth, and the heroines spend too much time being rescued.

Final Thoughts

The steps mimic the journey of life: the innocent child enters adolescence and thus finds himself battling his father for dominance as he struggles to find his place in the world. Only upon defeating the father and facing his dark side, can the teen reach adulthood. Meanwhile, the father eventually steps down, relinquishing his role as ruler to become a sage and teacher for the next generation, his grandchildren. In each case, characters can either accept their role, or die fighting it. Even those, like Dumbledore, who willingly learn each lesson, must submit to death in the end, once they've started the younger generation across the gap from innocence to the hero's quest.

---

[1] J.K. Rowling, "J.K. Rowling and the Live Chat," *Bloomsbury.com, Accio Quote!* 30 July 2007. http://www.accio-quote.org/articles/2007/0730-bloomsbury-chat.html.

[2] J. K Rowling, *Harry Potter and the Deathly Hallows,* (USA: Scholastic, Inc, 2007), 40.

[3] Ibid., 574.

[4] Ibid., 745.

[5] J. K Rowling, *Harry Potter and the Half-Blood Prince,* (USA: Scholastic, Inc, 2005), 149.

[6] Ibid., 585.

[7] Rowling, *Deathly Hallows,* 746.

[8] J.K. Rowling "Draco Malfoy," *Pottermore.* https://www.reddit.com/r/PottermoreWritings/comments/3l9s25/draco_malfoy_part_2_of_2.

[9] Rowling, *Half-Blood Prince,* 592.

[10] Ibid., 593.

[11] Ibid., 586.

[12] J. K Rowling, *Harry Potter and the Order of the Phoenix.* (USA: Scholastic, Inc, 2003), 841.

[13] Rowling, *Half-Blood Prince,* 277.

[14] J.K. Rowling, "J.K. Rowling and the Live Chat."

[15] Rowling, *Half-Blood Prince,* 277.

[16] Ibid., 362.

[17] Rowling, "J.K. Rowling and the Live Chat."

[18] Ibid.

[19] Rowling, *Deathly Hallows*, 678.

[20] Ibid., 687.

[21] Rowling, "J.K. Rowling and the Live Chat."

[22] Rowling, *Deathly Hallows*, 740.

[23] Rowling, "J.K. Rowling and the Live Chat."

[24] Rowling, *Deathly Hallows*, 758.

[25] Rowling, "J.K. Rowling and the Live Chat."

[26] Rowling, *Order of the Phoenix*, 94.

[27] Ibid., 94.

[28] Ibid., 74.

[29] Rowling, *Deathly Hallows*, 718.

[30] Rowling, *Order of the Phoenix*, 95.

[31] Rowling, "J.K. Rowling and the Live Chat."

[32] Rowling, *Order of the Phoenix*, 692.

[33] Christine Schoefer, "Harry Potter's Girl Trouble," Salon.com, http://archive.salon.com/books/feature/2000/01/13/potter.

[34] Ibid.

[35] Ibid.

[36] Rowling, *Deathly Hallows*, 736.

CHAPTER 3: ALBUS, SCORPIUS, AND THE HERO'S JOURNEY

Harry Potter and the Cursed Child arrived in 2016, offering a second generation of heroes to take the classic journey. The play itself is giant and complex, with plenty of plot for both generations.

> Cynics have suggested the decision to split the play into two parts rather than one smacks of commercial exploitation, echoing the way the final book was broken in two on screen. But Cursed Child could only be told over the five hours that splitting it into two allows. It's a fiendishly complex narrative, and moves at a lick; the first two years of Albus's time at Hogwarts are told in the first fifteen minutes. Considering each of the books covers the course of a single year, this marks a radical change of approach.[1]

While the published version of the play is a bit sparse of description, the live version has plenty of special effects. "There are magic tricks, surprise reveals, quick-change transformations and an intricate set, built to look like layered iron railway arches. Stand-alone staircases spin around to replicate the magical building at Hogwarts; actors float on wires to simulate swimming; and the somersaults of one fight scene are aided by a large cast of almost-invisible, black-clad assistants whirling the protagonists about."[2]

In the first act, Albus and Scorpius bond on the train, paralleling Harry and Ron – with the alluring teen Delphi introduced later as the third in their trio. At the same time, the boys' membership in Slytherin makes this an anti-Ron and Harry story, the tale of the heroes of Slytherin and how they help mend the dark reputation of their house. For certainly, this is Albus and Scorpius's adventure:

> It's the younger cast that steal the show, especially Sam Clemmett as Albus and Anthony Boyle as Scorpius. The self-described pair of "losers" are recognizably human and distinct

from their family traits; Clemmett captures the frustration of the delicate and troubled Albus, and Boyle is both hilarious and heartbreaking as his bumbling, devoted friend Scorpius, whose blond thatch is the only sign of his Malfoy heritage."[3]

Harry Potter NextGen fanfiction, which sprang up after book seven, focused especially on Albus and Scorpius…often friends and sometimes lovers. The risk, of course, with so little information in canon, was to make the characters their fathers all over again. As critic Emily Roach explains in her essay on post-Epilogue fanfiction, "There is a danger that the popular Albus Severus/Scorpius pairing becomes too like Harry/Draco, but for the most part, established writers of this pairing shy away from that approach, wanting to explore more interesting dynamics."[4] The play likewise gives the boys new personalities.

Albus shares the heroism (and also bad choices) of his namesakes Albus and Severus. The names mean "white" and "severe." Thus, he's a white wizard fighting for goodness, but is also quite severe on his father, actually carrying on a similar animosity to the one Harry shared with Snape. As many fans observed when book seven was published, his initials are ASP, a snake, pointing him already towards Slytherin. His last name, Potter, marks him as the heir to James, Sr. and Harry, but there's more to him than the impulsive heroism that has him travel back in time. Albus Dumbledore carried much guilt for the past – Grindelwald's actions more than his own, just as young Albus is consumed by Harry's legacy. Severus Snape was a spare in James and Lily's relationship, always an outsider to the tight Gryffindor friendships, and Albus feels like the unnecessary child of the family, one who doesn't fit in.

Scorpio, in Greek myth, was the scorpion sent by the gods to stop a great hunter – Orion – who had planned to kill all life on earth. Scorpius parallels this as the nemesis sent to stop Delphi, and a chosen one as Harry is. Scorpions were guardians, meant to keep villains away from treasure and to preserve the natural order – another Scorpius and Delphi parallel. In Zodiac symbology, Scorpio as an immature form is a conniving serpent, but he is also a shapechanger. As he achieves higher thought, he transforms into an eagle, suggesting Scorpius's nerdy love of knowledge that he shares with the Ravenclaw students. Scorpio as a Zodiac sign, "corresponds to that period of the span of a man's life which lies under the threat of death."[5] Obviously, he faces death in the story and grows through the challenge.

It's unusual for a pair of characters to both undergo the hero's journey – often one does, or each becomes more like the other, but most stories don't split between protagonists…especially in Harry Potter's world. Albus seems framed as the story's main character, but an entire quarter of the book erases him from existence, leaving Scorpius to carry the adventure and discover his own hidden talents. Their friendship maintains a living existence as each boy learns and teaches the other. Nonetheless, the characters, including the adults, take turns in the spotlight.

Albus doesn't fit, as he feels disconnected with his larger-than-life father and impressive brother, but sets off for Hogwarts nonetheless. Hero's journey scholar Joseph Campbell explains, "In the first stage of this kind of adventure, the hero leaves the realm of the familiar, over which he has some measure of control, and comes to a threshold."[6] Even for a boy who's grown up with magic, Hogwarts with its train represents the magical world journey. Immediately, Albus befriends Scorpius, thus rejecting much of what his father stands for and yet valuing the deepest lesson of the original series – true, unprejudiced friendship. It's no wonder that the Sorting Hat promptly places him in Slytherin, emphasizing his different choices from Harry's. There, Albus steals James's invisibility cloak to dodge school bullies.[7] Symbolically, he's trying to be his father and brother, even climbing into their clothes. Nonetheless, bullying continues.

Then there's Scorpius, who quickly loses his mother and detaches from his father. Young adult critic Leila Sales explains, "Dead parents are so much a part of middle-grade and teen fiction at this point, it's not even the 'in' thing…It's just an accepted fact: kids in books are parentless."[8] This makes the child's leaving home much easier, without the emotional baggage. At the same time, for the boy, Campbell emphasizes finding a new role model. "The boy has to disengage himself from his mother, get his energy into himself, and then start forth,"[9] seeking his father figure and his identity as a grown adult.

Both boys grow up surrounded by baggage, as they realize each year at the train station. Back at the Ministry, Voldemort's legacy continues, thanks to the lingering time turners in their reality. These time turners symbolize a universe where no one can move on – where they're all still students on some level, battling a monster who's

47

long been killed.

By his third year, Albus is growing ever more distant from his father, to the point of their fateful quarrel. Having this conflict just as he starts out on his epic quest is perfectly normal. As Campbell describes it:

> What's running the show is what's coming from way down below. The period when one begins to realize that one isn't running the show is called adolescence, when a whole new system of requirements begins announcing itself from the body. The adolescent hasn't the slightest idea how to handle all this, and cannot but wonder what it is that's pushing him—or even more mysteriously, pushing her.[10]

When Albus fights with his father, he becomes desperate to prove himself. Then comes a prompting from outside. Campbell scholar Christopher Vogler explains, "The hero is presented with a problem, challenge, or adventure to undertake. Once presented with a Call to Adventure, she can no longer remain indefinitely in the comfort of the Ordinary World."[11]

Upon overhearing the alluring Delphi's pain at Cedric Diggory's loss, he's prompted, like many gallant knights, to rescue the endangered innocent and fix the mistakes of the past. However, he's still channeling a great deal of his father. Albus tells Scorpius, "Everyone talks about all the brave things Dad did. But he made some mistakes too. Some big mistakes, in fact. I want to set one of those mistakes right. I want us to save Cedric."[12] He sees himself in lost Cedric, another teen boy heroic Harry didn't value enough and allowed to be lost in the currents of fate. Harry lied to Amos Diggory about having a time turner, and he's lied to Albus "because he doesn't care," Albus insists.[13] For Albus, saving Cedric means saving himself.

As Farah Mendlesohn notes in *Rhetorics of Fantasy*, "portal fantasies [such as Alice's journey through a rabbit hole or Dorothy's to Oz] lead us gradually to the point where the protagonist knows his or her world enough to change it and to enter into that world's destiny."[14] The problem is that these boys don't truly understand their parents or the past of decades before. Thus when they time-travel, they make clumsy mistakes and destroy all that holds their world together, before they learn enough about their loved ones to recreate it.

A mission of saving Cedric suggests fixing the classic Potter stories. The three new friends polyjuice themselves into the original trio, emphasizing how this generation will embark on similar adventures. Readers revisit the Triwizarding Tournament, cheating to change the winners and losers. "Just like my dad did," Albus says of gillyweed.[15] But there's also the time turners, Dumbledore's Army, Lily's patronus. The show even revives Dumbledore and Snape. Most of all, the alternate worlds ask the big "What ifs" – what if the book four Yule Ball had gone differently? What if Neville hadn't survived to the Battle of Hogwarts? Fans get their wish list with a Snape-Umbridge duel and with Dumbledore confessing his love for Harry. Meanwhile, Harry's stalling on paperwork and Hermione's prodding him – just like when they were in school. The story may revisit the best moments of the Potterverse, but Albus and Scorpius feel obligated to fix their parents' mistakes, while Delphi bears a similar burden. None of their lives are their own. Thus the creators "have chosen spectacle over story, nostalgia over novelty and motion over emotion."[16]

> Using alternate-universe versions of the original settings gives these plays the air of high-quality fan fiction. Potter fans are one of the largest fan communities online and have written every permutation of love interest and plot twist into the world built by J K Rowling. Going back into Hogwarts in the 1990s is what they do. The use of time travel will also remind the more hardcore fans how much the world has moved on since the books were first published.[17]

This repeating cycle affects the older generation as much as the younger. "My son is fighting battles for us just as I had to for you," Harry tells Dumbledore's portrait. "And I have proved as bad a father to him as you were to me."[18] His is the midlife crisis quest, struggling to connect with the adolescent son who's rejected him. There's the balance of work and family, the spectrum of voices demanding attention. Hermione has a similar disconnect, telling Harry, "You know, Ron says he thinks I see more of my secretary, Ethel, than him. Do you think there's a point where we made a choice – parent of the year or Ministry official of the year?"[19]

When the epilogue to book seven was published, followed by Rowling's interviews in which she listed everyone's marriages, jobs, and children, there was plenty of fannish backlash.

All the characters conformed to heteronormative social

convention, as even wacky Luna Lovegood marries Rolf Scamander and has babies. Not a single character is identified as homosexual except the now-dead Dumbledore. Charlie Weasley is one of the very few characters who doesn't marry, though Rowling insists this is only because Charlie is "more interested in studying dragons than forming a romantic attachment."[20]

> The epilogue is not only problematic from a queer perspective. It continues the prejudice born out of house rivalries and both marginalizes and limits the agency of the female characters through the affirmation of "traditional gender roles." ... It is unfortunate that through the epilogue we see these traditional gender roles assumed by Harry's generation with all of the key characters married with children. Hermione at least does seem to have a career, but despite demonstrating academic brilliance during her time at Hogwarts, the epilogue Hermione is a wife and mother, the next generation Molly Weasley, and in the secondary canon of Rowling's interviews, Rowling tells us she is simply "pretty high up" in the Department of Magical Law Enforcement.[21]

Compared to Rowling's statement that "Harry and Ron utterly revolutionized the Auror Department...They are now the experts. It doesn't matter how old they are or what else they've done,"[22] Hermione loses out.

Notably, *Cursed Child* repairs this a bit – everyone's in a classic nuclear family, but Ron mostly stays home with the kids, while Hermione has been promoted to Minister of Magic. Ron is still a goofball, preferring the quiet life to their fast-paced environment, as Rowling's Quidditch story on *Pottermore* explains. Slanted journalist Rita Skeeter says of his history:

> In the immediate aftermath of the battle [of Hogwarts] Weasley, whose famous ginger hair appears to be thinning slightly, entered into employment with the Ministry of Magic alongside Potter, but left only two years later to co-manage the highly successful wizarding joke emporium Weasleys' Wizard Wheezes. Was he, as he stated at the time, 'delighted to assist my brother George with a business I've always loved'? Or had he had his fill of standing in Potter's shadow? Was the work of the Auror Department too much for a man who has admitted that the destruction of He Who Could Not Be Named's Horcruxes 'took its toll' on him? He shows no obvious signs of

mental illness from a distance, but the public is not allowed close enough to make a proper assessment. Is this suspicious?[23]

"Hermione and Ron (Noma Dumezweni and Paul Thornley) are afforded more opportunities by the narrative to have fun, and garner some of the biggest laughs of the plays."[24]

Meanwhile, Harry's having nightmares of Voldemort, and denying to Ginny that anything's wrong. The guilt of the past is returning as Amos Diggory remonstrates him for Cedric's death, and for not changing time to fix it. In this plot, his son is a shadow for him, acting on Harry's secret desires and struggling to save Cedric, something mature Harry knows is an impossible task. At the same time, Harry can't understand Albus, and finally blows up at him:

> It's telling that the biggest gasp in Part One came not from a twist of the plot or a moment of magic but during a blazing argument between Harry and Albus where the father firmly crosses a line. In these scenes between father and son, Jamie Parker as Harry captures a sort of tortured celebrity anxiety, suggesting his concerns about Albus's shortcomings are in part driven by ego, and in part an orphan's struggle to connect with his child.[25]

Draco tells Harry, "I think you have to make a choice – at a certain point – of the man you want to be. And I tell you that at that time you need a parent or a friend. And if you've learnt to hate your parent by then and have no friends…then you're all alone. And being alone – that's so hard. I was alone. And it sent me to a truly dark place. For a long time. Tom Riddle was also a lonely child. You may not understand that Harry but I do—and I think Ginny does too."[26] In book six, Snape was Draco's only support, and that only barely. There and in book seven he's seen crying alone or paralyzed with doubt, uncertain what kind of man to become. Rowling provides a bit of Draco's background on *Pottermore:*

> My British editor questioned the fact that Draco was so accomplished at Occlumency, which Harry (for all his ability in producing a Patronus so young) never mastered. I argued that it was perfectly consistent with Draco's character that he would find it easy to shut down emotion, to compartmentalise, and to deny essential parts of himself. Dumbledore tells Harry, at the

end of Order of the Phoenix, that it is an essential part of his humanity that he can feel such pain; with Draco, I was attempting to show that the denial of pain and the suppression of inner conflict can only lead to a damaged person (who is much more likely to inflict damage on other people).[27]

Now he, like Harry, wants to be a good parent and leave his son with a trusted friend. It seems he's truly grown from the angry teen at Hogwarts. Rowling concludes:

I imagine that Draco grew up to lead a modified version of his father's existence; independently wealthy, without any need to work, Draco inhabits Malfoy Manor with his wife and son. I see in his hobbies further confirmation of his dual nature. The collection of Dark artefacts harks back to family history, even though he keeps them in glass cases and does not use them. However, his strange interest in alchemical manuscripts, from which he never attempts to make a Philosopher's Stone, hints at a wish for something other than wealth, perhaps even the wish to be a better man. I have high hopes that he will raise Scorpius to be a much kinder and more tolerant Malfoy than he was in his own youth.[28]

In fact, their sons' friendship throws Harry and Draco into conflict, insecure as they both are about their failures as parents. The two find themselves dueling in Harry's kitchen, enraged at their own flaws, seen so clearly reflected in the other man.

Of course, Draco and Scorpius are also disconnected after the death of Scorpius's mother Astoria. After finishing her series, Rowling commented, "Scorpius has a lot going against him, not least that name. However, I think Scorpius would be an improvement on his father, whom misfortune has sobered!"[29]

Boyle's scenes with father Draco, portrayed by Alex Price as a swaggering cockney, mirror those between Albus and Harry, and build to their own moving conclusion. Just as Rowling's novels captured some of the challenges and joys of growing up, this story is about the bond between parents and their children-- appropriate, perhaps, now that the novels' original readers are themselves becoming parents.[30]

Like Harry, Draco quests to physically find his son and also to connect with him so they can rejoin as a family. However, both their sons are lost on their trip through time, ironically to the days of their fathers at Hogwarts.

"One of the most stunning effects is the simplest: when time shifts, the lighting wobbles to make the set tremble like a sub-woofer."[31] Thus the world is shaken, literally as well as figuratively. The entire story involves the journey to several alternate realities, worlds that mirror the "real" one. This is fitting as the hero's journey centers on facing the unexplored sides of the self one has always hidden away rather than nurtured. As Campbell notes:

> The unconscious sends all sorts of vapors, odd beings, terrors and deluding images up into the mind—whether in dream, broad daylight, or insanity; for the human kingdom, beneath the floor of the comparatively neat little dwelling that we call our consciousness, goes down into unexpected Aladdin caves. There not only jewels but also dangerous jinn abide: the inconvenient or resisted psychological powers that we have not thought or dared to integrate into our lives.[32]

The shadow, in psychology, is "aspects of oneself which are considered by the ego to be undesirable or not useful and are therefore relegated to the dark."[33] Memorably, Tom Riddle is much like orphaned, half-Muggle Harry, if Harry had made far different choices with his life.

Albus is trapped with Harry and James as his antagonists and also the ideal selves he can never become – foils always emphasizing his own flaws. Then he transfers into the first shadow world, where a sterner Harry forbids him to see Scorpius. The alternate Albus is a Gryffindor and conformist, so he gets to see what that life is like. However, he has no new friendships, no unexpected delights. He and his father still disagree. Hermione is an angry shrew of a teacher, her children have vanished, and this world is harsher, colder, without the friendship that sustains him.

As he shuts Scorpius out, then Scorpius convinces him they need each other, it's much more Albus's story than his friend's. Scorpius's language is all about his friend as he insists: "He will always be Harry Potter, you know that, right? And you will always be his son. And I know it's hard, and the other kids are awful, but you have to learn to be okay with that, because – there are worse things, okay?"[34]

Together, the boys turn their weakness into strength. Albus says, "You're right – we are losers. We're brilliant at losing and so we should be using our own knowledge here. Our own powers. Losers are taught to be losers. And there's only one way to teach a loser—we know that better than anyone—humiliation."[35] They humiliate Cedric in an attempt to repair the changes they've made.

In fact, Albus gets his wish fulfilment in the next world – a world where he makes Harry Potter no longer exist. Of course, this makes him vanish as well and leads to a world of terrors. Voldemort won the Battle for Hogwarts, with a rage-filled Cedric Diggory by his side. Neville Longbottom, the smallest hero of the original books, died, and thus never killed Nagini. This was the linchpin of everything.

With Albus vanished, the quest transfers to Scorpius and gives him his own chance to shine. Here he faces a strange shadow in the universe where Voldemort rules – his overachieving self. In the dark world he's skilled at Quidditch – transformed from geek to athlete. All the students stand in awe of him and reverentially call him the Scorpion King. Girls, especially Polly Chapman, line up to escort him to the ball. The cool kids want to spend time with him. This suggests all the possibilities that exist inside him – his whole life he's been accused of being Voldemort's son, a monster, so he's held back. But if he were confident, the "Scorpion King" from a family of winners, he could score at Quidditch and get the girls. However, this road not taken is one of selfishness, one where he not only would participate in genocide but set himself above his peers and intimidate them into doing his homework. Scorpius definitively rejects the world where he's a king, noting, "The world changes and we change with it. I am better off in this world. But the world is not better. And I don't want that."[36]

At the same time, he's disturbed by his dark world father's cruelty. This, he suspects, has always been part of Draco. "The 'Mudblood' death camps, the torture, the burning alive of those who oppose him. How much of that is you?" he demands.[37] His image of his father shatters as he realizes Draco doesn't resist evil in the dark world but embraces it, and has made himself Head of Magical Law Enforcement. When Draco pins him to the table he's truly frightened.

The questing young hero often finds his father is a force for evil (famously in *Star Wars*, though this also occurs in other tales). This signals that he must cut ties with his childhood hero and make his own path. Here, Snape is the one to act as mentor, advising Scorpius on how to fix the past and insisting on traveling with him. He also introduces Scorpius to dark world Hermione and Ron, rebels on the run. Outside and surrounded by Dementors, Snape tells Scorpius how to resist them and persuades him to think of his love for his friend. Though they're both on the edge of death, Snape manages to pass on the lesson he learned from loving Lily. At last, Snape sacrifices himself to save Scorpius, and also provides a Patronus to guide him. "Thank you for being my light in the darkness" is all Scorpius can say.[38]

When he returns to his own world, he's contrite but also much braver. "Ever since being in the scariest place imaginable I'm pretty much good with fear," he asserts.[39] Later, he even asks out Rose Granger-Weasley, and she calls him Scorpion King. As he considers Quidditch tryouts, he prepares to become the man he once only imagined. Still, Scorpius sees himself as the weak, unloved shadow, compared with the mighty Scorpion King. "I discovered another Scorpius, you know? Entitled, angry, mean—people were frightened of me. It feels like we were all tested and we all—failed."[40]

Granted, there are elements of the antihero's story here. Through their incompetent and arrogant bumbling, as McGonagall observes, the boys ensure Hermione and Ron's children never existed and then kill off Harry Potter and thousands of wizards and Muggles, ushering in an age of true darkness. They fix their mistakes, but this is a story of world-shaking hubris, brought low. Further, heroic Harry never trusted the villains in his own story – not Voldemort/Quirrell, not his many devotees, and not even borderline characters Snape, Draco, and Slughorn. Like Ginny did with Tom Riddle's diary, Albus trusts Delphi and hands her the key to all of existence.

Delphi is his inspiration, bringing him the quest, then offering him kisses on his cheeks before they embark, making him blush. However, she turns out to be a femme fatale. Her apparent kindness conceals a dark agenda. This too is typical of the journey.

> Shapeshifting lovers are common figures in myth, from swan maidens to frog princes. "We have all experienced relationships in which our partner is fickle, two-faced, bewilderingly changeable," Vogler explains (65). The hero's or heroine's lover is incomprehensible, shifting moods and desires faster than the protagonist can comprehend. The task is to penetrate these shapes and barriers, to find the true self within. Only then can a pair fully commit.[41]

The delphinium flower, Delphi's namesake, relates to the throat chakra, which is associated with self-expression and communication. Imbalances are caused by being unfaithful to oneself or others, not being heard, or not being able to express who one is, feeling afraid to talk about things, or having a lack of honesty. None of these are truly Delphi's problem, but all are issues Albus and Scorpius deal with. Thus she's a catalyst to help them communicate with their fathers.

Another catalyst is Slytherin House itself. Rowling adds on the subject of colors:

> The four Hogwarts houses have a loose association with the four elements, and their colours were chosen accordingly. Gryffindor (red and gold) is connected to fire; Slytherin (green and silver) to water; Hufflepuff (yellow and black, representing wheat and soil) to earth; and Ravenclaw (blue and bronze; sky and eagle feathers) to air. (Rowling, "Colours")

Harry embarked on a journey of courage and warfare, mastering his love and passionate anger, dueling with his enemies. By contrast, the Slytherins teach care and discipline, thought before action. This is a lesson heedless Albus must learn. Albus tells Harry, "Green is a soothing color, isn't it? I mean, the Gryffindor rooms are all well and good but the trouble with red is – it is said to send you a little mad— not that I'm casting aspersions" (202). Like him, Scorpius joins Slytherin, and there manages to find some peace.

Together the boys resolve to destroy the time-turner, but this plunges them into a new level of betrayal as Delphi turns on them both, taking them prisoner and forcing them back to the third Triwizarding challenge. There, she plans to humiliate Cedric and turn him into a Death Eater once more. Bindings carry the extra symbolism of being "bound to the world," emphasizing the boys' responsibility to save their universe.[42] This represents a new test for both boys. As she taunts Albus. "What on earth do you think you can do? A worldwide disappointment? A sore on your family name? A spare? You want to stop me hurting your only friend? Then do what you're told."[43]

It's no coincidence they're in the labyrinth, symbolizing the boys' confusion. A maze is a place of "initiation into sanctity, immortality, and absolute reality," preparing the heroes for the ultimate battle to come, in *Goblet of Fire* and here.[44] A labyrinth symbolizes being lost from higher thought, and needing to find one's way out, to reach the spirit. In the boys' case, they have both started doubting themselves and their rightness of purpose, even before Delphi derides them. This labyrinth endangers their entire universe, if Delphi can use it to turn the world evil again. However, since Delphi's name references the Oracle, this is her place of power – the tangle of confusion and despair teaming with monsters.

This is their moment of trial. "You wanted a test, Albus, this is it and we're going to pass it," Scorpio tells him determinedly. They agree to die to stop her. Campbell explains that in classic tales, "the hero is swallowed and taken into the abyss to be later resurrected – a variant of the death-and-resurrection theme."[45] This moment of facing death or actually dying (as Harry does in each book) represents crossing a threshold and accepting adult maturity.

Of course, Cedric intervenes, the shining hero who's like both boys' shadows – the perfect paragon they never were. They face him and offer him the one thing they'd like for themselves – a little message of love from their fathers. The universal truth here is that the good hero, representing the perfect ideal of love and heroism, must be sacrificed. All the boys have is their own messy families, ones with whom they will need to go back and live. Thus with their freedom, they find a new mission – stopping Delphi and allowing Cedric to die.

"No one can go through an experience at the edge of death without being changed in some way," warns Vogler.[46] Even for ordinary humans, after a near-death experience, "colors seem sharper, family and friends are more important, and time is more precious. The nearness of death makes life more real."[47]

Back in the normal world, waiting for Delphi to change their existence forever, the adults make their peace. All stand together before the Ministry and admit their hubris and flaws – even Draco. Dumbledore too comes to Harry and apologizes for the past, acknowledging that he should have offered his protégé love. Finally, Draco and Harry talk and Draco bares his soul – Scorpius's birth, his wife's death and his own secret hoarding of a time-turner. Significantly, Harry says, "Love blinds. We have both tried to give our sons, not what they needed, but what we needed. We've been so busy trying to rewrite our own pasts, we've blighted their present."[48]

Draco too comes to a catharsis. "It is exceptionally lonely, being Draco Malfoy," explains the adult left a widower and then an empty nester.[49] He has no friends, no siblings or cousins (except, apparently, Delphi herself). By contrast, the famous trio are seen visiting each other, their children becoming close, and Ginny elevated to part of the team. It must seem on some level as if they're taking his only child from him. Nonetheless, through the story, Draco comes to accept his son's choices and, more to the point, face the choices he once made himself. As the Ministry browbeats Hermione, he joins her on the platform where she addresses the crowd. "Hermione and Harry have done nothing wrong but try and protect us all. If they're guilty, then I am too," he announces.[50]

With his son lost, Harry finally confides his survivors' guilt in Ginny. "The Boy Who Lived. How many people have to die for the Boy who Lived?"[51] They start communicating better, with their despair broken up by a message from Albus, sent only because he knows his father so well, and knows where he will go on All Hallow's Eve.

After, Albus and Scorpius call for help from the past, with Albus asserting, "We get a message to my dad, he'll find a way to get back here. Even if he has to build a time-turner himself."[52] They send it through his baby blanket, which represents the comfort and security of a grown-up protecting a child. This imagery continues – when the cavalry comes, Albus curls up on a pew and goes to sleep in St. Jerome's church in the Sanctuary. Ginny, watching over her son, tells Harry that sometimes kids don't need the big gestures but the kindness of someone playing exploding snap with them. Thus Harry is reminded of the simplicity and purity of supportive love.

Traveling back to Godric's Hollow the night James and Lily were killed, Ron and Hermione make their own peace with Draco. Draco responds with "I'm being bossed around by Hermione Granger... And I'm mildly enjoying it."[53] Ron and Hermione also make peace with each other, reaffirming their commitment as they decide to renew their vows. Now reunited, the famous trio have no hesitation in including Draco in taking down Delphi. However, there is a further descent required.

To stop her, Harry must face his greatest demon – the fact that he could have been Voldemort, that he is on some level just as big a destroyer. "I – I know what it is to feel – like him. I know what it is to *be* him. It has to be me."[54] To face this, he transfigures into Voldemort, speaks Parseltongue, channels the monster's memories. In so doing, he turns his nightmares into a weapon against the enemy, using them instead of being used by them. After, he tells Albus, "The part of me that was Voldemort died a long time ago, but it wasn't enough to be physically rid of him – I had to be mentally rid of him. And that – is a lot to learn for a forty-year-old man."[55]

He has Delphi fooled until Harry's disguise cracks and she attacks. Here, tiny Albus is needed to clamber through the crawlspace and let their family in so they can all defeat Voldemort together. He is the gentler part of Harry, childish and small but still heroic and resourceful. "I've never fought alone, you see. And I never will," Harry says triumphantly as he takes Delphi down.[56] Ginny and Albus stand with him as they watch Voldemort kill Harry's parents and let the natural cycle continue.

On their quest through Slytherin House, learning from the Parseltongue Delphi, Albus and Scorpius actually discover the lesson of the snake – that the life cycle must continue without hindrance, that people can die, like the snake shedding its skin, but new growth and birth will always follow. "The serpent represents immortal energy and consciousness engaged in the field of time, constantly throwing off death and being born again."[57] Now they have the wisdom to allow life and death to take their course without interfering again.

---

[1] Theo Bosanquet, "Review: Harry Potter and the Cursed Child Works Serious Magic on the West End Stage," *Time.Com* (July 26, 2016): 1. Business Source Elite, EBSCOhost.

[2] Helen Lewis, "Pottering About." *New Statesman* 145, no. 5325 (July 29, 2016): 87. MasterFILE Premier, EBSCOhost.

[3] Bosanquet.

[4] Emily E. Roach, "Epilogue? What Epilogue? Re-Visioning the Canon with Fanon" in *Harry Potter, Still Recruiting: An Inner Look at Harry Potter Fandom*, ed. Valerie Estelle Frankel (USA: Zossima Press, 2012), 70.

[5] J.E. Cirlot, *A Dictionary of Symbols* (New York: Routledge, 1971), 280.

[6] Joseph Campbell, *The Hero with a Thousand Faces* (Princeton: Princeton University Press, 1973), 146.

[7] J.K. Rowling, Jack Thorne, and John Tiffany, *Harry Potter and the Cursed Child* (Crawfordsville, IN: Pottermore, 2016), 142.

[8] Leila Sales, "The Ol' Dead Dad Syndrome," *Publishers Weekly*, 20 Sept 2010. http://www.publishersweekly.com/pw/by-topic/columns-and-blogs/soapbox/article/44502-the-ol-dead-dad-syndrome.html.

[9] Joseph Campbell with Bill Moyers, *The Power of Myth*, Betty Sue Flowers, ed. (New York: Doubleday, 1988), 138.

[10] Ibid., 142.

[11] Christopher Vogler, *The Writer's Journey* (USA: Michael Wiese Productions, 1998), 15.

[12] Rowling, *Cursed Child* 53.

[13] Ibid., 53.

[14] Farah Mendlesohn, *Rhetorics of Fantasy* (USA: Wesleyan, 2008), xix.

[15] Rowling, *Cursed Child* 153.

[16] Lewis.

[17] Ibid.

[18] Rowling, *Cursed Child* 257.

[19] Ibid., 32.

[20] "J.K. Rowling Goes Beyond the Epilogue," *Beyond Hogwarts*, 2007, http://www.beyondhogwarts.com/harry-potter/articles/jk-rowling-goes-beyond-the-epilogue.html.

[21] Roach 63.

[22] "J.K. Rowling Goes Beyond the Epilogue."

[23] Skeeter, Rita. "Dumbledore's Army Reunites at Quidditch World Cup Final." *Pottermore,* 8 July 2014.

[24] Bosanquet.

[25] Ibid.

[26] Rowling, *Cursed Child* 136.

[27] J.K. Rowling, "Draco Malfoy," *Pottermore.* https://www.reddit.com/r/PottermoreWritings/comments/3l9s25/draco_malfoy_part_2_of_2.

[28] Ibid.

[29] J.K. Rowling, "J.K. Rowling and the Live Chat," *Bloomsbury.com, Accio Quote!* 30 July 2007. http://www.accio-quote.org/articles/2007/0730-bloomsbury-chat.html.

[30] Bosanquet.

[31] Lewis.

[32] Joseph Campbell, *The Hero with a Thousand Faces* (Princeton: Princeton University Press, 1973), 8

[33] Clarissa Pinkola Estés, *Women Who Run with the Wolves* (New York: Ballantine, 1992), 85.

[34] Rowling, *Cursed Child* 141.

[35] Ibid., 144.

[36] Ibid., 193.

[37] Ibid., 172.

[38] Ibid., 195.

[39] Ibid., 210.

[40] Ibid., 211.

[41] Valerie Estelle Frankel, *Buffy and the Heroine's Journey* (Jefferson, NC: McFarland and Co, 2012), 26.

[42] Cirlot 191.

[43] Rowling, *Cursed Child* 229.

[44] Cirlot 175.

[45] Campbell 146.

[46] Vogler 30.

[47] Ibid., 164.

[48] Rowling, *Cursed Child* 261.

[49] Ibid., 261.

[50] Ibid., 249.

[51] Ibid., 269.

[52] Ibid., 264.

[53] Ibid., 286.

[54] Rowling, *Cursed Child* 282.

[55] Ibid., 305.

[56] Ibid., 291.

[57] Joseph Campbell with Bill Moyers, *The Power of Myth*, ed. Betty Sue Flowers (New York: Doubleday, 1988), 45.

CHAPTER 4: *CURSED CHILD* AND THE ANTIHEROINE'S JOURNEY

Molly Weasley's battle with Bellatrix is delightful because it's a moment, not only of feminist empowerment, but of the heroine's journey, seen in many fantasy series but only touched on in this one.

> The true goal of the heroine is to become this archetypal, all-powerful mother. Thus, many heroines set out on rescue missions in order to restore their shattered families: a shy princess knits coats of nettles to save her six brothers from a lifetime as swans, Psyche quests for her vanished lover. Demeter forces herself into the realm of the dead to reclaim her daughter, while Isis scours the world for her husband's broken body. Little Gerda in Hans Christian Andersen's tale quests all the way to Finland to rescue her playmate from the unfeeling Snow Queen. This goal does not indicate by any means that the girls are trying to "stay at home" or "play house." Though they redeem beloved family members or potential husbands, these heroines work as hard as any fairytale hero. And they do it without swords.[1]

Molly Weasley as rescuing mother fits the archetype perfectly. Other nuances of the heroine's (and hero's) journey involve facing one's dark side and coming to understand it. In book seven, Hermione learns this lesson as she disguises herself as Bellatrix, even carrying her wand, and channels the brutal murderous side she's never explored deep within herself. As she barks orders and browbeats bank tellers, the Muggle-born teen is discovering what it means to be a respected, even terrifying adult. Sadly, the book deprives readers of seeing her destroy the Horcruxed Hufflepuff cup and facing her deepest fears, as Ron does in the forest.

Likewise, Ginny is taken over by the force of evil and nearly dies, but Harry her white knight contributes most of the heroism while she lies unconscious in the Chamber of Secrets. Thus while Harry (and other characters like Snape, Neville, and Draco) undergo the classic hero's journey, the heroine's journey gets only a quick brush. *Cursed Child* offers more, however, as Hermione and Ginny travel across time and space to rescue the next generation and also consider their actions as parents.

In this dramatic new medium, Hermione, Minister for Magic, must accept the new conflict upon them, as Harry dreams of Voldemort once again. The ruler represents the well-being of the land, creating an era of restoration, justice, and peace.[2] In the face of this, Hermione declares herself a strong Minister of Magic and emphasizes that if evil is coming, she won't hide from it like Fudge once did.[3] However, behind this determination is a lack of trust that nearly shatters the world forever. Her paranoia in keeping a forbidden Time-Turner and her foolishness in keeping it locked behind riddles in her bookshelf allows the events of the novel to take place. As McGonagall yells at her, "Your children didn't exist!" McGonagall is the mentor here, the last one who lived through Voldemort's first rise to power. "You're all so young. You have no idea how dark the wizarding wars got," she tells both generations at once.[4] She thus reminds them all to preserve the world for which so many gave their lives.

Hermione is suffering from a midlife crisis of a sort, one that has her eating toffees in childish fashion. She explains, "What can I say? My parents were dentists, I was bound to rebel at some point. Forty is leaving it a little late, but…"[5] She has little outlet in her life, with the Ministry demanding all of her time, so much that she leaves Ron to bring up the children. She tells Harry, "You know, Ron says he thinks I see more of my secretary, Ethel, than him."[6]

Near the story's end, Hermione faces the Ministry and confesses her foolhardiness, only to have her friends and family join her on the platform, all supporting her. When Ron, Ginny, Harry, and even Draco gather around her, she feels affirmed in her choices. After this, she doesn't hesitate to travel back in time to stop Voldemort and fix her mistake, setting the world right once more.

Hermione in *Cursed Child* doesn't actually meet the potential shadows of herself, but she becomes them, displaying these latent, undeveloped selves for the audience. First, Albus finds himself in an uptight, well-behaved world, where he became a Gryffindor as he was expected to and agrees to stop seeing Scorpius. Ron married the nice girl Padma rather than argumentative and tempestuous Hermione. This Hermione never became a wife or mother and, perhaps consequently, never became Minister of Magic. These story components suggest her world-saving strength is tied to her family. (The book does not explore how the Trio took down Voldemort differently with Ron dating Padma and Hermione disconnected from Ron. It appears events proceeded about the same, however.)

This world's Hermione, now a professor, is startlingly mean, docking point after point from Gryffindor, her old house, for "stupidity." The single life seems to have left Hermione angry and bitter. As she lectures the boys, she says, "If you can conjure a Patronus, you can protect yourself against the world. Which, in some of our cases, seems like a necessity sooner rather than later."[7] This comment suggests she's a master of the Patronus and can thus protect herself against all the world's emotions. In the hallway with Ron, he babbles, but, closed off as she is here, she barely allows a word to escape.

The dark world's Hermione is another shadow, not only for ignoring love. While the normal world's Hermione has become the establishment as Minister of Magic, she's left the teen rebel far behind, to the point where, like Harry, she's forgotten what it was like to be Albus and Severus. The play allows her to channel the lost freedom fighter once more. This Hermione, in hiding, boldly leaves her sanctuary to aid Scorpius with rewriting the Triwizarding Tournament to restore the timeline.

She saves the world from Voldemort and restores her reality quietly and elegantly, simply by blocking the boys' disruptive spells with shield charms. The shield is an ancient feminine symbol – steady, immoveable protection rather than flashy warfare. Then when the Dementors come, she gives herself up to them to save Scorpius, Ron, and Severus in a blinding act of bravery. "This is still Voldemort's world. And I am done with it," she declares.[8] When the monsters come, she doesn't even cast a Patronus, deciding, "Let's keep them here and give the boy the best chance we can."[9] Ron perishes beside her, sacrificing his life in the same heroism, and to die with the woman he loves. Nonetheless, their romance is even more tragic because they never fell in love and had a war wedding like Bill and Fleur or James and Lily. Instead, it seems without Harry they went through life as fellow warriors against Voldemort, but never truly embraced their mutual feelings. Normal world Hermione only hears about these other realities secondhand, but they do provoke a small change. After learning what her life might have been, she's eager to marry Ron all over again, reaffirming their commitment to each other.

Ginny and Hermione are foils through the seven books, ignored then desired love interests of the lead boys, and often sharing a room as the only girls at the World Cup or in the Order of the Phoenix. They're opposites in many ways, with Ginny as Quidditch player while Hermione is the intellectual and walking library of facts. Hermione goes straight into politics, extending her campaign for the House-Elves into working at the Department for the Regulation and Control of Magical Creatures and then on to other projects. As Rowling explains after the series concludes, "After a few years as a celebrated player for the Holyhead Harpies, Ginny retired to have her family and to become the Senior Quidditch correspondent at the Daily Prophet!"[10]

In *Cursed Child*, quiet, unassuming Ginny takes the mom role, running interference between Harry and Albus. Still, she protects her son during Harry's conflict with him, forcing Harry to see how stubborn he's been and apologize when he's wrong. She's his emotional side, telling him with great perception, "Harry, you have one of the greatest hearts of any wizard who ever lived, and I do not believe your heart told you to do this."[11]

At story's end, she travels back to Godric's Hollow to save her son, adding herself to the heroic trio. Questing to the tyrant's place of power is common for the heroine, emphasizing the restrictions of her male-centric world.

> Journeying here represents the heroine leaving the place of her feminine power to ascend to the prince's tower or mountain, where she faces her greatest trial far from her unconscious realm of magic. The Little Mermaid leaves the ocean and Demeter leaves her fields as both journey into the man's world—human civilization....When she journeys into the enemy's sphere, she's alone and vulnerable, cut off from her strongest supports.[12]

On their journey to the past, Ginny sits protectively over her sleeping son and tells Harry with great insight that kids just want support, instead of giant sacrifices and distant gestures. She explains:

> You know, after I'd opened the Chamber of Secrets – after Voldemort had bewitched me with that terrible diary and I'd almost destroyed everything…After I came out of hospital – everyone ignored me, shut me out – other than, that is, the boy who had everything – who came across the Gryffindor common room and challenged me to a game of Exploding Snap. People think they know all there is to know about you, but the best bits of you are – have always been – heroic in really quiet ways. My point is – after this is over, just remember if you could that sometimes people – but particularly children – just want someone to play Exploding Snap with.[13]

"This too is a powerful metaphor for the idea of saving the childSelf, the soul-self, from being lost again in the unconscious, forgetting who we are and what our work is," Estés explains of the child the heroine rescues and defends.[14] This is the tenuous inner voice from within, her own inner child, which hasn't been nurtured much during her time as a grown up, holding her family together.

> The heroine's goal is to become a complete mother, resplendent with power. If her family is shattered, by either grief or remarriage, she cannot become whole without assembling the pieces. …Sometimes claiming one's reward is a dramatic moment – seizing Tam Lin off his horse, or claiming the prince in marriage. Other times, it is the quieter love and acceptance which makes one a wife or mother in more than name. (Frankel, *From Girl to Goddess* 145)

When Harry transfigures into Voldemort Ginny gets to face "The man I love shrouded in the man I hate" and admits her past trauma at Voldemort's hands.[15] Ginny faces her demons as she and Albus commiserate about being taken in by evil. "That's what they're good at, Albus, catching innocents in their web," she says.[16] Thus she confronts and accepts her past, growing wiser through the journey.

Finally, there is the new character Delphini, named for the Oracle at Delphi, the center of the world and a womb symbol. The Oracle of Delphi was also called the Pythia, the serpent goddess. In the ancient world, people would journey there to learn their dark fates. Like Voldemort, she has a secret nickname – the Augurey, an oracle of darkness. In the dark world, Umbridge describes sending "dispatches to the Auguery" and calls Scorpio "highly valued" by her.[17]

Derived from the Greek word "delphis" (dolphin), the name also references the delphinium or larkspur, a bluebell-like flower. The delphinium is a symbol of infinite possibility, something Delphi embraces as she changes the past, or tries. Fascinatingly, it's believed that the most ancient use of delphinium flowers was for driving away scorpions…or Scorpius.

It's also the birth flower of July. While the new children's birthdays are unknown, July and warmth have always been linked with Harry, while Voldemort was born in December. Thus Delphi mirrors Harry here, emphasizing how she's questing for the same family and acceptance he's always sought.

Delphi's hair is blue and silver. Both are feminine colors, blue seen in the Virgin's cloak and the serenity of sea and sky. Her namesake, the delphinium flower, is likewise blue. Silver is the color of the ghostly, mystical side of the world. It represents the Otherworld: feminine moon and water magic.[18] Artemis' bow, the divine amulets of the Egyptians, and the sixth chakra, often called the "third-eye" of special perception, were all particularly feminine talismans. Thus both colors connect her with meditation, the occult, and the spiritual. However, all is twisted.

She's on an antihero's journey to bring back evil…also an antihero's journey because she's determined to prop up the long-dead Voldemort as ruler. She's dredging up the traditional male hierarchy rather than becoming a leader in her own right.

Many were shocked by Bellatrix's infidelity, though Rowling commented in 2007, "She took a pureblood husband, because that was what was expected of her, but her true love was always Voldemort."[19] Voldemort wasn't the sort to love anyone, but he could have chosen to have a child with Bellatrix to become who the Auguery is in the dark universe – his most loyal lieutenant and valued servant.

Like Harry Potter and Tom Riddle, Delphi grows up an unloved orphan struggling for a place to belong. Her guardian, Euphemia Rowle, was cruel and uncaring. "She only took me in for the gold!" Euphemia, meaning well-spoken, is an old-fashioned name, suggesting an emphasis on appearance rather than real love and warmth. Rowle is apparently a great Death Eater family.

Delphi begins her quest with the revelation of her parentage. "It was Rodolphus Lestrange, Bellatrix's loyal husband, who on return from Azkaban told me who I was and revealed the prophecy he thought I was destined to fulfill."[20] This prophecy offers a single chance to save her father from death: "When spares are spared when time is turned, when unseen children murder their fathers: Then will the Dark Lord return."[21] This prophecy becomes her mission, as often happens once the fateful words are pronounced.

She soon gets an augurey tattoo. "They're sinister-looking black birds that cry when rain's coming. Wizards used to believe that the Augurey's cry foretold death. When I was growing up my guardian kept one in a cage," she explains.[22] Of course, in ancient myth, "birds could be seen as messengers from the supernatural world and as mediators between god and humans."[23] As early as *Fantastic Beasts,* Dumbledore describes wizards trying to "interpret the mournful cries of the Augurey."[24] The greenish-black bird resembles a vulture, though it is known as the "Irish Phoenix."[25] In *Fantastic Beasts and Where to Find Them,* it's classified as harmless and thus is more mystical than terrible.

Ravens and crows, symbolically similar, often brought grim omens of the future, and might be Celtic war goddesses in disguise. "The Morrigan and the Badbh, could change at whim from human to raven form, squawking dreadful omens and terrifying armies by their presence."[26] "Ravens and crows, with their black plumage and their habit of feeding off dead things, were clearly seen as messengers from the Otherworld."[27] They are vicious carnivores, known for preying on the dead. "Those birds are cruel – hence the collective term 'an unkindness of ravens' – and scavenge on dead flesh, so they symbolize both the pitilessness and the carnage of war."[28]

> It appears to armies, reminding them that in war no one wins except death itself. The raven is an oracle, but again, most of its portents are negative and fear-inducing. The blackness, the cruel, tearing beak, glittering, pitiless eyes, and its predilection for dead flesh endowed the raven with this dark, sinister imagery.[29]

Odin used ravens as his messengers, and they were also thought be able to fly between the worlds of the living and the dead. Thus Delphi becomes a foretelling of death and warning for the Wizarding World. Auguries appear one other place in the Harry Potter mythos – in selecting Hogwarts students. As Pottermore explains:

> In a small locked tower, never visited by any student at Hogwarts, sits an ancient book that has not been touched by human hands since the four founders placed it there on completion of the castle. Beside the book, which is bound in peeling black dragon-hide, stands a small silver inkpot and from this protrudes a long, faded quill. These are the Quill of Acceptance and the Book of Admittance and they constitute the only process by which students are selected for Hogwarts School of Witchcraft and Wizardry.
>   At the precise moment that a child first exhibits signs of magic, the Quill, which is believed to have been taken from an Augurey, floats up out of its inkpot and attempts to inscribe the name of that child upon the pages of the Book (Augurey feathers are known to repel ink and the inkpot is empty; nobody has ever managed to analyse precisely what the silvery fluid flowing from the enchanted Quill is). [30]

Thus the birds also serve the forces of goodness (or at least ambiguity), sorting the magicians from the Muggles. There's much mystery surrounding the book and quill, as no one knows their precise criteria, but all are bound by it nonetheless.

Meanwhile, Delphi treasures her ominous tattoo. "It reminds me that the future is mine to make."[31] This echoes Nazi songs like "Tomorrow Belongs to Me," much as Voldemort's regime had many Nazi parallels.

Delphi preys on the elderly Amos Diggory, insinuating herself into his life as caretaker. This traditional feminine role is subverted by her evil agenda, provoking an increasingly creepy juxtaposition. She's a murderer of the innocent but also an exploiter of the elderly. In the room at St Oswalds, the adults discover her secret. St. Oswald is an interesting namesake, since it was Oswald's mission to add to the warlike glory of his father Ethelfrid and build up a great kingdom. Oswald had a greater dominion than any of his ancestors, and "he brought under his sway all the nations and provinces of Britain, which are divided into four languages, namely the Britons, the Picts, the Scots, and the English."[32] This is Delphi's great dream for herself and her father's empire – with symbolic parallels for the four Hogwarts houses.

Her talisman hidden in the room is an oil lamp, another classically feminine symbol that offers a guiding light in the darkness. It's "a symbol of intelligence and the spirit."[33] As her secret talisman, it parallels Voldemort's many Horcruxes, as well as the Chamber of Secrets that opens at his Parseltongue password. The Vestal Virgins also kept lamps burning constantly as a sign of faith, much as Delphi has in Voldemort. "The lamps of the ancients were shaped according to their function – profane, religious, or funeral—and to suit the nature of the god to whom they were dedicated."[34] With hers, Delphi maintains her worship of the darkness and of her father.

When they unscrew it, it whispers, "Welcome, Auguery" in Parseltongue.[35] Snakes are actually a feminine symbol too. Snakes "possessed a complex symbolism in the Romano-Celtic world, evoking images of water, fertility, death, and regeneration."[36]

> The association between snakes and renewal or healing came about because of their habit of sloughing their skin several times a year, apparently being reborn. The chthonic or death symbolism is self-evident: snakes are carnivorous and their method of poisoning their victims well-known. In addition, they are generally earthbound and can emerge from narrow crevices, seemingly from deep below the earth.[37]

> As Merlin Stone notes in her groundbreaking *When God Was a Woman,* "Despite the insistent, perhaps hopeful, assumption that the serpent must have been regarded as a phallic symbol, it appears to have been primarily revered as a female in the Near and Middle East and generally linked to wisdom and prophetic counsel." Sumerians worshipped the great Mother Serpent of Heaven, and the snake was found coiled around many Great Goddesses such as Asherah, Ishtar, Athena, and Hathor. The Minoan snake goddess likewise dominated Crete, leaving behind figures of woman and snake entwined. The snake tempted Eve, offered prophecies, allowed Cleopatra's triumph…The snake reflected the Great Goddess, changing from young to old and then cycling back to young as the world renewed in the spring. It contained the insight only known to priestesses of the time, and it shed its skin, like a woman birthing a new organism from itself.[38]

Only when the boys end their time-travel experiments and try to smash the time-turner does Delphi reveal who she truly is. She ties them both instantly in "luminous cords."[39] In ancient myth, cords bound the earth and heavens together and connected people's minds to reason. Ropes thus symbolize interconnection and bonds between body and spirit. They, like the umbilical cord, are a symbol of the divine mother. In Egypt, cords represented matriarchal law, in service to Maat, goddess of justice. In Greece, "Ariadne's thread leading Theseus through the Labyrinth (into the darkness and out again) represented the rebirth journey," a journey Delphi will force the boys to undergo.[40]

"Children, particularly male children, are so naturally pliant aren't they," Delphi smirks.[41] At once, she breaks each of their wands in a castration symbol. The magical sword is a masculine hero symbol, divinely endowed as a sacred trust. "Often the breaking or loss of the sword signaled the loss of royal authority or of heroic mana, and the hero's consequent death."[42]

She's a destroyer of the innocent, focusing on the heroic Cedric. She soon realizes the two boys are most vulnerable if she threatens and tortures their friends. She kills Craig Bowker Jr., emphasizing she's perfectly willing to murder students. He, like Cedric, was simply in the wrong place. Further, rewriting the past is the ultimate destruction of the lifecycle.

She describes herself: "I am the new past. I am the new future. I am the answer this world has been looking for."[43] As alpha and omega, she's a self-contained source. Nonetheless, she longs for connection. The classic heroine's journey involves rescuing family. This is Delphi's mission as she seeks her lost father. Her words fill the auditorium: "I will rebirth the Dark. I will bring my father back."[44] Of course, she also shares her father's agenda as villainess, telling the boys, "I want a return to pure and strong magic. I want to rebirth the dark."[45]

Nonetheless, following her father's mission instead of her own is a source of weakness. She even plans to be her father's lieutenant rather than a Dark Lord in her own right. "Voldemort will return and the Augurey will sit at his side," she insists.[46] Delphi also doesn't act directly, forcing the boys to act for her. She insists Albus must be the one to humiliate Cedric – the prophecy says Albus must restore her father, so she threatens Scorpius to make him comply. She adds, "I realized your weakness was the same as your father's: friendship."[47] Murdock notes that the heroine's journey "often includes a rejection of the feminine as defined as passive, manipulative, or non-productive."[48] Delphi, however, is all of these as she schemes in the background and then forces the boys to do her dirty work. Once more, she's giving in to the worst stereotypes of her gender.

As the heroes discover in Godric's Hollow, she's questing to find the father she never knew, in the hopes he'll complete her. Delphi finally achieves her quest when she comes to Voldemort and tells him, "I have devoted my life to being a child you could be proud of."[49] She abases herself, adding, "I am the Augurey to your Dark Lord, and I am ready to give all that I have to serve you."[50]

However, this perfect father doesn't exist, as revealed by the fact that when she meets him, he's actually her enemy, Harry Potter. He confronts her with the brutal truth: "You can't remake your life. You'll always be an orphan. That never leaves you."[51]

Harry and Delphi duel, her alone and him with his friends. "I've never fought alone, you see. And I never will," Harry says.[52] Like Voldemort, Delphi has never had friends or loved ones.

Crushed, she pleads to see her father just once or to have her memory wiped so she needn't suffer through the pain she's feeling. The heroine's journey, like the hero's, involves learning from loss and defeat. But angry, miserable Dephini rejects the chance to understand what Harry and his friends want to teach her. Together, the adults defeat the evil child and consign her to Azkaban beside her mother, the other murderer of the innocent. Delphi's journey is finished, and she has lost.

---

[1] Valerie Estelle Frankel, *From Girl to Goddess* (Jefferson, NC: McFarland and Co, 2010), 4.

[2] Farah Mendlesohn, *Rhetorics of Fantasy* (USA: Wesleyan, 2008), 3.

[3] J.K. Rowling, Jack Thorne, and John Tiffany, *Harry Potter and the Cursed Child* (Crawfordsville, IN: Pottermore, 2016), 67.

[4] Ibid., 201.

[5] Ibid., 31.

[6] Ibid., 32.

[7] Rowling, *Cursed Child* 126.

[8] Ibid., 191.

[9] Ibid., 192.

[10] J.K. Rowling, "J.K. Rowling and the Live Chat," *Bloomsbury.com, Accio Quote!* 30 July 2007. http://www.accio-quote.org/articles/2007/0730-bloomsbury-chat.html.

[11] Rowling, *Cursed Child* 128.

[12] Valerie Estelle Frankel, *Buffy and the Heroine's Journey* (Jefferson, NC: McFarland and Co, 2012), 60.

[13] Rowling, *Cursed Child* 277.

[14] Clarissa Pinkola Estés, *Women Who Run with the Wolves* (New York: Ballantine, 1992), 449-450.

[15] Rowling, *Cursed Child* 285.

[16] Ibid., 285.

[17] Ibid., 167.

[18] Barbara G. Walker, *The Woman's Dictionary of Symbols and Sacred Objects* (San Francisco:

Harper, 1988), 522.

[19] Rowling, "J.K. Rowling and the Live Chat."

[20] Rowling, *Cursed Child* 287.

[21] Ibid., 230.

[22] Ibid., 219.

[23] Miranda Green, *Animals in Celtic Life and Myth* (USA: Routledge, 1992), 181.

[24] Newt Scamander, *Fantastic Beasts and Where to Find Them* (New York: Scholastic, 2001), xiii

[25] Ibid., 5.

[26] Green 88.

[27] Ibid., 126.

[28] Ibid., 88.

[29] Green 181.

[30] J.K. Rowling, "The Quill of Acceptance and The Book of Admittance," *Pottermore*, 2015. https://www.reddit.com/r/PottermoreWritings/comments/3lxcol/the_quill_of_acceptance_and_the_book_of_admittance.

[31] Rowling, *Cursed Child* 219.

[32] The Venerable Bede. *New Advent Catholic Encyclopedia* (III, 6). http://www.newadvent.org/cathen/02384a.htm.

[33] J.E. Cirlot, *A Dictionary of Symbols* (New York: Routledge, 1971), 176.

[34] Ibid., 176.

[35] Rowling, *Cursed Child* 241.

[36] Green 182

[37] Green 182

[38] Frankel, *From Girl to Goddess* 69-70.

[39] Ibid., 220.

[40] Walker 130.

[41] Rowling, *Cursed Child* 220.

[42] Walker 31.

[43] Rowling, *Cursed Child* 220-221.

[44] Ibid., 242.

[45] Ibid., 227.

[46] Ibid., 230.

[47] Ibid., 230.

[48] Maureen Murdock, *The Heroine's Journey* (Boston: Shambhala, 1990), 6.

[49] Rowling, *Cursed Child* 287.
[50] Ibid., 287.
[51] Ibid., 292.
[52] Ibid., 291.

PART II: GREEK, BRITISH, AND WORLD MYTH

CHAPTER 5: WIZARD SCHOOLS AND THEIR FOLKLORE

Native American Controversy

"The Native American magical community and those of Europe and Africa had known about each other long before the immigration of European No-Majs in the seventeenth century."[1] The concept of these three cultures communicating as equals certainly contradicts historical attitudes, though it's a nice revision to show some enlightenment. Still, no details or other elaboration appears about this issue on *Pottermore*, leaving it vaguely reassuring but highly unlikely.

After she wrote about North American magic on *Pottermore*, complaints about cultural insensitivity barraged Rowling – always a risk when creating fantasy from living religions. "The legend of the Native American 'skin walker' – an evil witch or wizard that can transform into an animal at will – has its basis in fact. A legend grew up around the Native American Animagi, that they had sacrificed close family members to gain their powers of transformation."[2] This last line drew some annoyed criticism from fans. Scholar Adrienne Keene tweets why this is all so problematic.

> Dr. Adrienne Keene
> ✔ @NativeApprops
> It's not "your" world. It's our (real) Native world. And skin walker stories have context, roots, and reality.
> https://twitter.com/jk_rowling/sta[3]

As she continues on her blog *Native Appropriations*:

> What you do need to know is that the belief of these things (beings?) has a deep and powerful place in Navajo understandings of the world. It is connected to many other concepts and many other ceremonial understandings and lifeways. It is not just a scary story, or something to tell kids to

79

get them to behave, it's much deeper than that. My own community also has shape-shifters, but I'm not delving into that either.

What happens when Rowling pulls this in, is we as Native people are now opened up to a barrage of questions about these beliefs and traditions (take a look at my twitter mentions if you don't believe me)–but these are not things that need or should be discussed by outsiders. At all. I'm sorry if that seems "unfair," but that's how our cultures survive.[4]

The concept of Skinwalkers being retold as Animagi drew much heat. Yes, they are shapeshifters, but the legend is more complex. Even in *Twilight*, it was revealed that they *weren't* traditional werewolves out of European lore.

Most of the objections are that this is a living culture – no one is annoyed about Arthurian legend or Greek myth, but some of the legends here have religious significance. Rowling, without doing the depth of research some would have liked, dragged the legends into her world and retold them through a European context in which the wandless magic has weaknesses. "As the Native American Animagi and potion-makers demonstrated, wandless magic can attain great complexity, but Charms and Transfiguration are very difficult without one."[5] Keene continues:

This whole wandless magic thing is bugging me. So Rowling has said multiple times that it takes a lot more skill to perform magic without a wand (Dumbledore does it at several points in the books), but points out that wands are what basically *refines* magic. Wands are a European invention, so basically she's demonstrating Eurocentric superiority here–the introduction of European "technology" helps bring the Native wizards to a new level. AKA colonial narrative 101.[6]

"The Native American wizarding community was particularly gifted in animal and plant magic, its potions in particular being of a sophistication beyond much that was known in Europe."[7] This sentence is complimentary, but it too bears a trace of imperial condescension in the phrasing. Locals flock to the European-style school of Ilvermorny, but its founder Isolt Sayre isn't described as learning a single lesson from any of her neighboring tribes. She must have employed some of the locals as teachers, but this again goes unstated. Likewise, Sayre and her friends have no idea where to find magical plants. Why don't they ask the locals, if the wizards respect them as peers? Once again, not a single one of their recipes is seen enriching the culture that followed. Thus, Native Americans must learn European culture to prosper, even in this magical reimagining. Whatever ability they possessed in Rowling's fictional world appears mostly vanished by the 1920s. Genocide is barely touched on, except for a one sentence mention of the "conflict [that] developed between the immigrants and the Native American population."

Likewise, Rowling's description of the vaguely-described "Native American community" accepting and acclaiming some magic users as their "medicine men, or outstanding hunters" seems once again an example of grafting Native American culture onto a European base and interpreting it that way. Religious beliefs of many tribes are trivialized as "magic" in children's stories – a condescending and Eurocentric attitude. Rowling's post adds, "However, others were stigmatised for their beliefs, often on the basis that they were possessed by malevolent spirits."[8] Most tribes' tales really don't bear this out.

Others brought up the point that Rowling often uses the term "Native American," suggesting one massive culture uninterested in wands. Here and in Africa, that is a long list of different cultures dragged under one umbrella: "One of the largest fights in the world of representations is to recognize Native peoples and communities and cultures are diverse, complex, and vastly different from one another. There is no such thing as one 'Native American' anything. Even in a fictional wizarding world," Keene protests.[9]

> Oh @jk_rowling, there is no singular "Native American" community. Over 500 federally recognized tribes exist & you're doing us a disservice.
> — deadcool. (@nkdvs) March 8, 2016[10]

Frontier and Native American Magic

Amid this controversy came a new continent of magic, with fantastical creatures drawn from the New World rather than the old. While there's no good answer to the complex issues of appropriation and generalization, there's much to explore in Rowling's new mythology and its origins.

> Shikoba Wolfe, who was of Choctaw descent, was primarily famous for intricately carved wands containing Thunderbird tail feathers (the Thunderbird is a magical American bird closely related to the phoenix). Wolfe wands were generally held to be extremely powerful, though difficult to master. They were particularly prized by Transfigurers.[11]

Calling the mythic Thunderbird a sort of phoenix is more of the appropriation, but the creature itself is intriguing. Its legends are found from the east coast to the west. Rowling likely adapted the one from Algonquian legend, since in this cosmology, the Thunderbird controls the upper world while the underworld is controlled by the underwater panther or Great Horned Serpent. Rowling can be seen uniting these in her wizard school totems: the Horned Serpent, the Panther Wampus, the Thunderbird and the Pukwudgie.

As Rowling relates in her account of Isolt Sayre and her founding of the first American wizard school:

> The Hidebehind is a nocturnal, forest-dwelling spectre that preys on humanoid creatures. As the name suggests, it can contort itself to hide behind almost any object, concealing itself perfectly from hunters and victims alike. Its existence has been suspected by No-Majs, but they are no match for its powers. Only a witch or wizard is likely to survive an attack by a Hidebehind.[12]

Gruesome lumberjack tales of Wisconsin describe the Hide Behind (which has a habit of dodging behind trees) as a fearsome creature:

> This animal stands five feet and ten inches high and walks on its hind feet. It is of slender build and can easily hide behind a tree of medium size. Its body is completely covered with long hair so thick, that it is impossible to tell where the face is, if it has one, and it is a hopeless task to determine whether the animal is going or coming. It has a short forearm of great strength, with sharp, pointed talons able to pierce through heavy garments. Strange to relate, the meals of the hide-behind are composed of the bowels of human beings and the intestines of hell divers. After this vicious animal has partaken of a meal to his liking, he utters a demoniacal laugh. It disembowels its victim, bringing out the entrails, raising them to its head for the purpose of smelling them before eating. Should there be any scent of liquor in the

entrails, the animal will throw them back into the face of the victim and with a horrible laugh, vanish into the forest.[13]

Rowling then continues her tale of Isolt and the other local creatures she encountered:

> The Pukwudgie is also native to America: a short, grey-faced, large-eared creature distantly related to the European goblin. Fiercely independent, tricky and not over-fond of humankind (whether magical or mundane), it possesses its own powerful magic. Pukwudgies hunt with deadly, poisonous arrows and enjoy playing tricks on humans.
>
> The two creatures had met in the forest and the Hidebehind, which was of unusual size and strength, had not only succeeded in capturing the Pukwudgie, which was young and inexperienced, but had also been on the point of disembowelling him when Isolt cast the curse that made it flee. Unaware that the Pukwudgie, too, was exceptionally dangerous to humans, Isolt picked him up, carried him to her makeshift shelter and nursed him back to health.
>
> The Pukwudgie now declared himself bound to serve her until he had an opportunity to repay his debt. He considered it a great humiliation to be indebted to a young witch foolish enough to wander around in a strange country, where Pukwudgies or Hidebehinds might have attacked her at any moment, and her days were now filled with the Pukwudgie's grumbling as he trudged along at her heels.[14]

She named him William and he became her friend and guide. Meanwhile, he still avoided humankind. "It was against the beliefs of his kind to assist humankind, Isolt being the unfortunate exception because she had saved his life."[15]

According to *NativeLanguages.org*, an American mythology site:

> Pukwudgies are magical little people of the forest in Algonquian folklore, similar to European gnomes or fairies. Pukwudgie stories are told throughout the northeastern United States, southeastern Canada, and the Great Lakes region. However, their nature varies in the folklore of different tribes. In the Ojibwe and other Great Lakes tribes, the pukwudgie (or bagwajinini) is considered a mischievous but basically good-natured creature who plays tricks on people but is not dangerous. In the Abenaki and other northeast Algonquian tribes, a pukwudgie (or bokwjimen) can be dangerous, but only to people who treat him with disrespect. In the Wampanoag and other tribes of southern

> New England, pukwudgies are capricious and dangerous creatures who may play harmless tricks or even help a human neighbor, but are just as likely to steal children or commit deadly acts of sabotage.[16]

As tiny magical beings, their skills include appearing and disappearing, luring people to their deaths, and generating fire. They are fond of poison arrows, as seen in Rowling's story. Though she doesn't show it, they can transform into a walking porcupine.

> Pukwudgies are usually described as being knee-high or even smaller. Their name literally means 'person of the wilderness' and they are usually considered to be spirits of the forest. In some traditions, they have a sweet smell and are associated with flowers. Pukwudgies have magical powers which vary from tribe to tribe but may include the ability to turn invisible, confuse people or make them forget things, shapeshift into cougars or other dangerous animals, or bring harm to people by staring at them.[17]

Pukwudgies also control Tei-Pai-Wankas, which are believed to be the souls of people they have killed. Pukwudgies could mean trouble and were generally avoided. Isolt's friend William specifically insists he's helping her because of a debt...though he may have affection for the young wizard.

> Shawnee tradition has three figures that control weather. Each of these was created by the Grandmother Spirit and was so instructed not to cause harm to the Shawnee. One of these is Cyclone Person, a female face with braids of hair that cause tornadoes. She is given great respect by the Shawnee for not harming them. The Shawnee are not afraid of these storms. The second weather spirit which is actually four separate spirits is called the four winds. The four winds are often called upon to witness prayers, and they have colors associated with them. The winds were told by Grandmother Spirit to respect all women and not to stare at them. Shawnee women will pull their skirts up to their waist to embarrass the winds, thus causing clouds to retreat. The third spirit and most well-known are the Thunderbirds. The Thunderbirds cause storms when they fight with the Great Horned Serpent and other evil creatures. Lightning is caused by blinking their eyes. The Shawnee believe that the Thunderbirds guard the entrance to heaven and are

honored by Kispoko during the war dance as the patrons of war.[18]

Thunderbird is enormous enough to carry a killer whale in its talons as an eagle carries a fish. He brings the sound of thunder and in some cases lightning as well, a weapon they could hurl at their underwater adversaries. In some tribes, Thunderbirds are considered extremely sacred forces of nature, while in others, they are treated like unusually powerful members of the animal kingdom. A Potawatomi legend describes a battle between a thunderbird and a horned serpent.

Now regarding the Thunder Mountain in the western part of Marinette County: Thunder is a large bird like an Eagle, only much larger. And when this bird was created it was made to have power in order to defend us from the great serpents, who wanted to kill and eat the human race. It was also to moisten the earth for vegetation. Thunderers, we call these great birds. One of them is called Chequah. And the mountain we call Bikwaki, so Thunder Mountain is Chequah Bikwaki.

Many, many years have gone by since the Hill received its name. In the beginning of its Indian history the Thunderbirds used to make their nests here and sit on their two eggs until their young were hatched. Some Indians many years ago in the summer time visited the Hill and were surprised to find several pairs of young Thunders. It was always the custom with Indians to offer tobacco for friendship and safety.

And later on in another visit by the Indians a pond was discovered on the top of the Hill. And it was dangerous. The Serpent who lives under the Hill had caused this to be so that he could sun himself when the sky was clear. And on a sunny clear day he was sunning, probably asleep, when a lone Thunder discovered him and decided to catch him alive and carry him off. So the Thunder came down from the sky and caught the Serpent. The Thunder would carry him high. The Serpent, struggling, would carry the Thunder back down on the pond. At that time an Indian hunter who was passing happened to look to the top of the Hill and to his surprise saw the two struggling, and went up to witness the great fight. He was noticed by them, and the Thunderbird spoke and said, "My friend, help me, and shoot the Serpent with your arrow, and I will make you a great man!" The Serpent also spoke and said, "Help me, and shoot the Thunder, and I'll promise you my friendship to the end of all time!" The Indian did not know which one to help, so he shut his eyes and shot an arrow toward the fighters and shot the Thunder. That shot weakened the Thunder and he fell down and

> was taken under the Hill as a prisoner. The Thunderbird is still there, and the Hill is called Chequah Bikwaki. Whenever there is going to be a thunderstorm lightning is seen flashing from the Thunder Mountain.[19]

The creatures were natural enemies – one of the heavens and one, the underworld.

To the Muscogee people, the crystalline Horned Serpent lives underwater with a single, large crystal in its forehead. "Highly prized as aids in divination, these dazzling scales and crystals could be obtained only by a shaman purified for contact with the dangerous powers of the lower world."[20] The horns, called *chitto gab-by*, were used in medicine. "Fragments of the horns were said to resemble red sealing wax and could be obtained only with the greatest exposure to peril."[21]

Jackson Lewis, who imparted the tale, adds, "This snake lives in the water and has horns like the stag. It is not a bad snake....It does not harm human beings but seems to have a magnetic power over game."[22] It fits into the tradition that the Horned Serpent aids Isolt in her moments of need, especially with creating New World magic to protect her family. Nonetheless, she goes extremely short on the required ritual for gathering horn scrapings. In the legends, one needed particular spiritual training, as well as a rattle, green wood, a special scraping knife, a circle of buckskin to catch the scrapings, and sumac plants to feed the snake. This ritual required four special songs and much patience.[23] Local tribes used the horn fragments to empower themselves before battle or the hunt, painted below each eye. Extending their use to a magic wand seems somewhat in keeping.

The name *misiginebig* literally means Great Serpent in the Anishinabe languages. Tales include humans who breaks taboos and eat forbidden foods and are turned into water snakes with human heads, or women who take them as lovers and bear their children. Two origin stories from the Shawnee follow:

> The serpent lived in a lake. One day he wrapped himself around a large buck deer and took its head which he wore as a mask to fool his prey, this event was witnessed by two ravens. Another variation of this legend is that the creator was busy at work making the earth when he let a thought about himself escape. In doing this he gave the serpent an opportunity to harness this power and instill it into himself, making him very powerful. When

the creator realized this had happened he reached out toward the serpent and tried to recover this missing power. In doing so he only managed to capture the head of the serpent and separate it from his body. The headless body managed to slither away and return to the lake. Once there the serpent took the head of the deer to replace what he had lost. Shawnee elders say the serpent was killed and some of his flesh was carved off and is kept in the bundles of the five divisions. The flesh is still fresh and contains some energy stolen from the creator. Shawnee are warned to stay away from hollow logs and holes in the ground because the spirit of the serpent may lurk there. [24]

"As the embodiment of the Chaotic Force, the Horned Serpent and the Water Cougar are traditionally associated with the Lower World and particularly with floods and destruction. As principles of the Lower World, they stand in opposition to birds of the Upper World."[25] As the Panthers represent the water element, Thunderbirds are the air. Thus destructive flooding is the Horned Serpent's responsibility.

Both mythological and iconographic traditions attest to the relationship between the Horned Serpent and a lionlike being, sometimes called the Water Cougar." On metal collars, sometimes, the Horned Serpent bears the cougar's head, melding the two creatures into a hybrid being. It's described as having four footless legs, long hair, and a fish's tail.[26] The Water Panther or Water Lynx crosses a cougar and a dragon, with a long prehensile tail made of copper. The furry (or occasionally feathery) creature has horns or deer antlers and a sharp saw-toothed back. It roars or hisses in the sounds of storms or rushing rapids.

The Wampus Cat, another of the Ilvermorny totems, whose hair is used in wand cores, hails from the Appalachians. It resembles a mountain lion, but walks upright like a man. It may parallel the Water Panther, but comes from legends that are a bit more modern and Southerly.

In Missouri they call it a Gallywampus; in Arkansas it's the Whistling Wampus; in Appalachia it's just a plain old Wampus (or Wampas) cat. A half-dog, half-cat creature that can run erect or on all fours, it's rumored to be seen just after dark or right before dawn all throughout the Appalachians. But that's about all everyone agrees on. In non-Native American cultures it's a howling, evil creature, with yellow eyes that can supposedly pierce the hearts and souls of those unfortunate enough to cross its path, driving them to the edge of sanity.[27]

Like the Sasquatch, rumors of sightings abound. It's been seen throughout Northeast Tennessee, in Eastern Kentucky, in Virginia and West Virginia, and even on the campus at the University of Tennessee in Knoxville. One reteller shares three traditional Wampus accounts, all of them featuring the ties between the cats and the local women:

> There once was a young Cherokee woman who had a serious lack of trust for her husband. So one night, while the men of the tribe were hunting, she decided she'd sneak up and spy on the group. So she took the skin of a mountain lion, draped it over her head, and approached the group in the dark. Moments later, she was discovered, and taken to the medicine man, whose punishment was to make the lady wear the mountain lion's coat forever. Her spirit continues to wander the area, with her mortifying appearance etched in the nightmares of men, women, and children alike.
>
> An awful beast had been terrorizing the Cherokee for quite some time, when a young warrior summoned the courage to put an end to it. So he set out to destroy the beast, once and for all. But as he approached it, the beast turned and faced the warrior. As he looked upon the face of the beast, the warrior was instantly driven insane.
>> Vowing revenge, the warrior's wife set out to find the beast. She cloaked herself in the skin of a mountain lion, and sneaked up behind it. When the beast turned and saw her, he ran away, terrified, and was never seen again. But the spirit of the woman still roams the area, wearing the mask of the mountain lion.
>
> There once was an old woman who lived by herself in the hills of West Virginia. Rumor had it she was a witch, and that she sneaked around at night stealing and killing livestock. So one night, the townsfolk got fed up with losing their animals, and made plans to catch her in the act. And although they never actually caught her stealing cattle or sheep, they did catch her in the middle of her transformation from woman to cat. Startled, her metamorphosis stopped and she remained half-woman, half-cat forever.[28]

A few other monsters appear in Rowling's New World. The

Clabbert, sort of a monkey-frog cross from the American South, swings through trees and eats small lizards with "razor-sharp teeth."[29] The large pustule in the center of its forehead flashes red when there's danger. The Diricawl, which can vanish like a phoenix, was apparently mourned as the extinct Dodo bird.[30]

"William began to introduce Isolt to the magical creatures with which he was familiar. They took trips together to observe the frog-headed Hodags hunting, they fought a dragonish Snallygaster and watched newborn Wampus kittens playing in the dawn."[31] Hodags actually hail from loggers' tall tales from Wisconsin. While the men were burning a dead ox, "as the fire died down, there slowly issued from the great pile of ashes, a mystical animal, later to be known as the hodag."[32]

> The animal's back resembled that of a dinosaur, and his tail, which extended to an enormous length, had a spearlike end. Sharp spines, one and a half feet apart, lined the spinal column. The legs were short and massive and the claws were thick and curved, denoting great strength. The broad, furrowed forehead was covered with coarse, shaggy hair and bore two large horns. From the broad, muscular mouth, sharp, glistening white teeth protruded.
>
> This strange animal of the woods had an alert movement and the swish of his tail made the earth tremble. When he exhaled, an obnoxious odor penetrated the atmosphere for some distance.[33]

The men decided to entrap the creature with an ox as bait, and led it into the forest. "Then came a growl so deep, loud and sepulchral, that it fairly shook the earth, causing a vibration so great that it started a great shower of leaves and limbs from the giant trees."[34] Despite this, they persevered and, luring the beast into the pit they'd dug, captured it.

Like the medieval Germans, the lumberjacks considered the forest a place of terrors, with monsters waiting in the primordial darkness to swallow travelers. The apelike Argopelter inhabits hollow trees and hurls wooden splinters and branches at passerby. Some have described the creature as being so quick that it has never been seen. Another more frightening threat is the Rumtifusel, a flat creature with fur like a mink's that wraps itself around a stump or base of a tree trunk. When a traveler picks up the soft fur he sees lying their abandoned, it smothers the person and swallows him completely.

The Snallygaster was rumored to live around Maryland and Washington DC, going back to the days of German settlers in the 1730s. It's likely corrupted German from "schnell geiste," "quick spirit" like the gusts that slam doors, topple small objects, or scatter papers.[35] In 1909, the demon returned as hysterical accounts filled the papers. "The first person to see it, James Harding, described it as having enormous wings, a long sharp beak, claws like steel, and one eye in the middle of its forehead. He said it made shrill screeching noises and looked like a cross between a tiger and a vampire."[36] "The February 1909 article claims that a man had been seized by the winged creature, which proceeded to sink its teeth into his jugular, drain his body of blood and casually drop it off a hillside."[37] Sightings of the Snallygaster created such a commotion that President Theodore Roosevelt apparently considered postponing a trip to Europe so that he could hunt the creature. Seven-pointed stars, which reputedly repel the Snallygaster, can still be seen painted on local barns. "The area was no stranger to strange happenings: Settled by German immigrants in the early 1700s, it was riddled with stories of menacing creatures and assorted ghouls. But no tale sunk its claws into the imagination of the community quite like that of the Snallygaster."[38]

"Some protective instinct told Isolt to save the Horned Serpent cores only for her two adoptive sons and she and James learned to use a variety of other cores, including Wampus hair, Snallygaster heartstring and Jackalope antlers."[39] The Jackalope is a fabled jackrabbit with antelope horns (and the squashing of these words gives it its name). In real life, the creature appears to have evolved as a taxidermy joke. Throughout the Midwest one can find postcards, statues, and other jokes. Tall tales mostly dwell on the danger hunters found themselves in from cornered beasts.

"After the Great Sasquatch Rebellion of 1892 (for full details, see Ortiz O'Flaherty's highly-acclaimed book Big Foot's Last Stand), MACUSA headquarters was relocated for the fifth time in its history, moving from Washington to New York," Rowling writes.[40] Another creature in Shawnee tradition is the Misignwa, a guardian of the forest who protects other creatures. Misignwa carvings have been found on poles in the village squares, in council houses and carved into pipes until the 19th century. Many equate them with the Bigfoot or

Sasquatch. The Misignwa watches all hunters and if they are disrespectful or waste the animals they've killed, he will cause them to have an accident as punishment. "During the Bread Dance the Shawnee have a man who dresses in a suit of bearskin, wearing a wooden mask and carrying a cane and turtle shell rattle to impersonate Misignwa. This impersonator will seek out children who are disruptive and frighten them, hence teaching them a valuable lesson."[41]

> Thiago Quintana caused ripples through the magical world when his sleek and usually lengthy wands began entering the market, each encasing a single translucent spine from the back of the White River Monsters of Arkansas and producing spells of force and elegance. Fears about over-fishing of the monsters were assuaged when it was proven that Quintana alone knew the secret of luring them, a secret he guarded jealously until his death, at which point wands containing White River Monster spines ceased production.[42]

The White River Monster is one of Arkansas's most popular mysteries. Since 1915, along the White River near Newport in Jackson County, the monster has appeared over the decades and become a local legend. Bramlett Bateman, owner of a plantation near the river, saw the monster in 1937 and described it as having gray skin and being "as wide as a car and three cars long."[43]

> In 1971, the sightings began again when someone reported seeing a gray creature with a horn sticking out from its forehead. Other witnesses described it as having a spiny back twenty feet long. Later, a trail of three-toed, fourteen-inch prints was found in the White River area. Crushed vegetation and broken trees were evidence that something large had passed by, and it was assumed that the tracks were Whitey's.[44]

In 1973, Senator Robert Harvey established the White River Monster Refuge within which it was illegal to harm the creature. That seemed to put an end to the matter.

> Violetta Beauvais, the famous wandmaker of New Orleans, refused for many years to divulge the secret core of her wands, which were always made of swamp mayhaw wood. Eventually it was discovered that they contained hair of the rougarou, the dangerous dog-headed monster that prowled Louisiana

swamps. It was often said of Beauvais wands that they took to Dark magic like vampires to blood, yet many an American wizarding hero of the 1920s went into battle armed only with a Beauvais wand, and President Picquery herself was known to possess one. [45]

The rougarou of New Orleans, many think, is a corruption of "Loup Garou," the French word for werewolf. The rougarou most often is described as a creature with a human body and the head of a wolf or dog, similar to some versions of the werewolf legend. In the Cajun variant, the creature is said to prowl the swamps around Acadiana and Greater New Orleans. When stabbed or killed, he returns to human form. Wolves are not native to Louisiana, so many times the animal form is that of dogs, pigs or cattle, generally white in color. The creatures add to the supernatural terrors of New Orleans, a city shrouded in dark mists.

Ilvermorny School of Witchcraft and Wizardry

The North American school of magic, Ilvermorny, is on Mount Greylock, in the Berkshires of western Massachusetts. The founders, two parents and two adopted children, each named a House after their favorite magical beast.

For Chadwick, an intelligent but often temperamental boy, it was the Thunderbird that can create storms as it flies. For argumentative but fiercely loyal Webster, it was the Wampus, a magical panther-like creature that was fast, strong and almost impossible to kill. For Isolt, it was, of course, the Horned Serpent that she still visited and with which she felt a strange sense of kinship.

When asked what his favourite creature was, James was at a loss. The only No-Maj in the family was unable to consort with the magical creatures the others had begun to know well.

Finally, he named the Pukwudgie, because the stories his wife told of curmudgeonly William always made him laugh.

Thus were the four houses of Ilvermorny created, and while the four originators did not yet know it, much of their own characters leaked into the houses they had so light-heartedly named. [46]

Wands and wand-carrying were permitted to all wizards in Europe back to 1692, thanks to the wizards' persecution. [47] In the United States, however, MACUSA has forbidden this in an effort to preserve secrecy.

Mount Greylock itself has an interesting history. Before the Europeans arrived, the Mahican people dwelt there – James Fenimore Cooper based his novel, *The Last of the Mohicans*, on them. The mountain was known to 18th century English settlers as *Grand Hoosuc(k)*. The present name of Greylock first appeared in print about 1819, and may reference its appearance, as it often has a gray cloud, or lock of gray mist upon his head. It might also reference Chief Gray Lock (1670-1750) of the Western Abenaki Missisquoi, who conducted guerrilla raids into Vermont and western Massachusetts. It certainly suggests a misty head of hair rising over the land, shrouded in mystery.

Timothy Dwight IV, President of Yale University, climbed Greylock in 1799 and writes in *Travels in New England and New York*:

> [The mountain] is the highest land in the state…Its southeastern front is extensively visible throughout Berkshire, and from high elevations in the states of New Hampshire, New York, Vermont, and Connecticut at very great distances…During a great part of the year, it is either embosomed or capped by clouds, and indicates to the surrounding inhabitants the changes of weather with not a little exactness.[48]

In May 1831 the first wooden meteorological observatory, "Griffin's Tower," was built there by students from nearby Williams College. By the mid-19th century, many visitors were hiking up the mountain trails. Among them were writers and artists inspired by the mountain scene: Nathaniel Hawthorne, Herman Melville, Oliver Wendell Holmes, William Cullen Bryant, and Henry David Thoreau. Of course, Rowling has now joined their company.

Isolt Sayre's Story

Isolt Sayre, founder of Ilvermorny, has interesting symbolism. She was adopted by her wicked aunt Gormlaith Gaunt, whose family obviously features in the Voldemort legend. At the same time, Isolt has a name as mythic as Ginny's Guinevere, and she's descended from "the famous Irish witch Morrigan, an Animagus whose creature form was a crow" – actually a goddess in Celtic myth. Her story takes much from classic fairytales, the Greek myth of the Gordian Knot, dream symbolism, and Childe Ballads, soon carrying over to incorporate American tall tales and Iroquois legend as well. Many of these stories have deep symbolism and significance, adding lovely shadings to this epic tale of romance and revenge.

Isolt Sayre is named for Isolde or Iseult, heroine of a tragic romance. In the service of his uncle, King Mark, Tristan goes to win the damsel Isolde and kills Morald, her intended bridegroom. He's desperately wounded, but Isolde saves him, only learning later that he was the killer, which causes some strife between them. When he fulfills the condition of killing a dragon, she boards his ship to Cornwall. On the journey, however, they share a love potion and are immediately consumed by overpowering lust. They have an affair on the voyage, but Isolde still marries Mark when they arrive. Her secret love for Tristan continues, in an affair that parallels Lancelot, and Guinevere's. Tristan is finally banished and weds another woman, "Isolde of the White Hands," of Brittany, who resembles his love, "Isolde the Fair." Finally, he is wounded and dies – his true love Isolde sadly arrives too late to save him. Rowling's character brings a touch of this epic romance to the story, but like Ginny, is loyal to her family and thus achieves a happy ending.

"Her father, William Sayre, was a direct descendant of the famous Irish witch Morrigan, an Animagus whose creature form was a crow. William nicknamed his daughter 'Morrigan' for her affinity for all natural things when she was young."[49] Morrigan was a Celtic battle goddess, who indeed transformed into a crow. Through classic literature, she and her sisters have great powers over the elements:

> Then the *Badb*, and *Macha*, and *Morrigu* went to the hill of hostage-taking, the tulach which heavy hosts frequented, to Temhair (Tara), and they shed druidically formed showers, and fog-sustaining shower-clouds, and poured down from the air, about the heads of the warriors, enormous masses of fire, and streams of red blood; and they did not permit the Fir-Bolgs to scatter or separate for the space of three days and three nights.[50]

In the battle of Magh-Rath it is the "gray-haired *Morrigu*" (scald-crow), that shouts victory over the head of one hero, as another sings:

> "Over his head is shrieking
> A lean hag, quickly hopping

Over the points of their weapons and shields—
She is the gray-haired *Morrigu*."[51]

Rowling more commonly names her characters for ancient gods than insists they were gods (see chapter six), but the Celtic myth fits logically into her Animagi magic. Thus Isolt is twice over a figure of Celtic legend, though she leaves the old world to recreate herself in the new.

"Isolt Sayre was born around 1603 and spent her earliest childhood in the valley of Coomloughra, County Kerry, in Ireland. She was the offspring of two pure-blood wizarding families."[52] At age five however, she lost both her parents in a fire set by her mother's estranged sister, Gormlaith Gaunt. Gormlaith then took her to the valley of Coomcallee, or "Hag's Glen," and raised her there to value only purebloods, as a descendent of the great Salazar Slytherin.

As Isolt grows up, raised by the cruel Gormlaith Gaunt, she's a Rapunzel figure. Their home's name is clear enough, and Gormlaith casts herself as the wicked witch straight from stories:

> Gormlaith set herself to be the model she thought Isolt needed by forcing the child to watch, as she cursed and jinxed any Muggle or animal that strayed too near their cottage. The community soon learned to avoid the place where Gormlaith lived, and from then on the only contact Isolt had with the villagers she had once been friends with, was when local boys threw stones at her as she played in the garden.[53]

Mimicking the Rapunzel witch, Gormlaith refused to allow Isolt to go to Hogwarts, where she would learn less biased lessons. Until age seventeen, she kept her niece penned up at home. Rapunzel is the story of the girl not ready to grow up, who lives a safe, confined life in the tower.

> While this archetypal Terrible Mother seems adversarial, she, like the prince and other characters, is enacting the young princess's sublimated desires, walling her up in a tower or hiding her behind a hedge of brambles. "You mustn't leave yet, you mustn't grow up," the crone cackles. "Stay and be my daughter longer—aren't we happy?" And they are. The child grows up under the mother's influence; she is the source of all love, nourishment, comfort. This overwhelming authority is difficult to escape. In fact, the mother often reinforces this, sometimes

95

unconsciously. "I'm going to have to keep taking care of you. You'll always need me," she says. However, this protector is too demanding, too all encompassing; if she wishes to survive and grow independently, the princess must break away.[54]

This, Isolt does, seeking the excitement, romance, and destiny-breaking of her namesake. "At last the young woman developed sufficient skill and courage to escape by stealing her aunt's wand, for she had never been permitted her own. The only other object that Isolt took with her was a gold brooch in the shape of a Gordian Knot that had once belonged to her mother. Isolt then fled the country."[55]

The Gordion Knot is a famous old myth of the Greek fisherman-turned-king Gordius, who created the unsolvable knot with hidden ends. A prophecy sprang up that whoever untied it would conquer all of Asia. Alexander the Great, not much for finesse, sliced it open then did just that. Symbolically, "to cut the knot was to transfer the pure idea of achievement and victory to the plane of war and of existence."[56] Thus Isolt carries with her an unsolvable puzzle – how to teach herself new beliefs in a new land.

A knotted cord represents a closed ring and is thus protective. The Gordion Knot "is a long-standing symbol of the labyrinth, arising out of the chaotic and inextricable tangle of the cords with which it was tied. To undo the knot was equivalent to finding the 'Centre' which forms such an important part of all mystic thought."[57] Isolt, on a heroine's journey quest to find her purpose, thus is a closed knot waiting for her to solve the mystery of her destiny. She also has powers she hasn't yet explored. Some of these powers are tied to the wand, apparently the one wielded by Salazar Slytherin. Isolt is a true heir, gifted with Parseltongue. However, just as she is filled with untapped potential, her wand is as well, and can be commanded to sleep through a passed down magical word.

"Isolt cut off her hair. Masquerading as a Muggle boy called Elias Story, she set sail for the New World on the Mayflower in 1620."[58] Historically, there were about a hundred passengers, include one James Steward, who features later in Rowling's tale. No Elias Story or Boot family are seen on the land grant list, but since all snuck away from the Colonists, this is accounted for. Of the Mayflower passengers, half died during the first winter of scurvy, pneumonia, and tuberculosis.

To reach the new world, Isolt traveled with the Puritans, who were seeking religious freedom. Of course, they were also intolerant of anything they considered heretical, and they were the ones to murder women accused of witchcraft in the Salem Witch Trials. As the *Pottermore* site explains, "Their religious beliefs made them deeply intolerant of any trace of magic. The Puritans were happy to accuse each other of occult activity on the slenderest evidence, and New World witches and wizards were right to be extremely wary of them."[59] Thus she could not share herself with her fellow travelers and promptly left them behind.

She soon discovered local magical creatures, saving a goblinlike Pukwudgie from a ghostly Hidebehind. They became quite close and she named him William. Though she didn't tell him this, she began communicating with the local great horned river serpent, whom she understood through Parseltongue. The serpent told her, "Until I am part of your family, your family is doomed."

Discovering lost children Webster and Chadwick Boot, whose parents had been killed by the same Hidebehind, Isolt saved them. She found they were magical children, and soon met their adult friend from the Plymouth settlement, the stonemason James Steward. He injured himself with one of the Boot parents' broken wands, and Isolt began caring for him too. They fell in love and were married. Isolt christened their new home "Ilvermorny" after her childhood home, once more transplanting the British name but giving it a happier destiny in the new world.

As the boys grew up, Isolt promised she would make them their own wizard school. As Chadwick's eleventh birthday approached, she dreamed of the Horned Serpent and went to it, where it allowed her to shave a long shard from its horn. She and James worked together to make their son an ash wand "of exceptional power," then did the same for Webster in time. Their home-turned-school expanded, welcoming the local Native American tribes and European settlers alike. Isolt also had twin girls: Martha, named for James's late mother, and Rionach, named for Isolt's.

One night, Gormlaith came, preying on the most helpless twins and planning to raise them as she had raised Isolt. In the heroine's journey, the evil witch preys on the most helpless. Just as Isolt or other central heroines protect innocents in danger, the witch corrupts and destroys them.

Gormlaith incapacitated Isolt's wand with her Slytherin password and sent its owner into a magical sleep. However, like Voldemort, she discounted those she shouldn't have. Teen Chadwick and Webster awoke to their wands emitting a low musical note, "exactly as the Horned Serpent sounds danger." The boys tried to wake their parents, but failing, dueled the evil witch.

> Two onto one made her job more difficult: moreover, the twin cores of the Boot boys' wands, when used together against a common enemy, increased their power tenfold. Even so, Gormlaith's magic was strong and Dark enough to match them. Now the duel reached extraordinary proportions, Gormlaith still laughing and promising them mercy if they could prove their pure-blood credentials, Chadwick and Webster determined to stop her reaching their family. The brothers were driven back inside Ilvermorny: walls cracked and windows shattered, but still Isolt and James slept, until the baby girls lying upstairs woke and screamed in fear.
>
> It was this that pierced the enchantment lying over Isolt and James. Rage and magic could not wake them, but the terrified screams of their daughters broke the curse Gormlaith had laid upon them, which, like Gormlaith herself, took no account of the power of love. Isolt screamed at James to go to the girls: she ran to assist her adoptive sons, Slytherin's wand in her hand.[60]

When Gormlaith reached the girls' room, James stood before the crib, much as Lily Potter did. Touching the same primal, parental love, Isolt cried mindlessly for her father, and William the Pukwudgie appeared to slay her enemy. As with Hogwarts, it seems help will always be given at Ilvermorny to those who ask for it. "The old witch had indulged in all manner of Dark magic in an attempt to make herself invincible, and these curses now reacted with the Pukwudgie's venom, causing her to become as solid and as brittle as coal before shattering into a thousand pieces." As with Voldemort, her life-prolonging curses don't save her, only make her end more gruesome. Symbolically, she has no power over the new family, and their defiance causes her to crumble and blow away. Slytherin's wand remained inactive and Isolt and James buried it outside the grounds.

> Within a year an unknown species of snakewood tree had grown out of the earth on the spot where the wand was buried. It resisted all attempts to prune or kill it, but after several years the leaves were found to contain powerful medicinal properties. This tree seemed testament to the fact that Slytherin's wand, like his

scattered descendants, encompassed both noble and ignoble. The very best of him seemed to have migrated to America.[61]

Once again, Isolt's family reimagines the myths of old Britain to protect their family in the New World.

Since Martha marries into the Pocomtuc tribe and Chadwick weds a Mexican Healer called Josefina Calderon, they emphasize rational diversity and acceptance. James is joint Headmaster of the school, perhaps the only Muggle with such a role. It makes sense that this is the story of a Muggle hero (not just Muggle born, but truly Muggle), since it takes place in America, land of new opportunity. Likewise the increased diversity is an American hallmark. "As might be expected of a school part-founded by a No-Maj, Ilvermorny has the reputation of being one of the most democratic, least elitist of all the great wizarding schools," the website concludes.

> Pure-blood families, who were well-informed through wizarding newspapers about the activities of both Puritans and Scourers, rarely left for America. This meant a far higher percentage of No-Maj-born witches and wizards in the New World than elsewhere. While these witches and wizards often went on to marry and found their own all-magical families, the pure-blood ideology that has dogged much of Europe's magical history has gained far less traction in America.[62]

Isolt thus fulfilled her dream – not attending Hogwarts but building her own school. All Ilvermorny students' robes are fastened by a gold Gordian Knot, and her Gordion Knot symbol dominates the room where the Sorting happens, encouraging each student to find his or her potential.

> It is sometimes said of the Ilvermorny houses that they represent the whole witch or wizard: the mind is represented by Horned Serpent; the body, Wampus; the heart, Pukwudgie and the soul, Thunderbird. Others say that Horned Serpent favours scholars, Wampus, warriors, Pukwudgie, healers and Thunderbird, adventurers.

All these are united in Isolt's small family, who united to become great heroes and saviors.

Castelobruxo

Castelobruxo, the Brazilian school for magic, means "Castle of Witches." It appears a ruin to Muggle eyes, but is actually "an imposing square edifice of golden rock, often compared to a temple." There is no particular El Dorado in Brazilian myth to be confused with this; one assumes it simply fits the setting. In Western tradition "the mountain-symbol appears in the legend of the Grail" as the height of salvation.[63] Likewise a gleaming castle of gold can mean spiritual deliverance as well as earthly reward. It transforms children into witches and wizards, training them in mystical understanding as well as heroism.

The local legends of Caipora have been co-opted into Rowling's Wizarding World. The Tupi (from the coastal rainforests) and Guarani (from Southern Brazil and Paraguay) tell of the Caipora, whom Rowling describes as "small and furry spirit-beings who are extraordinarily mischievous and tricky, and who emerge under cover of night to watch over the students and the creatures who live in the forest." Apparently they're comparable to Peeves but more numerous.

In the ancient legends, the Caipora is a tiny dark-skinned figure with a long black mane, perpetually smoking cigars. Others paint him as a fox-headed animal spirit. Like the legendary Curupira, he may have backwards-facing feet to confuse trackers. The Caipora famously guards the forest and avenges it when hunters get too arrogant or cruel. The related Pombero (a short, hairy, ugly man with broad feet) can imitate the sounds of various forest creatures and protect birds with his whistles. Sometimes he snatches children and licks them, wrapping them in climbing plants or drowning them in rivers. Both are most often harmless troublemakers who bewilder hunters in the forest or scatter cattle and steal food. Some people leave them gifts like cigars or honey.

The Caipora also appear during Rowling's account of the World Cup on *Pottermore*. Quidditch in fact is immensely popular in South America, where the Peruvian warlocks take the lead.[64] Ginny Potter reports:

> The stadium is full and the noise is deafening. We await the arrival of both team's mascots, who will put on a pre-match show. The Bulgarians, of course, bring their celebrated dancing troupe of Veelas, which constitutes a major reason for the

team's popularity, at least with men. Brazil's Curupiras have already caused a great deal of mischief so far this tournament but are similarly popular, mostly with children. Security wizards stand by all around the perimeter in case of trouble.[65]

As Ginny adds, "And here come the Curupiras with their bright red hair and back-to-front feet. Tumbling, performing acrobatics, stealing hats from fans and generally creating mayhem, the stadium is greatly enjoying their antics." She finishes: "The opening ceremony concludes with an interesting Veela/Curupira pyramid formation. If several back to front feet found themselves in the Veela's eyes, the latter have resisted the temptation to transform into the terrifying Harpy-like form that gave many children – myself included – nightmares after their 1994 display."[66] Thus, the Caipora have a great deal added to their mythology here.

Mahoutokoro

Mahoutokoro, in Japan, is the smallest attended wizarding school. The name means "Place of Magic," and offers the students careful training from a young age, before they begin boarding there. "While day students, wizarding children are flown back and forth to their homes every day on the backs of a flock of giant storm petrels." Its association with storms makes the storm petrel a bird of bad omen, which foretell or cause bad weather. (The Albatross of the famed poem is related.) The birds are also linked with witchcraft, since the petrel's dark reputation led to the old name of *witch*.[67] Oddly, however, this is British mythology, not Japanese.

In most Asian and Middle Eastern countries, flying carpets are more popular than broomsticks.[68] In Japan, nonetheless, Quidditch is gaining popularity. This suggests a Western tradition taking over the country, as several are today.

Japan has many demons (*Oni*) and related creatures in its cosmology, including *Yōkai* (ghosts), *Tengu* (dog spirits), *Kitsune* (fox tricksters), smoke monsters, fire creatures, shapechanging badgers, soul-sucking plants, and lake monsters. *Fantastic Beasts* specifically mentions the Kappa, which famously loses the strengthening water kept in a bowl-like depression in its head if it's tricked into bowing.[69]

"The ornate and exquisite palace of Mahoutokoro is made of mutton-fat jade, and stands on the topmost point of the 'uninhabited' (or so Muggles think) Volcanic island of Minami Iwo Jima."

Mountains link with "loftiness of spirit"[70] as well as the world axis, and thus, ultimate truth. In many religions, the gods dwell there.

Meanwhile, nephrite jade appears from a translucent white to very light yellow form, called *mutton fat* jade in China (another cross cultural mash-up, though it's not clear who's contributing this description). In ancient China, jade, considered the "imperial gem," was more precious than silver or gold, and was used to create many ceremonial or decorative objects along with amulets and grave goods. Jade objects represented the power of the old Chinese rulers. Thus, they were made for ceremonial and ritual purposes as well as in a sign of intellectual power.

"According to the Chinese tradition, jade possess an essential quality of immorality as of right. Hence, it figured in rites and invocations from the third millennium before our era."[71] An entire palace of it would indeed be priceless as well as striking.

Students are presented with enchanted robes when they arrive, which grow in size as they do, and which gradually change colour as the learning of their wearer increases, beginning a faint pink colour and becoming (if top grades are achieved in every magical subject) gold. If the robes turn white, this is an indication that the student has betrayed the Japanese wizard's code and adopted illegal practices (which in Europe we call 'Dark' magic) or broken the International Statute of Secrecy. To 'turn white' is a terrible disgrace, which results in instant expulsion from the school and trial at the Japanese Ministry for Magic.

Of course, white is the color of death and mourning in Japan. Pink, a universal sunrise color, suggests new beginnings, allowing the wearer to progress through darker, more striking hues. Gold is universally prized as the essence of the sun, but in the east it is also the sacred or imperial yellow, worn only by royalty and the spiritually ascended. In Japan, it further suggests courage, beauty and refinement, and aristocratic elegance.

Uagadou

Although Africa has a number of smaller wizarding schools (for advice on locating these, see introductory paragraph), there is only one that has stood the test of time (at least a thousand years) and achieved an enviable international reputation:

Uagadou. The largest of all wizarding schools, it welcomes students from all over the enormous continent. The only address ever given is "Mountains of the Moon"; visitors speak of a stunning edifice carved out of the mountainside and shrouded in mist, so that it sometimes appears simply to float in mid-air.

In alchemy, the hollow mountain is the "philosopher's oven" within which magic happens. The inside of a mountain is often the fairyland under the hill, the mythic underworld. "Mountains of the Moon" meanwhile, references a legendary mountain range in east Africa that forms the source of the Nile River. The story comes from a merchant named Diogenes, who reported that he had traveled inland from Rhapta in East Africa for twenty-five days and had found the source of Nile flowing from a group of massive mountains into a series of large lakes. Because of their snowcapped whiteness, they were called the Mountains of the Moon. Many explorers searched for them and placed them on maps. The Rwenzori Mountains, shrouded in mists, may be this fabled place. Modern stories and poems have referenced these mountains – Edgar Allan Poe's 1849 poem "Eldorado" or a song in *The Hobbit*. Likewise, a 1937 Bengali adventure novel by Bibhutibhushan Bandyopadhyay has this name.

Rowling writes, "Much (some would say all) magic originated in Africa, and Uagadou graduates are especially well versed in Astronomy, Alchemy and Self-Transfiguration." *Quidditch through the Ages* says much the same. These categories aren't chosen at random. Historically, there have been several classes of magicians on the continent. In South Africa, the "thakathi" is a wicked person who operates in secret to harm others. The more benevolent "sangoma" is a diviner or fortune-teller, often hired to detect illness, predict the future, or identify a criminal. The "inyanga," usually translated as "witch doctor," heals and provides magical talismans. Among the Zulu and other Bantu speaking peoples, "witch smellers" tracked and caught evil witches in the area. Vodoun is a traditional religion of coastal West Africa, from Nigeria to Ghana, which emphasizes the power of the spirits or *loa* in everyday life. Some people, skilled at spirit possession, act as mediums to communicate with the *loa*. Much of this is still practiced today.

Quidditch through the Ages mentions the Ethiopian team the Gimbi Giant-Slayers, suggesting giants are a threat in their country.[72] Animals mentioned in *Fantastic Beasts and Where to Find Them* include the Runespoor, from Burkina Faso – a three-headed serpent beloved by dark wizards that's given to disagreement with itself.[73] There's also the Tebo, an invisible warthog from Congo and Zaire, and the Erumpent, a rhino-like creature whose horn can explode (seen in Xenophilius's collection). Of course, having creatures whose hides, horns, etc., are useful to wizards worldwide seems another mark of imperialism as they would attract European hunters.

Books of African myth and folklore mention many creatures – Inkanyamba is a huge carnivorous eel that can control the weather in South Africa. Ninki Nanka, which lives in the Gambia River, is something of a water dragon. Jengu are merfolk from Cameroon. The kishi is a two-faced demon in Angola, with one man's head and one hyena's. Tokoloshe is an evil-spirited gremlin in Zulu mythology. The ones in *Fantastic Beasts* appear invented by Rowling, however.

One exception is the Nundo, which, according to *Fantastic Beasts*, may be the most dangerous beast in the world. It's a giant leopard "whose breath causes disease virulent enough to eliminate entire villages."[74] Rumors of an enormous grey feline the size of a donkey have spread through Tanzania since the early 1900s, though the beast itself has eluded hunters.

In the new film *Fantastic Beasts,* Newt, needing a distraction, throws a small object, which unfurls into a lovely peacock blue, winged creature. *Pottermore* calls it "A large, butterfly-like creature that emerges from a small object, possibly a cocoon."[75] It might be a brilliantly colorful African Fwooper – whose song drives people to insanity[76] – but it's actually the Swooping Evil. (The same bird flies in to make up the "S" in the word "Beasts" from the movie titles.) One assumes its frightening swooping and scary face help frighten all its natural enemies.

The broomstick comes from Europe but is slowly catching on in Africa, along with the sport of Quidditch.[77] Likewise, "the wand is a European invention, and while African witches and wizards have adopted it as a useful tool in the last century, many spells are cast simply by pointing the finger or through hand gestures." Like Rowling's Native Americans, her Africans have sophisticated hand magic but no superior competition to a wand. And like them, they later adopt the wand and thus take on European ways.

Students receive notice that they have gained entrance at Uagadou from Dream Messengers, sent by the headmaster or headmistress of the day. The Dream Messenger will appear to the children as they sleep and will leave a token, usually an inscribed stone, which is found in the child's hand on waking.

The ancient Egyptians believed that dreams were messages from the gods, and 1300 years before Christ, produced the earliest dream book with over 200 of those messages. The Zulu people regard dreams as messages from ancestors rather than gods, offering guidance in their day to day existence. In some African tribes, dream life is as important as waking life. After dream battles, some warriors wake up with sore arm muscles assuming that they have been wielding their clubs during the night.

---

[1] J.K. Rowling, "Fourteenth Century – Seventeenth Century," "History of Magic in North America," *Pottermore*.
https://www.pottermore.com/collection-episodic/history-of-magic-in-north-america-en.

[2] Ibid.

[3] Sarah Begley, "J.K. Rowling Accused of Cultural Appropriation in her Depiction of Native American Wizards," *Time*, 9 Mar 2016.
http://time.com/4252247/j-k-rowling-criticism-native-american-wizards.

4 Adrienne Keene, "Magic in North America Part 1: Ugh," *Native Appropriations*, 8 Mar 2016.
http://nativeappropriations.com/2016/03/magic-in-north-america-part-1-ugh.html.

[5] "Fourteenth Century – Seventeenth Century."

[6] Keene.

[7] Rowling, "Fourteenth Century – Seventeenth Century."

[8] Rowling, "Fourteenth Century – Seventeenth Century."

[9] Keene.

[10] Begley.

[11] J.K. Rowling, "1920s Wizarding America." "History of Magic in North America," *Pottermore*. https://www.pottermore.com/collection-episodic/history-of-magic-in-north-america-en.

[12] J.K. Rowling, "Ilvermorny School of Witchcraft and Wizardry." *Pottermore*. https://www.pottermore.com/writing-by-jk-rowling/ilvermorny.

[13] Lake Shore Kearney, "The Hide Behind," *The Hodag and Other Tales of the Logging Camps*. (Madison, WI: Democrat Printing Company, 1928), 54-55.
http://www.lumberwoods.com/hodagthebook.htm.

[14] Rowling, "Ilvermorny School."

[15] Ibid.

[16] "Puckwudgie," *NativeLanguages.org*. http://www.native-languages.org/pukwudgie.htm.

[17] Ibid.

[18] "Shawnee Mythology." http://www.bigorrin.org/archive123.htm

[19] "Thunder Mountain," *NativeLanguages.org.* http://www.native-languages.org/thunderbird.htm

[20] Bill Grantham, *Creation Myths and Legends of the Creek Indians,* (Gainesville: University of Florida Press, 2002), 25.

[21] Ibid., 25.

[22] Ibid., 25.

[23] Ibid., 25-26.

[24] "Shawnee Mythology."

[25] Grantham 27.

[26] Ibid., 27.

[27] Dave Tabler, "The Story of the Wampus Cat," *Appalachian History,* 6 Oct 2014. http://www.appalachianhistory.net/2014/10/story-of-wampus-cat.html.

[28] "The Wampus Cat: Kills Animals, Steals Children, Smells Awful," *Sunny Tennessee,* 30 May 2011. https://sunnytennessee.wordpress.com/2011/05/30/the-wampus-cat-kills-animals-steals-children-smells-awful.

[29] Newt Scamander, *Fantastic Beasts and Where to Find Them* (New York: Scholastic, 2001), 14.

[30] Ibid, 17.

[31] Rowling, "Ilvermorny School."

[32] Lake Shore Kearney, "The Hodag" *The Hodag and Other Tales of the Logging Camps,* (Madison, WI: Democrat Printing Company, 1928),11. http://www.lumberwoods.com/hodagthebook.htm.

[33] Ibid., 12.

[34] Ibid., 15.

[35] Timothy L. Cannon and Nancy F. Whitmore, "The Snallygaster," *From Ghosts and Legends of Frederick County.* http://wesclark.com/jw/snallygaster.html.

[36] Ibid.

[37] Susan Fair, "Mountain Monster: The Snallygaster," *Blue Ridge County,* 1 Jan 2012. http://blueridgecountry.com/archive/favorites/snallygaster-monster.

[38] Ibid.

[39] Rowling, "Ilvermorny School."

[40] Rowling, "1920s Wizarding America."

[41] "Shawnee Mythology."

[42] Rowling, "1920s Wizarding America."

[43] "White River Monster," *The Encyclopedia of Arkansas History and Culture.* http://www.encyclopediaofarkansas.net/encyclopedia/entry-detail.aspx?entryID=2790

[44] Ibid.

[45] Rowling, "1920s Wizarding America."

[46] Rowling, "Ilvermorny School."

[47] Whisp, *Quidditch through the Ages,* 55.

[48] Timothy Dwight IV. *Travels in New England and New York,* ed. Barbara Miller Solomon. (Cambridge, Massachusetts: The Belknap Press of Harvard University Press, 1969).

[49] Ibid.

[50] W.M. Hennessy, "The Ancient Irish Goddess of War," *Revue Celtique* 1 (1870): 32–37, *The Internet Sacred Text Archive,* http://www.sacredtexts.com/neu/celt/aigw/aigw01.htm.

[51] Ibid.

[52] Rowling, "Ilvermorny School."

[53] Ibid.

[54] Valerie Estelle Frankel, *From Girl to Goddess* (Jefferson, NC: McFarland and Co, 2010), 29.

[55] Rowling, "Ilvermorny School."

[56] J.E. Cirlot, *A Dictionary of Symbols* (New York: Routledge, 1971), 173.

[57] Ibid., 173.

[58] Rowling, "Ilvermorny School."

[59] Rowling, "Fourteenth Century – Seventeenth Century."

[60] Ibid.

[61] Ibid.

[62] J.K. Rowling, "Seventeenth Century and Beyond." "History of Magic in North America," *Pottermore.* https://www.pottermore.com/collection-episodic/history-of-magic-in-north-america-en.

[63] Cirlot 221.

[64] Whisp, *Quidditch through the Ages* 85.

[65] Rita Skeeter, "Dumbledore's Army Reunites at Quidditch World Cup Final." *Pottermore,* 8 July 2014.

[66] Ibid.

[67] William Burley Lockwood, *Oxford Book of British Bird Names* (Oxford: Oxford University Press, 1984).

[68] Whisp, *Quidditch through the Ages* 86.

[69] Scamander, *Fantastic Beasts* 43.

[70] Cirlot 219.

[71] Ibid., 161.

[72] Whisp, *Quidditch through the Ages* 81.

[73] Scamander, *Fantastic Beasts* 72.

[74] Ibid., 58.

[75] J.K. Rowling, "Swooping Evil," *Pottermore.com* https://www.pottermore.com/explore-the-story/swooping-evil.

[76] Scamander, *Fantastic Beasts* 31.

[77] Whisp, *Quidditch through the Ages* 80.

CHAPTER 6: THE PANTHEON AMONG HOGWARTS PROFESSORS

All pantheons of ancient mythologies have similar archetypes: There's Zeus, Odin, or Enlil, the father god. Demeter, Hathor, or Chicomecoatl, goddess of the harvest. The Hogwarts teachers as they sit along their long table reflect these archetypes, from Dumbledore to Professor Sprout. Argus Filch is guardian of the gates at Hogwarts, Minerva is its font of wisdom. Dolores Umbridge might be Eris, Goddess of Discord. Slughorn is rather a Dionysus figure, obsessed with hedonism and selfishness. Dour Snape, always excluded, has many correspondences to Hades as he lurks underground. Other teachers seem better linked to other traditions: Professor Flitwick is a clever crafter figure like the dwarf and goblin crafters in Norse myth. The vulturelike Madam Pince has echoes in Thoth, the bird-headed Egyptian god of lore and wisdom. But which archetypes are missing from the "Hogwarts Pantheon"? With names like Minerva, Argus, Pomona, Silvanus, Septima, and Sybill, are they just reenacting the Roman gods, or are there other, closer correspondences?

Some archetypes are better found in the students: The goddess of love and beauty, present in every culture, corresponds best to Fleur and her Veela friends, while Harry, of course, is the culture hero. The sacrificed maiden like Persephone appears as Ginny in book two or Fleur in book four. Hermione is frequently compared to Hermes the messenger and provider of sacred gifts, while Luna's name links her to Artemis, the shining moon goddess.

There is frequently a traitor among the pantheon, like Prometheus or Loki. Similarly, there is a traitor at Hogwarts each year, from Quirrell to Barty Crouch Jr.

Exploring all these archetypes can deepen our understanding of the characters when the Hogwarts pantheon is revealed as a chorus of quibbling gods and Harry their appointed hero.

Greek Myth

Dumbledore, in his thronelike chair, certainly resembles Zeus, head of the Pantheon. They share the absolute rulership and also various attributes like the snowy beard and arcane wisdom. In the pantheon of Hogwarts professors, Minerva, the Athena character, is certainly a surrogate daughter as well as the source of wisdom. Pomona Sprout works as Demeter, the harvest goddess whose concoctions can save mankind. Filius Flitwick, the clever crafter, parallels Hermes. Hephaestus the misshapen smith can be seen in one-eyed, one-legged Mad-Eye Moody, who is gruff but generous to his friends. Meanwhile, Moody's first name, Alastor, was an epithet (title) of Zeus. It meant the avenger of evil deeds, specifically, familial bloodshed. It was also an epithet of the Furies, who avenged crimes. This is an excellent name for an Auror, especially considering the events of book four. The outcast, the dour god who always seemed to lose in Olympian contests, was Hades, banished to the gloomy underground, much like Professor Snape.

Dionysus spent all his time enjoying drunken pleasures and convincing mortals to do the same. This irresponsible figure is a good match for Horace Slughorn. Helga Hufflepuff is Hestia, modest guardian of the hearth. Dolores Umbridge, stirring up animosity everywhere, parallels Eris, goddess of Discord. Gilderoy Lockhart, admittedly, is a more awkward fit as Aphrodite the love goddess, though her handsome, sacrificed paramour Adonis may be about right. Hagrid parallels well with Pan the satyr of the forest.

Argus Filch, lower in rank than the professors, is famously named for the many-eyed guardian Argus, whom Hera employed to watch Zeus's paramour, Io. When Hermes tricked and killed him, Hera set his many eyes on the peacock's tail. Of course, the tricksters of Hogwarts, Fred and George, spend much of their time outwitting Filch, though they stop long before murder.

Sybill Trelawney is the oracle priestess or Greek Sibyl, from which she gets her name. Of course, in the series she's the Cassandra figure, who offers dire prophecies but is never actually believed. Sybill Trelawney's great-great-grandmother, a more reliable seer, was even named Cassandra in homage. "Cassandra's gift had been much diluted over ensuing generations, although Sybill inherited more than she knew," Rowling writes.[1] She adds:

'Trelawney' is a very old name, suggestive of Sybill's over-reliance on her ancestry when seeking to impress. There is a beautiful old Cornish song featuring the name (' The Song of the Western Men'). Sybill's first name is a homonym of 'Sibyl', which was a female clairvoyant in ancient times. My American editor wanted me to use 'Sibyl', but I preferred my version, because while it keeps the reference to the august clairvoyants of old, it is really no more than a variant on the unfashionable female name 'Sybil'. Professor Trelawney, I felt, did not really qualify as a 'Sibyl'.[2]

Correspondences

Dumbledore	Zeus, Father god
Minerva McGonagall	Athena, goddess of wisdom
Filius Flitwick	Hermes the clever crafter
Horace Slughorn	Dionysus the drunken hedonist
Severus Snape	Hades the despised underworld god
Pomona Sprout	Demeter, harvest goddess
Alecto and Amycus Carrow	The Furies, who punish traitors
Dolores Umbridge	Eris, goddess of discord
Argus Filch	Argus the guardian
Gilderoy Lockhart	Aphrodite, love goddess
Mad-Eye Moody	Hephaestus the misshapen smith
Sybill Trelawny	The Oracle
Charity Burbage	Prometheus
Hagrid	Pan the forest demigod
Firenze	Chiron the centaur
Helga Hufflepuff	Hestia, guardian of the hearth
Rolanda Hooch	Iris the rainbow messenger
Quirinus Quirrell	Minos

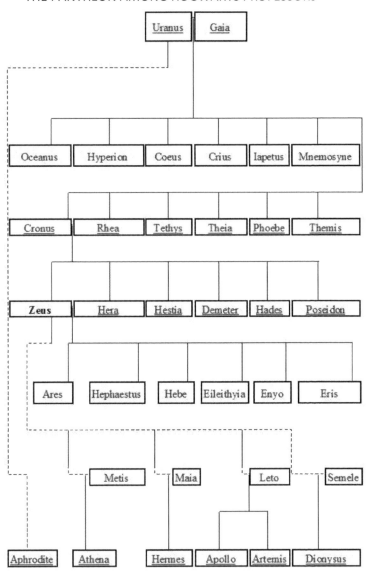

Amycus and Alecto are the Death Eater twins who torture students in book seven. Alecto "the implacable or unceasing anger" is one of the Erinyes, or Furies, in Greek mythology. It was their job to leave the underworld and torture mankind with cruel glee on behalf of the gods. Amycus, the son of Poseidon and Melia in Greek myth, was a boxer and King of the Bebryces. When the Argonauts landed on the coast of his dominions, he challenged the bravest of them to a boxing match. Polydeuces, who accepted the challenge, killed him. Likewise, Amycus Carrow challenges the brave Gryffindors to fights all the time. Upon the tomb of Amycus there grew a laurel, would make people fight when they encountered it. Thus he's like a male Eris or Fury.

The twins torture Charity Burbage, the Muggle Studies professor. She strongly parallels Prometheus, the Titan who declared himself a friend of mankind and brought them fire. The new regime, in his story, the Greek gods, caught him and bound him to a rock where an eagle came and tore at his liver each day, until Hercules managed to free him. In Greek and Roman mythology, Hygieia, was the goddess of health and sanitation, daughter of Asclepius. Madame Pomfrey matches her. Quirrell, meanwhile, parallels Minos, the man who became arrogant and dared to challenge the gods. They tormented him with a monster, the Minotaur, and when the hero Theseus arrived, he destroyed both the monster and the king's empire.

The Next Generation

Specifically, there were two generations of Olympian gods – Zeus's siblings and Zeus's children. The Harry Potter series too is split between teacher heroes and student heroes, emphasizing the gifts of the younger generation. Among the children, there are many parallels with Zeus's children. If sunny red-headed Ron is Apollo, the sun, then Luna is of course the mad, distant moon (appropriately for her name). Hermione is the messenger Hermes. Draco, Crabbe, and Goyle are the angry war god Ares and his sons and cronies Phobos and Deimos. Fleur is Aphrodite, goddess of love, who entices all with her beauty. Ginny is undoubtedly Persephone, the sacrificed maiden in *Chamber of Secrets* whose loss could destroy their world (bringing eternal winter or shutting down the school). Fred and George parallel many Greek hero-twins: Castor and Pollux (brothers to Helen of Troy), sons of the West Wind Calaïs and Zetes, or the Argonauts

Ascalaphus and Ialmenus.

Finally, Harry, the central hero, shares much with the heroes of classical myth. His closest parallel is, however, Hercules – the half god half man with a long list of impossible labors. As with the Pantheons, much of this may be archetypal – more a lesson about skills any hero must learn than about Harry's deliberate correspondences with Hercules. Nonetheless, his famous labors match well with Harry's tasks and the lessons they offer, both over the seven book series and in his *Deathly Hallows* Horcrux hunt.

Labor One – Nemean Lion – Hercules strangles the beast and wears its skin for the rest of his labors. Harry's first major test is battling the troll. The reward – Hermione's friendship – is something he carries forever. The first villain in *Deathly Hallows* is Voldemort, trying to stop him from escaping. All these require a bit of cleverness as brute force isn't enough to win the day. These battles test the hero's courage, but emphasize that worse is coming.

Labor Two – Lernean Hydra – Hercules needs his nephew Iolaus to help him burn the neck of each Hydra head after he slices it off. Fighting the Hornback in *Goblet of Fire*, Harry swoops and dodges the reptilian creature, with outside help from his broom and Hermione's Summoning Charm. Likewise, he sneaks through the Ministry to get to Umbridge in *Deathly Hallows*, Hermione and Ron aiding him. All this tests his clever resourcefulness and willingness to ask his friends for help.

Labor Three – Cerynitian Hind – Hercules must capture it alive, an unusually delicate task. Through the series, Harry learns potions and transfiguration, all very dexterous work. In the final book, the Sword of Gryffindor has a gentle doe guardian, testing his courage as he follows it then dives into the frozen lake. Care and caution are key here.

Labor Four – Erymanthian Boar – In this test, Hercules's teacher Chiron is accidentally killed. Thus the loss of his beloved mentor is the true trial, as Hercules advances to independence and continues his tests. For Harry, this is paralleled in the loss of Sirius, Dumbledore, and other friends, many of whom perish in book seven.

Labor Five – Stables of Augeas – Famously, as Hercules shoveled, the stable filled even faster. This endless, impossible task is paralleled in Harry's Horcrux search with its interminable camping. On the way he discovers the locket he's found is a fake, loses the Sword of Gryffindor, and has numerous setbacks. Before this, he has homework and classes, along with many impossible tasks for someone his age like the Triwizarding Tournament and creating a Patronus. All teach patience and determination.

Labor Six – Stymphalian Birds – These were shrieking swarms of nasty creatures. This echoes the horde of keys guarding the Philosopher's Stone and also the giant deadly snake in Godric's Hollow. Both test dexterity.

Labor Seven – Cretan Bull – Facing the vast empire of Minos and traveling far from familiar territory added to Hercules's trials here. For Harry, this reflects in entering the Ministry, Knockturn Alley, the Hall of Prophecies, the graveyard, and other menacing places. In *Deathly Hallows*, there's more of this, from Godric's Hollow to camping in the countryside. The true test is winning the day in places of isolation and adversity.

Labor Eight – Mares of Diomedes – Hercules rescues Queen Alcestis from death himself as a favor to her husband. Likewise, Harry battles the basilisk to rescue Ginny, and then frees Dobby. He also rescues Mrs. Cattermole from the Ministry. The heroism here is defending the weak, even while on grandiose quests to defeat evil.

Labor Nine – Belt of Hippolyte – This mission calls for tact: the queen of the Amazons surrenders the belt freely when Hercules charms her. Learning the same finesse, Harry convinces Cho to join the DA, and finally wins Cho's then Ginny's affection. Later on, Harry persuades Kreacher to trust him and retrieves the locket.

Labor Ten – Cattle of Geryon – Heated by the Sun, Hercules bends his bow at Helios himself, threatening to strike down a god. The gods of the wizarding world are not only evil Voldemort, but also the Ministry, as seen in Fudge and his allies. Harry indeed resists all the Ministers of Magic and their representatives, the highest authorities. Both heroes emphasize that when authority is arbitrarily cast over them, they have no need to show deference.

Labor Eleven – Apples of Hesperides – Hercules wrestles Antaeus, who gets his powers from earth, and kills him in midair. Exploiting the villain's own power to destroy him is the penultimate test. Similarly, Harry exploits Umbridge's greed, Wormtail's honor, Voldemort's superiority, and more to defeat them. In the last book, Harry uses the Horcruxes, Elder Wand, and his mother's protection (which are all supposed to safeguard Voldemort) to defeat him.

Labor Twelve – Hound of Hades – This is the greatest test of all for Hercules, and for Harry in book seven – facing death in the deepest pit or the Forbidden Forest. Of course, in book one, this monster dog is reimagined as Fluffy, the three-headed dog, guarding the path down to Voldemort.

More Greek Myth

Merope Gaunt, Voldemort's mother, has a striking name from Greek myth. One Merope was one of the seven Pleiades, star nymphs in the sky and a daughter of the titan Atlas. She married King Sisyphus, the man who cheated death multiple times, and was punished by the gods to eternally roll a bolder up a hill. Merope was said to have been so ashamed of her husband's crimes that she hid her face, when the seventh star of the Pleiades vanished from the heavens. Her name means "with face turned" from *meros* + *ops*.

> "Atlas by Pleione or an Oceanitide (Oceanid) had twelve daughters...Their names are as follows: Electra, Alcyone, Celaeno, Merope...Of these, they say Electra does not appear, because of the death of Dardanus and the loss of Troy. Others think that Merope appears to blush because she had a mortal as husband, though the others had gods. Driven from the band of her sisters because of this, she wears her hair long in grief, and is called a comet, or *longodes* because she trails out for a long distance, or *xiphias* because she shows the shape of a sword-point. This star, too, portends grief."[3]

Merope of the Heliades was one of the five daughters of Helios and Clymene the Oceanid. The most famous member of this family was her brother Phaeton. Wanting to prove himself son of the sun titan, he drove the sun god's chariot and scorched the earth, so the gods killed him. All his sisters grieved so long, the gods turned them into poplar trees weeping tears of amber.

Another Merope was the daughter of King Cypselus of Arcadia, who married King Cresphontes of Messenia. "Polyphontes, one of the true Heraclids, came to the throne and took to wife, against her will, Merope, the wife of the murdered man."[4] When her husband was murdered and she was forced to wed the new king, she sent away her son Aepytus and had him trained him in vengeance…but nearly slew him by mistake when Aepytus gained entry to the court by claiming to be his own murderer. At last, mother and son succeeded in punishing their enemy. (Euripides' lost tragedy *Cresphontes* is based on this myth).

Another Merope was daughter (or in some versions wife) to King Oenopion of Chios, son of Princess Ariadne and Dionysus. The hunter Orion broke guest-right (in itself a sacred law) and assaulted Merope, so Oenopion stabbed out his eyes and banished him.

> And Artemis slew Orion in Delos. They say that he was of gigantic stature and born of the earth; but Pherecydes says that he was a son of Poseidon and Euryale. Poseidon bestowed on him the power of striding across the sea. He first married Side, whom Hera cast into Hades because she rivalled herself in beauty. Afterwards he went to Chios and wooed Merope, daughter of Oenopion. But Oenopion made him drunk, put out his eyes as he slept, and cast him on the beach. But he went to the smithy of Hephaestus, and snatching up a lad set him on his shoulders and bade him lead him to the sunrise. Being come thither he was healed by the sun's rays, and having recovered his sight he hastened with all speed against Oenopion. But for him Poseidon had made ready a house under the earth constructed by Hephaestus.[5]

A few rare versions tell this as an incest story, with Merope as Orion's mother.

Bridging on this, the name Merope also belonged to the adoptive mother of Oedipus, who killed his birth father and wed his birth mother. Thus these connections brand every Merope as an innocent victim but the close family of some very bad men. Sisyphus tried to cheat death and live forever. Oedipus defied the gods' natural laws by killing his father and marrying his mother, Aepytus killed his stepfather and claimed to have murdered himself, and Phaeton nearly destroyed the world when he tried to fly the sun god's chariot. Orion assaulted his hostess, or in a few versions, his own stepmother. All four of these men defied the laws of the gods in unholy and unnatural fashion, and all were punished.

There are more names from Greek myth, including Hermione. Greek Hermione was the daughter of Helen of Troy, a lovely princess fought over as marriage bait by the sons of Agamemnon and Achilles. Thus there's little connection here. Hermione, also used by Shakespeare to name his betrayed queen in *A Winter's Tale,* became a popular English name. Thus, unlike the other Greek appellations, hers may come from the English tradition. She's also been compared to the helpful messenger Hermes. Likewise, Hermes, Percy's owl, is named, appropriately, for the messenger god, as this is his job. Even Galatea Merrythought, DADA professor in Voldemort's day, is named for the mythological woman sculpted to her creator's purpose, much as Voldemort planned to do with the Dark Arts position.[6]

Fantastic Beasts and Where to Find Them presents griffons, winged horses, manticores, hippocampuses, and sphinxes, animals which are occasionally referenced in the main series. It also links merfolk with the Greek sirens. Of course, hippogriffs and centaurs play major roles in the series itself. *Fantastic Beasts* adds that the mythical chimera (a terrible beast that combines fire-breathing lion, goat, and snake) only was slain once "and the unlucky wizard concerned fell to his death from the winged horse,"[7] a Belleraphon reference.

Xenophilius Lovegood has a name which, down to its Greek roots, means "a lover of foreign things." Rowling adds in *Short Stories from Hogwarts of Heroism, Hardship and Dangerous Hobbies*, "A very great variety of first names are given to children by their wizard parents, some of them being what we might think of as Muggle names (e.g. James, Harry, Ronald), others giving a distinct flavour of the personality or destiny of the bearer (e.g. Xenophilius, Remus, Alecto)."[8]

She notes that these "destined names" are actually chosen after consulting with fortune tellers explaining, "A certain sector of magical society, however, follows the ancient wizarding practice of consulting a Naming Seer, who (usually for a hefty payment of gold) will predict the child's future and suggest an appropriate moniker."[9] Presumably, this is why Remus Lupin is so-named before he's even bitten.

Roman Gods and Star Names

Pomona Sprout is named for the Roman goddess of fruit and agriculture, while Minerva, of course, is the Roman goddess of wisdom. Aurora was the goddess of the dawn, who gives her name to Aurora Sinistra, professor of Astronomy. (Sinistra means left, and witchcraft is often known as the left-hand-path.) Hagrid inherits his job from Silvanus Kettleburn, whose first name is shared with a Roman forest god similar to the Greek Pan. "Like Hagrid after him, he was prone to underestimating the risks involved in caring for creatures such as Occamys, Grindylows and Fire Crabs, and once famously caused the Great Hall to catch fire after enchanting an Ashwinder to play the Worm in a play of 'The Fountain of Fair Fortune'."[10]

Septima Vector teaches Arithmancy. Of course, a vector is a mathematical element, while Septima means "seven," a math reference combined with the most magical number. Helga Hufflepuff, already compared to modest Hestia, gains more political power as Vesta, a sacred figure whose female devotees ruled the political stage. It should not be forgotten that she was a powerful founder, not just a homebody. Albus Dumbledore's first name means "white," casting him as a blessed saint and good wizard. Rowling adds on the subject of colors:

> Colours also played their part in the naming of Hagrid and Dumbledore, whose first names are Rubeus (red) and Albus (white) respectively. The choice was a nod to alchemy, which is so important in the first Harry Potter book, where 'the red' and 'the white' are essential mystical components of the process. The symbolism of the colours in this context has mystic meaning, representing different stages of the alchemic process (which many people associate with a spiritual transformation). Where my two characters were concerned, I named them for the alchemical colours to convey their opposing but complementary natures: red meaning passion (or emotion); white for asceticism; Hagrid being the earthy, warm and physical man, lord of the forest; Dumbledore the spiritual theoretician, brilliant, idealised and somewhat detached. Each is a necessary counterpoint to the other as Harry seeks father figures in his new world. (Rowling, "Colours")

Quirinus Quirrell comes from Roman myth as well. Quirinus ("spear") was an early god, most likely a Sabine god of war. When the

Romans settled there, they absorbed the cult of Quirinus into their early belief system, and by the end of the first century BC Quirinus was considered to be the deified Romulus. The tarot symbol or Celtic hallow of the spear echoes the elder wand, and Quirrell harbors a great evil through his arrogance. Quirinus was also an epithet of Janus, the two-faced god. With Voldemort on his back, the reference seems more than coincidental. "Janus is a symbol of wholeness – of the desire to master all things."[11] Voldemort certainly shares this ambition though he discounts much in his search for power.

Remus Lupin gets his name from the mythic twins Romulus and Remus. The pair were abandoned as babies and raised by a she-wolf. After this, Romulus grew up to slay Remus and then founded the city of Rome. Remus has the wolf connection (likewise, "lupine" means "wolflike"), but is also a victim, one preyed upon by stronger adversaries like Fenrir Greyback. This of course mirrors the fate of Rowling's character.

Lucius Malfoy is a name that's Latin for light, but this parallels him well with Lucifer, the light-bearer who rebelled against the dictates of heaven and preferred to rule the dark side than serve the light. *The Tales of Beedle the Bard* mention "Brutus Malfoy, editor of Warlock at War, an anti-Muggle periodical," who "perpetuated the stereotype that a Muggle-lover was about as magical as a Squib." In 1675, Brutus wrote: "This we may state with certainty: any wizard who shows fondness for the society of Muggles is of low intelligence, with magic so feeble and pitiful that he can only feel himself superior if surrounded by Muggle pigmen." Certainly, he is a "brutal" man, and thus this Roman name well fits his character.

Greco-Roman star names are common in Sirius's family, though naming him for the Dog-Star seems more than coincidence: There's also Bellatrix Lestrange, Alphard Black, Arcturus Black, Pollux Black, and Regulus Black. Constellation names include Draco Malfoy, his son Scorpius Malfoy, Andromeda Tonks, Cassiopeia Black, Cygnus Black, and Orion Black. Somewhere in the family tree is Phoebe Black – named for the Greek Titaness of the Moon or for Artemis herself.

Narcissa Malfoy's name comes from the Greek myth of Narcissus, who fell in love with his own reflection. The name suggests self-centeredness. Draco means "dragon," but it also belongs to the first lawgiver of ancient Athens, from whom the term draconian (severe) is derived. It also fits well with the Black tradition of Greek star names – Draco is a constellation in the far northern sky.

The star names of Sirius and his family are Latin-based and largely significant. Sirius is the brightest star in the night sky, and thus comes from the Ancient Greek for "glowing" or "scorcher." Sirius is also known colloquially as the "dog star," thanks to its prominence in its constellation Canis Major (Greater Dog). Its rising marked the "dog days" of summer for the ancient Greeks, The dog parallel is obvious, and in fact, he transforms into a black dog with a "blackened" name. Still, one should also notice the contradictory elements of his description as glowing against the blackness.

His brother Regulus takes his name from the star Alpha Leonis, the brightest star in the constellation of Leo and one of the brightest in the night sky. He too shines against the darkness as he takes his own stand against evil in the last days of his life. The lion suggests bravery and steadfastness. Regulus is Latin for 'prince' or 'little king' – presumably how he was treated by his Slytherin parents. "I hated the lot of them: my parents with their pure-blood mania, convinced that to be a Black made you practically royal... my idiot brother, soft enough to believe them... that's him. He was younger than me, and a much better son, as I was constantly reminded," Sirius complains.[12]

His middle name, Arcturus, from Ancient Greek, means "Guardian of the Bear." This, the fourth brightest star in the sky, is the brightest star in the constellation of Boötes (the Plowman), next to Ursa Major and Ursa Minor, the Greater and Lesser Bears. (The ancient Greeks saw the "Big Dipper" as a cart with oxen.) According to one version, Boötes was a son of Demeter and inventor of the plow. In another, he's Icarius, tutored in winemaking by Dionysus, whose neighbors killed him when they were startled by the intoxicating effects. This last seems to fit better as Voldemort trained him with impressive skills, all of which branded him a Death Eater. Regulus appears named for his great-uncle, also named Regulus, and his paternal grandfather, Arcturus. Thus he follows the family tradition more than his brother.

Their parents were Orion and Walburga Black. The latter is named for St. Walburga of England (presumably she married into this family of star names, rather than having one herself). Walburga became an abbess, but more significantly, she is often called the first female author of both England and Germany. She may thus be a personal hero of Rowling's.

The constellations Scorpio and Orion are tied since, in myth, the great hunter Orion boasted to his lover the goddess Artemis that he would kill every animal on earth. This was too great an act of destruction, so the earth goddess Gaia, or perhaps Artemis herself sent a scorpion to sting him to death. The pair battled and the scorpion killed him. Zeus raised both characters to the heavens, where Scorpio became a Zodiac sign. Every winter Orion hunts in the sky, but every summer he flees as the constellation of the scorpion comes. Orion, like Phaeton, served the forces of destruction as was destroyed by them – a clear theme for a Death Eater.

"There's Phineas Nigellus…my great-great-grandfather, see?… least popular Headmaster Hogwarts ever had," Sirius says, foreshadowing the Headmaster's portrait.[13] Both his names are classically British, but he named his sons Sirius, Cygnus, and Arcturus, committing to the star constellation names.

Cygnus is a northern constellation, deriving its name from the Latinized Greek word for swan. Zeus disguised himself as a swan to seduce Helen of Troy's mother, or in some tales, Orpheus or King Cygnus is the origin for the constellation. In Ovid's *Metamorphoses*, there are three people named Cygnus, all of whom are transformed into swans. There's Cycnus, brother of tragic Phaeton, who couldn't stop grieving but spent all his days diving into the river to collect Phaeton's bones and give him a proper burial. There's a boy from Tempe who commits suicide, but is transformed into a swan and flies away, and the invulnerable son of Neptune, who is defeated by Achilles in the Trojan War, but saved by transformation.

Pollux (Sirius's maternal grandfather) was the hero-twin of Castor, brother to Helen of Troy. The two heroes make the constellation Gemini (Latin, "the twins"). Alphard, is the brightest star in the constellation of Hydra. It's known as "The Solitary One" and either this or its affiliation with Hydra might define the character, Sirius's uncle who left him "a decent bit of gold."[14] Tellingly, astronomer Tycho Brahe dubbed it Cor Hydræ, Latin for "the heart of the snake."

In this family, there's also Andromeda Tonks and her daughter Nymphadora. Greek nymphs were beautiful, magical maidens, known for shapeshifting between human and nature forms, like trees or rivers (thus offering a link for Tonks). They generally aided heroes rather than performing great deeds themselves. Andromeda was likewise a beautiful princess rescued by the hero Perseus, who mostly furthered the hero's story rather than her own. This suggests that her Muggle husband Ted Tonks was a true hero. Cassiopeia Black is named for Andromeda's mother, a vain woman whose boast of her daughter's beauty led to her sacrifice. It's a name much like Narcissa.

Continuing through their family, Bellatrix is Latin for "female warrior" and was called the Amazon Star. It's the third brightest star in Orion's belt. Certainly, the root of "bel" means war, as in belligerent. Thus it's a fitting name for the angry character. *Harry Potter and the Cursed Child* introduces her supposed daughter, Delphini, named for the Oracle at Delphi. This was the Greek center of the world where people traveled to learn their dark fates. Her name relates to her title of Augurey, an oracle of darkness.

Judeo-Christian

Anthony Goldstein, Ravenclaw, has a distinctly Jewish last name, and Rowling tweeted at one point that he is indeed Jewish.[15] Bathsheda Babbling also has a Jewish-derived name, but she teaches Ancient Runes. Little more is known of her. Of course, these runes might also be Jewish.

"For one thing, the lack of common words for chemical concepts and processes, as well as the need for secrecy, led alchemists to borrow the terms and symbols of biblical and pagan mythology, astrology, kabbalah, and other mystic and esoteric fields; so that the even the plainest chemical recipe ended up reading like an abstruse magic incantation," Libatius Borage, teacher of Advanced Potion-Making, is quoted as saying in the film *Half-Blood Prince*. Thus many ancient traditions appear in the wizards' magic. Kabbalah is Jewish mysticism, which incorporates *sphirot*, or levels of enlightenment.

In the Hebrew alphabet, letters all have symbolic meanings, with links to alchemy and tarot.[16] To many medieval occultists, Biblical Hebrew was considered the original tongue, or language of Adam. Thus many believed this was the same language used by God and Angels in the formation and direction of the universe.

During the Renaissance, many famed occultists and crypto-graphers experimented with rediscovering Adam's language in pursuit of spiritual and magical power. In the early 1500s, Heinrich Cornelius Agrippa wrote his *Three Books of Occult Philosophy*, in which he recorded three of the earliest Medieval/Renaissance examples of divine writing: Celestial, Malachim (Angelic), and Passing the River with alphabets given for encoding Divine Names upon talismans. All were related to

Hebrew. An obscure alchemical text called the *Voarchadumia*, from the mid-1500s, created an Alphabet of Enoch, closer to Latin letters. The Angelical alphabet later recorded by Queen Elizabeth's astrologer Dr. John Dee and his scryer Edward Kelley is related, and helped found much of Western occultism such as the Order of the Golden Dawn. Hogwarts runes may derive from these as easily as from Norse sources.

The English wizards celebrate Christmas at Hogwarts with twelve towering Christmas trees in the Great Hall, enchanted snow, and suits of armor singing carols. There's also a grand dinner for those who stay over break:

> Harry had never in all his life had such a Christmas dinner. A hundred fat, roast turkeys; mountains of roast and boiled potatoes; platters of chipolatas; tureens of buttered peas, silver boats of thick, rich gravy and cranberry sauce – and stacks of wizard crackers every few feet along the table... Harry pulled a wizard cracker with Fred and it didn't just bang, it went off with a blast like a cannon and engulfed them all in a cloud of blue smoke, while from the inside exploded a rear admiral's hat and several live, white mice.[17]

Much more direct religious references appear in book seven. Albus Dumbledore places a Bible verse on the tomb of his mother and sister: "Where your treasure is, there will your heart be also." This suggests that he's Christian or values the Bible's teachings. On Harry's parents' graves at Godric's Hollow he sees "The last enemy that shall be destroyed is death," a reference to 1 Corinthians 15:26. "They're very British books, so on a very practical note Harry was going to find biblical quotations on tombstones," Rowling explained. "[But] I think those two particular quotations he finds on the tombstones at Godric's Hollow, they sum up – they almost epitomize the whole series."[18]

The book also begins with two religiously-themed epigraphs – one pagan from *The Libation Bearers* by the Greek playwright Aeschylus, which calls on the gods to "bless the children." The other is more Christian from William Penn's *More Fruits of Solitude*, which speaks of death as but "crossing the world, as friends do the seas." Both reflect the themes of the series, especially the final book.

Rowling was raised Christian in the Anglican Church and currently attends the Church of Scotland. Of course, many Christian leaders and organizations, such as the US-based Focus on the Family, had famously condemned the series. Pope Benedict XVI, then Cardinal Joseph Ratzinger, wrote that their "subtle seductions, which act unnoticed...deeply distort Christianity in the soul before it can grow properly."[19]

However, the books had a dramatic turnaround with all the Christian symbolism and Bible quotes of the final books. Most importantly, Harry sacrifices his life to save his community, then resurrects, in a clear Jesus parallel. He also, as "Master of Death," resurrects his loved ones in the Forbidden Forest. "To me, [the religious parallels have] always been obvious," Rowling said. "But I never wanted to talk too openly about it because I thought it might show people who just wanted the story where we were going."[20] Certainly, she underwent six books of controversy (most of it aimed around children performing spells) before her great revelation.

Norse

From this culture, the crafts and creatures appear, but names less so (excepting Fenrir Greyback, named for Fenrir, the Norse superwolf who will swallow the world at Ragnarok). From the nine worlds of the Norse world tree we get giants, trolls, and goblins. The latter were clever crafters known for their superb handiwork. Likewise, the runes Hermione studies are likely Norse, the most popular kind today.

The word "rune" derives from the Indo-European root *ru*, "mystery or secret." Today's runes are usually Norse (a tradition which influenced ancient Britain, certainly), with alphabetic meanings as well as symbolic ones. The Norse god Odin was said to have traded his eye for this language, which was adapted into Tolkien's *Lord of the Rings* and other fantasy works. Today, some people use these letters for spell casting and meditation. As the *Internet Book of Shadows* describes modern runes:

> In the most mundane sense, runes are an alphabet much as our own alphabet and others such as the Greek and Cyrillic alphabets. Each rune represents a sound and was/is used to write words with.
> But that is in the most MUNDANE of senses.
> Runes were used long before the concept of writing was around. Each rune is an archetype of a force. People had concepts for such things as Fire, Honour, Birth, et.al. and each

of these concepts were given names to make them easier for us
to comprehend.

...

> Runes can be used for fortune telling. They can be drawn
> and placed and read much like tarot cards. The can be cast or
> strewn and the relationship of groupings, distance and angles
> and patterns formed will tell the caster what he wishes to know.
> Runes are also entities in and of themselves. Much like the
> angels, princes, demons, sylphs, undines and watchtowers of
> the ceremonial magician, each rune can be invoked or evoked
> and the power harnessed to work one's will to enlighten the
> intellect. They are a fantastic meditation tool and will always
> increase one's knowledge.[21]

Hermione is rarely seen using them, though the book of Beedle the
Bard Dumbledore leaves her is written in them, suggesting
information he wishes kept secret from unenlightened eyes. (Runes
weren't actually used historically to communicate the British language,
only as mystical codes and symbols.)

In Norse cosmology, there are all the classic characters of the
pantheon – Heimdall, the handsome gold-toothed guardian of the
rainbow bridge leading to Asgard, the home of the Gods, parallels
Argus. Frigga, Odin's wife, is the All-Mother, protector of children
and teller of the future, a bit like Trelawney. Madam Hooch might be
Freya, feather-cloaked leader of the flying Valkyries. She has many
amazing female protégés like Angelina and Ginny.

Still, most correspondences between professors and Norse gods
are only those of obvious archetypes – father god, nature mother, and
so on. In addition, the fact that the male gods are warriors and
goddesses embody fertility and beauty make the correspondences a
bit weaker here. Still, the Prose Edda, source of much of our
knowledge of the Norse gods, has a few pieces of telling description.

"Odin is the greatest and oldest of the Æsir." The patriarch is
Dumbledore; both sacrifice a great deal for wisdom – Odin his eye
and Dumbledore his loved ones then his hand. Thor, the greatest of
Odin's sons, is a brawling warrior, but the next, Baldur, is the
brightest and most beautiful, sacrificed to save humanity. Harry is the
best parallel, unless one is a Cedric fan.

"Bragi is the name of another of the asas. He is famous for his
wisdom, eloquence and flowing speech." Flitwick has some echoes,
though he's closer to the clever crafting dwarves. "Hoder who is
blind, but exceedingly strong; and the gods would wish that this *asa*

never needed to be named, for the work of his hand will long be kept in memory both by gods and men." Misled, he killed the handsome, eloquent Baldur, just as Mad-Eye Moody's form is used to betray Cedric and Harry.

Finally, "there is yet one who is numbered among the *asas*, but whom some call the backbiter of the *asas*. He is the originator of deceit, and the disgrace of all gods and men. His name is Loki." Loki, contentious and set apart, the traitor, has Snape parallels…

Among the goddesses, "The ninth is Var. She hears the oaths and troths that men and women plight to each other. Hence such vows are called *vars*, and she takes vengeance on those who break their promises." This corresponds with the Unbreakable Vow, which dominates the sixth book.

"The tenth is Vör, who is so wise and searching that nothing can be concealed from her. It is a saying that a woman becomes *vor* (ware) of what she becomes wise." Perhaps McGonagall knows more than she's telling, as she's certainly the goddess of wisdom in the series.

"The eleventh is Syn, who guards the door of the hall, and closes it against those who are not to enter. In trials she guards those suits in which anyone tries to make use of falsehood. Hence is the saying that '*syn* is set against it,' when anyone tries to deny ought." The guardian who protects against liars seems much like the Fat Lady, whose portrait defends the Gryffindor common room.

"The twelfth is Hlin, who guards those men whom Frigg wants to protect from any danger. Hence is the saying that he *hlins* who is forewarned." Lily, Harry's protector, certainly parallels her as a heaven-sent guardian.

Celtic

The Greek pantheon lacks the animal gods echoed in Hagrid, Lupin, Firenze, and other teachers. For these, we must go to Celtic Epona or Rhiannon, Lithuanian Medeina, Hindu Sarama, or a host of Egyptian and Native American animal-spirits. The Celts especially have particular links to the animal gods, including Rudiobus, the god of horses and a link for Rubeus Hagrid. Rudiobus's name means "red" with the Latinized masculine ending *us*; making his name "He of the Red Zeal," or "He of the Red [Battle] Frenzy." Thus Rudianus is a "bearsark," a berserker, one who is filled with the red mist of rage in battle, the perfect warrior god.

Celtic Rosmerta is "The Great Provider," goddess of fertility and wealth. Her symbol is a cornucopia, or horn of plenty. Meanwhile, Balor of the Evil Eye may parallel Mad-Eye Moody. Balor's eye, ruined in an accident, is so hideous that he only opens it to kill his enemies with its terrible venom. Also, there's the crone Cailleach, who guarded her underworld with a monstrous gatekeeper dog named Dormarth "Death's Door" and brewed regeneration and prophecy in her cauldron. Sybill Trelawney only has teacups, but is obsessed with the Grim in a subtle parallel. Another correspondence for her is Corra, Goddess of Prophecy, transcendent knowledge, and transitions. The rune stones, crystal balls, and tarot cards were her symbols.

There are other, subtler correspondences, with Filius Flitwick as Sucellos, the Celtic 'good striker' and smith god. Unusually, the Celts has a *male* love god, Angus Og, who corresponds with Gilderoy Lockhart. The terrible Hogwarts team of Dolores Umbridge and the Carrows parallel the triple war goddesses Badb/Madb/Macha who would cheer on carnage and shriek their bloodlust on the battlefield.

Nuada of the Silver Hand was the first king of the Tuatha Dé Danann (fairyfolk), who brought his tribe to Ireland and contended with its inhabitants for possession of the island. An enemy sliced off his left hand at the wrist. Because sacred law decreed that a king of the Dé Danann had to be whole in body and mind, the maimed Nuada was forced to step down as ruler of the gods. However, the people needed him, so the Dé Danann physician Dian Cecht fashioned a magical silver hand, which worked as well as the flesh one, and enabled Nuada to take back his throne. This of course finds a parallel in Peter Pettigrew's replacement hand. It's not Peter's hand that makes him unworthy, though the missing finger betrays his identity; it's Harry's mercy for him that makes him truly corrupted as he serves Voldemort. When Harry challenges him in book seven, reminding Peter he once saved his life, the hand strikes back, serving the godlike Voldemort to the end. Thus magical gifts often have a catch.

The Dagda, Celtic earth god and All Father, had a few Dumbledore parallels. Though he was a formidable fighter, he shared Dumbledore's humility and simple tastes, dressing in a brown tunic and hooded cape. He was god of the arts, knowledge, magic, music, prophecy, prosperity, and regeneration. Dumbledore offers much knowledge, magic, and prophecy through the series, along with traces of these other gifts. The Dagda mingled life and death, with a club that could slay nine men with one end and bring back life with the other and a pair of swine, one of which was perpetually roasting, the other perpetually growing. His other talismans were the bottomless cauldron of plenty, one of the original Hallows, and a harp with which he controlled the seasons – this is seen in the symbolism of Hogwarts with its indoor snows or night skies. In perhaps the most striking image, the Dagda had four great palaces under hollow hills, much like the Hogwarts houses.

Lugh, the Irish and Welsh god of harpers, healing, poets, smiths, sorcerers, and waters, bears the symbol of a white stag. Thus he's linked with Snape, and both symbolize Lugh's classic themes – healing, reincarnation, prophecy, knowledge, and revenge. Lugh quested for a wife but a curse prohibited him from having an earthly wife, so his uncles made him one out of flowers and named her Blodeuwedd. She betrayed him, and she and her lover, Gronw Pebr, plotted Llew's death. James Potter and Lily run off together, betraying Snape, from his point of view.

"The Horned One," Cernunnos, is a Celtic god of fertility, life, animals, wealth, and the underworld. Cernunnos is depicted with the antlers of a stag, thus corresponding with James Potter. Each year, the Horned God is born at the winter solstice, marries the goddess at the spring festival of Beltane, and dies at the summer solstice. Each year he continues the cycle of death, rebirth and reincarnation, emphasizing the connection between life and death and the power of the natural cycle. James Potter's spirit returns from death several times, in photographs and stories and most often through Harry's stag Patronus. As the death god, Cernunnos leads the wild hunt at Samhain, the holiday on which James Potter was killed. "Hunted animals were sometimes perceived as messengers of the Otherworld powers, the means of bringing living humans, either directly or indirectly, to the underworld." [22] Stags, especially white stags, were associated with shapechanging as they were often messengers from the fairy world.[23] "It is possible that Cernunnos was a skin-turner or shape-shifter, able to vary his outward form from human to animal at will."[24]

Egyptian

In Egypt, Dumbledore corresponds to the father god as always. However, when Osiris was prematurely murdered by his brother Set, he was avenged by his heroic son Horus. After he died, his wife Isis searched the world for the pieces of his body, rather like a Horcrux hunt. Besides this, most teachers correspond to obvious archetypes: Minerva McGonagall reflects Ma'at, goddess of truth, balance, order, law, morality, and justice. Poppy Pomfrey corresponds to Serket, goddess of healing stings and bites, and Pomona Sprout to Hathor, goddess of life and growing things.

Once again, there are the dark, rejected members of the Pantheon, in this case Set, brother and betrayer of Osiris, and god of the desert, storms, darkness and chaos, who corresponds best to Voldemort. Dolores Umbridge works as Nephthys, the dark despised rejected goddess, wife of Set.

Two closer correspondences appear in Irma Pince, always described as "vulturelike" as she guards the library. Nekhbet, the white vulture, was a protective goddess. Likewise, Mrs. Norris, the cat always keeping watch, is Bast, the cat goddess of protection.

Hindu

The Hindu goddess Parvati, wife of Shiva, is known for her bravery. Her name derives from the Sanskrit/Hindi word *Parvat*, mountain – something unmovably strong. "Padma" means "sacred lotus" and is a name of Saraswati, goddess of intellect. If Rowling wanted to name the two Indian students as the "perfect Gryffindor" and "perfect Ravenclaw," and then sort them into those houses, these names were good choices. It's no coincidence that Parvati's favorite subject is Divination, reflecting Hindu belief in "Kundali," which contains all the details and secrets of a person's past, present and future

The third Indian name in the series goes to Nagini. Voldemort's snake is roughly twelve feet long and thick as a man's thigh.[25] *Naga* means male snake in Sanskrit, and *nagin* is the female snake in Hindi and Urdu. Nag and Nagini are also the villainous snakes in the British children's book *Rikki Tikki Tavi*.

Conclusion

Two archetypes are absent: There is no queen equal to Dumbledore (McGonagall is accurately cast as Minerva since she acts as more of a daughter-subordinate to Dumbledore). Hogwarts is also notable for its lack of warriors, except among the Death Eaters who take over the school. (Mad-Eye has a small role but works better as maimed Hephaestus.) Hogwarts is clearly a place of higher thought rather than brutality, but they surrender to dark forces for several months of the final book.

There are also basically no marriages or couples among the teachers, and Rowling's descriptions on *Pottermore* reveal romantic tragedies in some of the teachers' pasts, isolating them. The love goddess is absent (though Fleur has a small role), and love potions always go horribly awry. Finally, the great mother goddess is absent (mothers Molly and Lily are exiled from the school and have limited power). However, as the heroes grow up and take their place in *Cursed Child*, a shift appears: McGonagall rules the school and adults Hermione and Ginny do more to establish themselves as warrior-mothers, fighting to defend their families.

---

[1] J.K. Rowling, *Short Stories from Hogwarts of Heroism, Hardship and Dangerous Hobbies* Pottermore, Kindle Locations 483-485.

[2] Ibid., Kindle Locations 508-512.

[3] Pseudo-Hyginus, "Fabulae." *The Myths of Hyginus,* trans. Mary Grant, (Lawrence, Kansas: University of Kansas Publications), 192.

[4] Apollodorus. *The Library of Greek Mythology,* trans. Keith Aldrich. (Lawrence, Kansas: Coronado Press, 1975), ii. 8. § 5.

[5] Ibid., i. 4. § 3

[6] J. K Rowling, *Harry Potter and the Half-Blood Prince,* (USA: Scholastic, Inc, 2005), 432.

[7] Newt Scamander, *Fantastic Beasts and Where to Find Them* (New York: Scholastic, 2001), 12.

[8] Rowling, *Short Stories,* Kindle Locations 518-520.

[9] Ibid., Kindle Locations 523-524.

[10] Ibid., Kindle Locations 546-547.

[11] J.E. Cirlot, *A Dictionary of Symbols* (New York: Routledge, 1971), 161.

[12] Rowling, *Order of the Phoenix* 112.

[13] Ibid., 113.

[14] Ibid., 111.

[15] Alexis Rhiannon, "J.K. Rowling's Response to Whether There Were LGBT Kids at Hogwarts Will Melt Your Heart," *Crushable,* 18 Dec. 2014. http://www.crushable.com/2014/12/18/entertainment/lgbt-jewish-kids-at-

hogwarts-j-k-rowling-confirms-harry-potter.

¹⁶ Cirlot 183.

¹⁷ J. K Rowling, *Harry Potter and the Philosopher's Stone* (London: Bloomsbury Publishing Plc, 1997), 203.

¹⁸ "Harry Potter Author Reveals Books' Christian Allegory, her Struggling Faith," *Christian Today,* 19 Oct 2007. http://www.christiantoday.com/article/harry.potter.author.reveals.books.ch ristian.allegory.her.struggling.faith/14052.htm

¹⁹ Ibid.

²⁰ Ibid.

²¹ Lokrien. "What Are Runes." *Internet Book of Shadows,* 1999. *The Sacred Texts Archive.* http://www.sacred-texts.com/bos/bos064.htm

²² Miranda Green, *Animals in Celtic Life and Myth* (USA: Routledge, 1992), 164.

²³ Ibid., 168.

²⁴ Ibid., 234.

²⁵ Rowling, *Goblet of Fire* 122.

CHAPTER 7: REINVENTING EVE: BIBLE AND ARTHURIAN MYTH REBORN IN *HARRY POTTER* AND *HIS DARK MATERIALS*

Modern fantasy takes its roots in older legends: epic myths, fireside tales, and Bible stories. The roots of a name, a hero's talisman, a moment's treason or loyalty: all allude deeper, strengthening the modern stories through allegory. The Harry Potter books and the contemporary children's trilogy *His Dark Materials* (1995-2000) are no exception. Harry Potter is the foretold British king, determined to repair the betrayals and failures of King Arthur and usher in a new golden age. Just as Arthur's world is ending, Harry's is just beginning to flourish. Likewise, Lyra quests for knowledge through her alethiometer, gladly falling as Eve did and losing her heaven-sent grace. Yet for Lyra, this is a triumph: the gift of growing into adulthood even with the losses and sorrows it encompasses. In both cases, the protagonists destroy the old regime in a glorious revolution of ascending adulthood and power, casting Eve and King Arthur both as heroes reborn.

Reenacting King Arthur: Names in Harry Potter

King Arthur faces betrayal from all his closest allies: wife, best friend, son, and sister. His story encompasses the end of a golden age and the destruction of magic, as age robs him of his kingdom. Harry Potter mirrors his story, but Harry is growing into kingship, not losing it. His heroic journey takes him through gaining worthier friends than Arthur's and rising in power, until Harry's story ends with triumph rather than defeat. This reflection of Arthurian mythos is reborn most strongly in character names: Ginevra, Arthur,

Voldemort, and Percival.

Before Lancelot was later added to the story by Chrétien de Troyes, Guinevere was depicted as a powerful queen, ruling independently and named for the Welsh triple goddess, Gwenhwyfar. "Having been informed by JKR on her website that Ginny is short for Ginevra, not Virginia, we have only to note that Ginevra is Italian for Guinevere to realize that, as Guinevere was meant for King Arthur, so Ginny is the only one fit to be Harry's queen," essayist Tim Lambarski notes.[1] Thus, Ginny Weasley is a powerful heroine and suitable partner for Harry, the hero-king. She defends Harry from criticism and self-doubt:

> When Malfoy claims that Harry is always making the front page, she bursts out, "Leave him alone, he didn't want all that!" In *Chamber of Secrets*, Rowling has set up a connection between Harry and Ginny by making her the only other student of their time to be confronted by Riddle/Voldemort and experience the Dark Lord inside her head.[2]

This proves invaluable in book five, when Ginny uses her experience to convince Harry he's not becoming Voldemort. "You don't know anyone but me who's been possessed by You-Know-Who, and I can tell you how it feels,"[3] she says angrily. Book five shows her as Quidditch seeker like Cho: both of Harry's girlfriends are his equals on the playing field as well as in life. She's talented in Dumbledore's Army, which she names, and her "Bat-bogey hex" gets her an invitation to the prestigious Slugg Club, based solely on her talent. Ginny, of course, remains steadfastly loyal in the series, rather than committing the treason that brings down King Arthur's kingdom. She willingly stays in safety at Hogwarts, rather than distracting Harry or becoming a hostage for Voldemort. When they part, she only says, "I knew this would happen in the end. I knew you wouldn't be happy unless you were fighting Voldemort. Maybe that's why I like you so much."[4]

Arthur Weasley, her father, is a hero of the Order of the Phoenix, unquestionably brave and loyal, undisputed ruler of the enormous Weasley family. His children Ginny and Percy (Percival) emphasize the King Arthur connection once more. Further, Rowling stated in an interview that he was supposed to die in book five.[5] This death would have marked the end of safety and a stable kingdom, forcing the next generation (in the form of Harry and his friends) to restore the lost

Camelot of the Wizarding World. Lacking the tragic sense of Arthur's tellers, Rowling preserves Arthur Weasley, allowing him to defend a Camelot shaken by Percy Weasley's betrayal yet unfallen.

Voldemort is very much the Mordred character, and not just because of the "Mor" (death) root they share. Voldemort created Harry as his nemesis by forming an unnatural Horcrux from his attempted murder, while King Arthur created Mordred through his incestuous union with a half-sister. These rulers and their creations struggle for power throughout the story: one leads the forces of light, and the other, forces of death and destruction. Only through an epic battle can the war finally end in a metaphor for the son growing into adulthood, supplanting the high king, his father. King Arthur cannot return to childhood and hold the throne forever; thus, he can only stop his successor, Mordred, through mutual destruction. Harry, however, destroys Voldemort's regime forever, setting himself in place as a future Auror and new protector of the Wizarding World.

Albus Percival Wulfric Brian Dumbledore offers five names to readers. Albus means white, suggesting spirituality and altruism, while a Dumbledore is a mythic bumblebee. But what of the other names?

Percival, of course, offers the Arthurian link. He was a valiant fighter who quested for the grail (or in Harry Potter's world, the Horcruxes) but failed in his goal. His teenage protégé Galahad succeeded, through immaculate faith and goodness. Clear parallels appear here with the Dumbledore-Harry relationship. Galahad dies as he grasps the grail, just as Harry dies just after uniting the Deathly Hallows. Still, the protection of Harry's blood binds him to life, allowing him to return as mankind's savior. Percival Dumbledore (father to Albus) and his namesake, Percy Weasley, likewise appear as knights who fail, but leave others to battle and complete the great quest against Voldemort.

Wulfric and Brian are both names of British Catholic saints: Wulfric of Haselbury was a hermit and miracle worker. Blessed Brian Lacey was one of the London Martyrs of 1591.[6] This connection to sainthood and martyrdom suggests pure righteousness, but an altruism lacking the practicality to finish the war. Dumbledore indeed becomes a martyr, willingly sacrificing his life in order to save his students, Draco and Harry, among others. In her essay on love in the series, Catherine Danielson describes this death as a godlike release from his human form, adding, "Dumbledore knew that when he was no longer confined to his physical body, his power would be greater."[7] As with religious saints, Dumbledore's selfless devotion takes its reward as spiritual ascension. In Arthurian legend, Merlin likewise safeguards and instructs Arthur, all the while knowing he will fall to Morgan Le Fay's duplicity. Snape apparently betrays Dumbledore, striking the killing blow in the lightning-struck tower. Yet as we later learn, he is assisting in suicide, rather than committing treachery. "He [Dumbledore] chose his own manner of dying, chose it months before he died, arranged the whole thing with the man you thought was your servant,"[8] Harry tells Voldemort before defeating him in their duel. While Arthur finally dies, abandoned by his mentor's magic, Snape's loyalty and Dumbledore's trust ensure Harry keeps the Elder Wand, the world's deadliest weapon.

Casting Harry as Arthur with a touch of Galahad emphasizes his heroic role, but this charming fantasy repairs the tragedy and betrayal of the Arthurian Saga. Ron, the best friend, stays loyal to Harry (though many readers expected a three-way catastrophe over Hermione), and Ginny never betrays him. Finally, Dumbledore and his "betrayer" work together, to ensure Harry masters the Elder Wand and defeats his enemy. Rather than losing Camelot forever, Harry preserves it, destroying the evil Mordred forever.

Pullman's Names and The Biblical Pagan Dichotomy

The Golden Compass, of course, offers Biblical names but also Greek ones, reminiscent of not only the Greek Orthodox church but also the beloved pagan myths of Zeus and his Pantheon. These symbolize the great struggle reborn: paganism or Church, freedom or obedience? Each character in the series is torn between religion and independence, skepticism and faithful obedience. Many characters have hidden motivations, such as Mrs. Coulter's love for Lyra or Lord Asriel's willingness to sacrifice a child. And nearly every character switches allegiance. Too, each character is split into human and dæmon with two sets of desires and personalities. As Lyra struggles to choose a side: Church or fallen Eve and "Republic of Heaven," these mixed allusions reflect her confusion and shed doubt on her entire world.

All this ambiguity is symbolized by the dæmon each character has, a part of the soul, yet with different thoughts and opinions. "A dæmon is a visible, external part of a person that represents facets of the person's character"[9] writes Tony Watkins, author of *Dark Matter: Shedding Light on Phillip Pullman's Trilogy* His Dark Materials. While strong Lord Asriel has a leopard and crafty Mrs. Coulter, a monkey, the dæmons more often represent a hidden or contradictory part of the personality. When Lyra first meets Will Parry, she wishes to see his dæmon to know what secrets he's hiding. However, Will, perhaps the most forthright character, cannot see his dæmon for most of the story. Mrs. Coulter speaks sweetly to Lyra while her monkey brutally attacks Lyra's dæmon. And almost all dæmons are the opposite gender from their owners. A dæmon acts more as a devil's advocate, or angel on one's shoulder than the agenda-free soul. Sally Vincent adds, "It is your guardian angel, your confidante, your conscience, your representative."[10] This sensation that all characters are split in two: male and female, doer and questioner, emphasizes the characters' moral confusion.

Lyra's dæmon, Panteleimon, evokes St. Panteleimon of the Orthodox Churches: "'Panta' means 'all' in Greek, and 'eleison' means 'have mercy' in Greek, thus Panteleimon means 'all merciful.'"[11] Here he sounds angelic, but Lyra calls him Pan, a nickname that evokes the crafty and mysterious satyr of Greek myth. So dear little Pan the shapechanger is part Orthodox saint, part pagan mischief-maker. He is the "all merciful" one that can intercede between Lyra and God, yet he can be selfish and dismissive: the first time we see him, he suggests Lyra not save Asriel from the poison— hardly a merciful act. This myriad of contradictions always surrounds the shapeshifter, keeping him neither one thing nor, the other, especially for very long. This mirrors the confusion of Lyra's task: deciding whom to trust when her parents betray her, the Church experiments on children, and only society's outcasts can protect her.

Lyra herself splits into sinner and saint, angel and dæmon, liar and defender of truth. At the beginning, Lyra is very much a flawed, immature character, worthy of her Eve parallels. Many notice the lexical link between Lyra and "liar," her biggest hobby. Self-centered and egocentric, "she does whatever she finds to be fun, and is only obedient so she can avoid being punished," as one critic comments.[12] She tells Roger incredible stories, and lies bold-faced about Dust to all who ask. Iorek Byrnison names her Silvertongue when she fools Iofur Raknison, the King of the Bears, by telling him that she is a dæmon and that she is willing to change sides for the "strongest bear." Clearly the name refers to her skill at lying, reminiscent of Eve who fell to the snake's lying words.

Still, as Lyra calls herself a dæmon, she is reconciling her two selves. Before Iofur Raknison, her dæmon is hidden and she must play the role of a complete person. She is no longer divided into human and dæmon, Lyra and Pan: now she has taken on both roles and thus claimed power over her innate wisdom, the elusive male shifting part of her personality she can now fully understand. Thus armed, she can leave Pan behind and descend into the land of death itself. Once the harpies there attack her for lying, she realizes she's lost her gift: "I can't tell lies...it's all I can do, and it doesn't work!"[13] The next story she tells, the true story of the world of the living, wins the harpies to her side. There her silver-tongued gift changes to something far more profound—the truth that frees all those trapped in death. She has become liar and seer, both shown through the name of Silvertongue. As another critic ironically comments, "Little lying Lyra is the one who's going to help save the world(s) through truth."[14]

Will, it's been noted, has more "will" than most people. Like the Biblical Adam, "earth," he's a simple primal character with a simple primal name. When we first meet him, he has a cat named Moxie, and later, a dæmon named Kirjava (Finnish for "multi-colored"). These animal sidekicks reveal Will's hidden side through contrast: they exhibit the traits he lacks. In the beginning, Will lives at home with his mother, going to school and awaiting his father's return. In danger, he hides. He indeed lacks "moxie," as shown by the brave cat beside him, foreshadowing his future demon. By the time Kirjava has arrived, Will has grown into resolute strength: he bears the subtle knife which trembles and then finally breaks when his resolve is divided. Thus, his "multi-colored" dæmon is again his hidden side; as the bearer of the Subtle Knife, wielder of the greatest will, cannot afford to be multi-faceted.

The name of Lord Asriel relates to the Hebrew Ashriel, who, in the Jewish and Muslim tradition is the Angel of Death, who separates souls from their bodies.[15] The Koran, however, regards him as helpful rather than demonic.[16] In English, Asriel is an anagram of Israel, which means "struggles with God." Lord Asriel is the Lucifer figure, who rebels against God and is cast from heaven. Like Lucifer, he is beautiful and proud, commanding the scholars of Oxford and winning Lyra's unquestioning loyalty in her childhood. He is charismatic yet dangerous, offering Lyra sanctuary is one moment, and murdering her friend Roger in the next. His window opens the world to atmospheric anomalies and chaos. Though technically on Lyra's side through his rebellion, his morals are ambiguous and he doesn't mind committing a few murders. Nonetheless, he rejects the Church's fears of Dust and "sin," as he understands that sin is the joy of life.

Lord Asriel's dæmon is Stelmaria, a beautiful, powerful snow leopard. The Latin roots, "Stel—Maria" mean "Star Mary," associated with the Star of Bethlehem and the Nativity. Thus the Lucifer figure is constantly shadowed by Mary, light to his innate cruelty. Asriel is Lyra's father (though he nearly sacrifices her at the end of *The Golden Compass*) and Stelmaria a divine mother-protector. As Asriel is the Authority's adversary, Stelmaria's name suggests his greatest divine follower. In this way, the leopard's innate nobility helps to conceal Asriel's treachery and cruelty until his murder of Roger at the end of *The Golden Compass*.

Mary Malone's name suggests Mary, the saintly mother of Jesus and female figurehead of the Church: protective, mothering, and angelically innocent. Yet she is a fallen angel. Once a nun, she has become an atheist, turning from a devout believer in the Church to its antagonist. Her apparent sinfulness evokes Mary Magdalene, a fallen woman who devotes herself to Jesus, as Mary Malone does to Lyra. Yet the alethiometer has identified her as the one who will play the serpent to Lyra's Eve.

Mary Malone's dæmon, the alpine chough, is a "black bird with red legs and a bright yellow beak, slightly curved. A bird of the mountains."[17] Birds, the dæmons of choice for Serafina Pekkala and all the other witches, symbolize air spirits and even the divine soul itself. Birds offer prophetic knowledge in Pagan myth; in the Bible they offer redemption and peace. Though cast as the serpent, Mary has saved the world by preserving Dust and defying the angels. Mary is a woman of the earth, shaping the world with her knowledge of Dust and how its loss threatens nature. Her hidden dæmon, however, is a spiritual creature of heavenly enlightenment. When Serafina helps her see her dæmon, Mary reconciles her two halves and reaches this accord between seeking wisdom and finding it.

All these ambiguities and contradictions between pagan and Christian values echo a world in torment, as angels and Dust vie for dominance. Lying leads Lyra to divine wisdom, just as Mary, the serpent, can save the world. Throughout, every character has a dæmon, offering more contradictions, as each dæmon has all the characteristics his or her master lacks. As Lyra struggles to trust through lies, betrayals, and endless moral confusion, she must reconcile these conflicting beliefs to rescue many many worlds from destruction.

The Hallows of Britain in Welsh and Irish Myth

King Arthur's realm is decaying, and his quest for the Holy Grail, rather than saving it, dooms all his knights to obscurity and death. In fact, all Arthur's treasures, from the mystic Excalibur to his thirteen hallows, fail to preserve Camelot. Arthur quests for kingship, but such a material power is transient, as magic departs the world forever. Harry Potter's tale, however, is growing into adulthood and thus earning power and magical treasures. "While Lord Voldemort has been disintegrating himself [by splitting his soul into Horcruxes], Harry has with each new year at Hogwarts integrated more and more into himself: knowledge, memories, courage, friendships, and most of all, love. With each new memory added, he becomes more than he was before, even as Voldemort is becoming less," says author and commentator Pegg Kerr.[18] Each year he gains spells and treasures, like Sirius's mirror and the Sorting Hat, which help him to summon loved ones. The Goblet of Fire, the grail-like object Harry quests for, is the only item (through its portkey magic) that can save him from Voldemort's evil. These treasures reflect his growing spirituality and power. "Harry, like Arthur, is 'The Chosen One,' the child of destiny. As Arthur was the only one who could pull the sword from the stone, so Harry is the only one who could pull the Sorcerer's Stone from his pocket."[19] Though Harry keeps few of the Deathly Hallows, nearly identical to many of Arthur's treasures, he uses them heroically to preserve the Wizarding World.

The Tuatha de Danaan were said to have brought four treasures to Ireland from the Otherworld. The Spear of Victory wins every battle, while the Sword of Light always destroys its target. The Cauldron of Plenty produces food enough to feed a kingdom. The Stone of Destiny confers kingship, much like the ancient Scottish Stone of Scone or a myriad of thrones, crowns, orbs, and scepters.[20] These four symbols appear in the climax of the Arthurian grail quest, and later became the suits on Tarot cards, and then modern spades, clubs, hearts, and diamonds, echoing through *The Tain*, *The Mabinogion*, and many other Celtic epics.

The Spear of Victory descends through Rowling intact, transmographied into the similar-looking Elder Wand that defeats all opponents. However, the other Hallows have been massively changed. Why? Harry's destiny lies in defeating death, rather than in kingship, as is apparent when Harry gravitates instantly toward the Resurrection Stone.[21] Thus, he quests to destroy the Horcruxes, unnatural defeaters of death created by soul-maiming, something only the depraved Voldemort would attempt.

The Hallows of Britain

The Earliest Hallows	Powers	Later Hallows	Tarot Symbol	Grail Hallows	Rowling
Shining spear of Lugh	Provides victory in any fight	The Pole of Combat	Spear or Wand	Crucifixion Spear	Elder Wand
Sword of Nuadu	Always destroys its target	The Sword of Light	Sword	Broken Sword	Godric's Sword
Cauldron of Dagda	Provides endless food	The Cauldron of Cure	Cup	The Grail	Hermione's Beaded Bag
Stone of Fal	Confers kingship	The Stone of Destiny	Pentacle	Platter or Stone	Resurrection Stone

Harry's power comes from repeatedly surviving Voldemort's Avada Kedavra: as a baby, in book four's graveyard, and in book seven's ultimate test of courage and sacrifice. In each case, his skill evading death gives him the power to resist or defeat Voldemort, finally destroying him forever in the climax of *Deathly Hallows*. Harry's test is to literally defy death, not to sit on a throne, and so that is the power the Resurrection Stone grants him. As Rowling said in an interview, "As Dumbledore explains, the real master of Death accepts that he must die, and that there are much worse things in the world of the living. It is not about striving for immortality, but about accepting mortality."[22] Thus the stone sends James, Remus, Sirius, and Lily to protect him and it only comes to Harry when he willingly surrenders his life to destroy Voldemort. "I am about to die,"[23] he whispers, summoning the power for his greatest adventure of all: death itself. King Arthur's task is to rule Camelot, never surrendering it, even to Mordred. Thus, Arthur wins in the end, having defeated the evil usurper, though the deed costs his own life. Harry quests to master death, and he likewise succeeds – thanks to his magical blood, bequeathed by his dying mother and stolen by Voldemort in the graveyard, Voldemort has lost the power to kill him. At the same time, Harry's death and resurrection has extended his protection over everyone at Hogwarts. "You won't be killing anyone else tonight," he says. "I was ready to die to stop you from hurting these people."[24] Now Harry, master of death, can save all his friends from dying. Even before the final duel, he has truly conquered death in a way Voldemort never manages.

Harry likewise doesn't feed and care for subjects, only defends those in need. In fact, the teens' lack of food and supplies is a major plot device, as the teens suffer depravation and unending depression while hiding in the forest. While "magic can't provide food," they rely on books, information, and rumors from Hogwarts, all available from Hermione's beaded bag. Though their equivalent to the cauldron doesn't nourish them, it lets them accomplish their quest.

Harry needs a sword of unavoidable destruction, but to murder Voldemort's Horcruxes, not people. In fact, Harry, as master of life, never uses it to attack another person at all.

Harry's "Sword of Light" is indeed powerful, but, like the original Arthurian Hallows, descends from the gods (or at least the founders of their world like Godric Gryffindor), only to protect those worthy of its magic. "It must be taken under conditions of need and valor"[25] and it only appears when a worthy person summons it. "Much like a magic wand, the sword of Gryffindor appears to be almost sentient, responding to appeals for help by Gryffindor's chosen successors; and, similar to a wand, part of its magic is that it imbibes that which strengthens it, which can then be used against enemies."[26] Further, the sword emphasizes the wielder's warrior spirit, as only Dumbledore, Neville and Harry, the male heroes, wield it.

Rowling acknowledges the sword's ties to the hallows and also to Excalibur, the sword that can only be drawn by the worthy king. Likewise, Harry must draw the sword from the hat and then the frozen pond, an allusion to the Arthurian Lady of the Lake. Rowling explains:

There have been many enchanted swords in folklore. The Sword of Nuadu, part of the four legendary treasures of Tuatha Dé Danann, was invincible when drawn. Gryffindor's sword owes something to the legend of Excalibur, the sword of King Arthur, which in some legends must be drawn from a stone by the rightful king. The idea of fitness to carry the sword is echoed in the sword of Gryffindor's return to worthy members of its true owner's house.[27]

These four hallows, thus, have changed into the prized Elder Wand and Resurrection Stone, along with the beaded bag and Sword of Gryffindor used over and over throughout book seven. Obviously, one item is missing from this collection: the third hallow of Harry's invisibility cloak. This one is less of a plot point, useful but always in Harry's possession. Perhaps it is not surprising that the humblest of these, the one he's had and used all along, comes from a more modern list.

Later Arthurian legend lists thirteen treasures, many of which seem to have evolved from the previous four. The treasures could only be used by the King or his representative in battle. Six of the thirteen provide food or drink (something our trio would've welcomed). The others are more interesting, as they likewise offer a number of Deathly Hallows parallels. Dyrnwyn, the sword of Rhydderch Hael, would burst into flame if drawn by any man but its owner. While it is a blade in the original myth, a clearer parallel with the series is Fiendfyre: the unworthy Crabbe casts it and he and the tiara Horcrux are destroyed by its unstoppable force. Also new to book seven is Apparating, since all three teens have passed their tests and left the confines of Hogwarts. This new power is much like "the chariot of Morgan Mwynvawr: whoever sat in it would be immediately wheresoever he wished." [28] The Halter of Clydno Eiddyn lets the owner call any horse, just as Harry uses Sirius's mirror to summon Dobby and rescue, while the Whetstone of Tudwal Tudclud kills any man it wounds, rather like the total destruction inflicted by Gryffindor's Sword. The next two appear many times in Harry Potter: One is the chessboard that plays by itself, a favorite pastime of Ron's. The other is a coat that identifies those of noble birth, paralleling the Sorting Hat and its uncanny ability to choose one's Hogwarts house. The thirteenth hallow is Arthur's Mantle, an invisibility cloak and the parallel for the third Deathly Hallow.[29]

Highlights of The Thirteen Treasures of Britain

The Arthurian Hallows	The Mantle of Arthur	The Whetstone of Tudwal Tudglyd	The Chariot of Morgan the Wealthy	Dyrnwyn, Sword of Rhydderch
Ability	Makes the wearer invisible	Ensures death follows wounding.	Travels at great speed to any location.	Bursts into flame.
Rowling	Invisibility cloak	Godric's Sword	Apparition	Fiendfyre

The Arthurian Hallows	The Coat of Padarn Red-Coat	Chess-board of Gwend-dolau	Halter of Clydno Eiddyn	Other Arthurian Hallows
Ability	Identifies those of noble birth.	Plays by itself.	Summons any horse into it.	Produce and prepare food and drink
Rowling	Sorting Hat	Wizard Chess	Sirius's Mirror	Beaded Bag

Between the Hallows, the spare wands, the new spells, and other items (Sorting Hat, Sword of Godric Gryffindor, beaded bag, basilisk fangs) Harry has at least thirteen treasures aiding him on his sacred quest to destroy Voldemort. Only King Arthur or one appointed in his stead could wield these treasures, just as only Harry, the symbolic king, or those whom he's appointed to aid him (as he confides his task to Ron, Hermione, and Neville) can destroy the Horcruxes. Dumbledore's greed for the Resurrection Ring overcomes his caution: "I lost my head, Harry," he says. "I quite forgot it was now a Horcrux, that the ring was sure to carry a curse."[30] He wears it, desperate to see his family, and the ring unleashes a fatal trap. Likewise, Crabbe's overzealous use of Fiendfyre destroys a Horcrux but himself as well. Harry destroys three portions of Voldemort's soul, and his three friends, with his encouragement, each destroy one, thus fulfilling book seven's goal.

Dumbledore withholds knowledge of the Hallows because Harry has to prove himself worthy. Likewise, the sword can only appear to Neville and Harry as a test. Dumbledore must realize that being appointed is not enough: only those imbued with kingship can succeed. Thus when Harry appoints his friends to help him destroy Horcruxes, they, especially Neville, do what he cannot and make the quest succeed. When Harry loses his magic sword, Neville draws it from the Sorting Hat and wields it, proving himself a worthy successor to Harry.

Compass, Knife, and Spyglass

Peter's sword of knighthood, given by Father Christmas. Excalibur, Sting, Andrúil, the Sword of Gryffindor – every hero caries a blade destined to win his battle against the evil overlord. In fact, Will Parry's blade destroys the greatest overlord of them all: the Authority himself. The gentler alethiometer and amber spyglass, by comparison, help the heroines to channel the feminine power of the unconscious, leading them to likewise reject the Church. All three defy their religion and "fall," but this fall is not Eve's failure: it is the trilogy's triumph.

As a boy hero, Will receives the most dangerous gift of all: the knife that cuts anything. The cliff-ghasts call it the Æsahættr, or God-destroyer, for its prophesized mission. Everything in existence must succumb to the blade, which, in turn, has chosen Will to bear it. The hero generally pits his magic sword against the tyrannical ruler of the world, in this case, the Authority. By defeating evil, the young hero can begin a benevolent reign over a newer, better kingdom. Many readers are shocked that the tyrant here is portrayed as God, whereas others can't accept that a rigid, decrepit angel with delusions of grandeur even deserves the association. Fantasy writer Kay Kenyon asks, "How could this so-called God doom billions of the dead to a horrifying underworld that forcibly exiles them from their own souls, for crying out loud? Kill the Old Man, put Him out of His misery."[31] Whatever the Authority's true identity, as chosen wielder of the knife, Will is the only one with the power to destroy him. After much travail, Will uses the Subtle Knife to slice apart the Authority's protective crystal. "In the open air, there was nothing to stop the wind from damaging him, and to their dismay, his form began to loosen and dissolve. Only a few moments later he had vanished completely."[32] The wind blows him away, thus completing the prophecy.

Lyra's "golden compass" or alethiometer, like most heroines' talismans, is nonviolent, offering advice and wisdom away from the battlefield. At the same time, it is completely reliable, offering unwavering intelligence that only Lyra can decipher. Its truth forms a powerful counterpoint to Lyra's lies, teaching her through example how magical honesty can be. "Lies have a place, Pullman tells us. But ultimately, it's truth that is important, particularly inner truth, being truthful to yourself."[33] As Lyra uses the alethiometer, her morality grows. She searches for Roger and finally rescues him. Likewise, she offers compassion to Iorek Byrnison and helps him retake his kingdom. At last, "she and Will sacrifice their own happiness for the ghosts of friends and strangers alike,"[34] thus ascending to the highest moral level of all. This grasp of morality, the journey from innocence to wisdom, is condemned by the Church. They would rather kill her to keep her loyal to the Authority than let her evolve to a point where she rejects his design and frees the ghosts trapped in the land of the dead. Lyra, rejecting the Church, devotes herself to the alethiometer which speaks to her in the voice of Dust—pure consciousness. This is the voice of responsibility and adulthood, urging her to grow up.

Many heroines have gifts of prophecy or foreknowledge, gifts linked with the unconscious, or mystic feminine power. Lyra can read the alethiometer if she gazes at in "a particularly lazy way, as she thought of it."[35] Don Debrandt, author of "His Dark Pharmaceuticals" describes this particular lazy way as "The same kind of unfocused state that many people find to be when they get their most creative ideas.[36] Thus, the alethiometer trains Lyra in tapping into her unconscious, the power of the feminine. When she relaxes, she opens her mind to Dust and a deeper consciousness, moving toward enlightenment and knowledge.

Lyra, as Eve reborn, must abandon the world of faith, childhood, and unquestioning obedience: She ends the epic as an adult who has lost her grace for reading the alethiometer. Likewise, Pan, brushed with a "lover's touch" can no longer change form. But leaving Eden isn't a loss, it's growth, and Lyra and Pan celebrate it in this vein. Even the pain of losing Will is worth the price of saving the world forever. Lyra's choice frees the ghosts trapped in torment; no longer suffocated by their own unchanging garden, they're free to go forth and merge with nature, embracing life's unending cycle as they continue their journey. This is the exodus from Eden: a time of rebirth and triumphant change.

Surrounded by technology and computers, Mary Malone can only help the primitive Mulefa by embracing a more primitive, true way of seeing: her spyglass of amber sap. Thus the amber spyglass is made from the most natural of materials: tree sap and seed pod oil, with a bamboo tube holding the plates apart. In fact, it starts out as a mirror in an experiment to try capturing Dust and help the Mulefa save the dying wheel-pod trees. Mary Malone uses it as a lens to discover the truth behind the dying trees: Dust is being deflected rather than drifting down naturally. Only Dust's restoration will restore the balance.

"In order to create the amber spyglass, Dr. Mary Malone realizes she will have to cultivate the same unfocused state of mind Lyra uses to read the alethiometer,"[37] Debrandt notes. Again, this helps a heroine tap the font of feminine creativity: the unconscious. Often mirrors represent the soul – the hidden self or doppelganger. When Mary looks through the spyglass for answers, she's truly abandoning obedience to the stale, domineering Church and even her beloved science: she's asking her soul for the truth. Through inquiry, rather than blind faith, she learns Dust's secrets.

Dust, original sin as the Church thinks, preserves nature rather than destroying it. Likewise, Eve's fall from innocence into consciousness is not the horror they think it. The Mulefa tell Mary their own version of the Eden story thusly: The snake advises a young Mulefa to "Put your foot through the hole in the seedpod where I was playing and you will become wise."[38] Upon doing so, the young Mulefa woman shares it with her kindred. "They discovered that they knew who they were, they knew they were Mulefa and not grazers. They gave each other names."[39] As one critic puts it, "Consciousness, for these creatures, is not a source of shame and guilt, but of joy. Pullman strongly suggests that to fall from innocence is not to become guilty, but simply to become conscious of responsibility as a sentient and moral being."[40] Thus armed with knowledge (like Lyra with her alethiometer), Mary can battle to save the gentle Mulefa, and nature too.

The Church condemns Eve's fall as sin, and tries to kill Lyra rather than let her fall to Mary's temptation. However, the alethiometer and spyglass save them, offering unflinching truth. When Lyra falls, it's not because of a lie. The Dust made up of love, joy, creativity and inspiration is not evil: it's the source of nature and growth, and the power behind both compass and spyglass. Only by Will's wielding his knife to destroy the restrictive Authority can Lyra joyously "fall," casting aside her innocence in favor of growing up. She frees the tormented souls of the dead, falls in love, and feels her dæmon settle. A life of innocence has no comparison.

Lyra's Biblical fall is an act of joy and growth: she surrenders to the power of truth, rather than despair and damnation. Likewise, Harry's Camelot builds a new wizarding world free of corruption. This is the story of Harry's triumph, in which he grows to adulthood and battles death in order to become an inspiring leader, not a failing king besieged by betrayal. Both Pullman and Rowling redress these ancient legends, turning sin and entropy into a renaissance of rebirth, delighting young readers throughout the world.

---

[1] Tim Lambarski, "Ginny Weasley: A Gryffindor and a Match for Harry," *The Harry Potter Lexicon*, http://www.hp-lexicon.org/essays/essay-ginny-weasley.html.

[2] Ibid.

[3] J. K Rowling, *Harry Potter and the Order of the Phoenix*, (USA: Scholastic, Inc, 2003), 23.

[4] J. K Rowling, *Harry Potter and the Half-Blood Prince*, (USA: Scholastic, Inc, 2005), 647.

[5] Meredith Vieira, "JK Rowling One-On-One: Part One," *Today Show* (NBC), 26 July 2007.

[6] *Catholic.org*, "Saints and Angels," *Catholic.org*, http://www.catholic.org/saints.

[7] Catherine Danielson, "Harry's Loves, Harry's Hates: A New Key to Their Mysteries, or, The Dumbledore Code," in *Lumos 2006: A Harry Potter Symposium*, 2006 [CD-ROM] OmniPress, 15.

[8] J. K Rowling, *Harry Potter and the Deathly Hallows*, (USA: Scholastic, Inc, 2007), 740.

[9] Tony Watkins, *Dark Matter: Shedding Light on Phillip Pullman's Trilogy "His Dark Materials,"* (USA: InterVarsity Press, 2004), 113.

[10] Sally Vincent. "Driven by Daemons." *Guardian*, Manchester, England. Nov 10, 2001.

[11]"Pantalaimon," Srafopedia: The "His Dark Materials" Encyclopedia, http://www.hisdarkmaterials.org/srafopedia/index.php/Pantalaimon.

[12] Kim Dolgin, "Coming of Age in Svalbard, and Beyond," in *Navigating The Golden Compass*, ed. Glenn Yeffeth (USA: BenBella Books, 2004), 75.

[13] Phillip Pullman, *The Amber Spyglass* (USA: Dell Laurel-Leaf, 2000), 263.

[14] Carole Wilkinson, "Pants on Fire" in *The World of the Golden Compass: The Otherworldly Ride Continues*, ed. Scott Westerfeld (USA: Borders Group Inc, 2007), 5-14, 8.

[15] Lois Gresh, *Exploring Philip Pullman's His Dark Materials*, (USA: St. Martin's Griffin, 2007), 49.

[16] Sophie Masson, "Lord Asriel: Dad from Hell or Heroic Rebel?" in *The World of the Golden Compass: The Otherworldly Ride Continues*, ed. Scott Westerfeld (USA: Borders Group Inc, 2007), 35-36.

[17] Pullman, *The Amber Spyglass*, 453.

[18] Pegg Kerr, "A Shining Silver Thread: Memory and Identity in the Harry Potter Novels" in *Lumos 2006: A Harry Potter Symposium*, 2006 [CD-ROM] OmniPress, 13.

[19] Lambarski, "Ginny Weasley"

[20] Ella Young, *Celtic Wonder Tales*, (USA: Sacred Texts, 1910), http://www.sacred-texts.com/neu/celt/cwt/cwt08.htm

[21] Rowling, *Deathly Hallows*, 414.

[22] J.K. Rowling, interview by author, "Bloomsbury Live Chat with J.K. Rowling," July 30, 2007, Webchat, http://www.bloomsbury.com/jkrevent.

[23] Rowling, *Deathly Hallows*, 698.

[24] Ibid., 738.

[25] Ibid., 689.

[26] Rowling, J.K. *Hogwarts: An Incomplete and Unreliable Guide*. (USA: Pottermore, 2016), Kindle Locations 528-530.

[27] Ibid., Kindle Locations 531-534.

[28] Lady Charlotte Guest, "Notes to Kilhwch and Olwen," *The Mabinogion* Vol. II, trans. Charlotte Schreiber (USA: Google Book Search, 2006), 353-4.

[29] Guest, "Notes to Kilhwch and Olwen."

[30] Rowling, *Deathly Hallows*, 719.

[31] Kay Kenyon, "Reading by Flashlight" in *Navigating The Golden Compass*, ed. Glenn Yeffeth (USA: BenBella Books, 2004), 104.

[32] Pullman. The Amber Spyglass, 367.

[33] Wilkinson, "Pants on Fire," 13.

[34] Dolgin, "Coming of Age in Svalbard," 76.

[35] Phillip Pullman, *The Golden Compass*, (New York: Alfred A. Knopf, 1995), 174.

[36] Don Debrandt, "His Dark Pharmaceuticals" in *Navigating The Golden Compass*, ed. Glenn Yeffeth (USA: BenBella Books, 2004), 35.

[37] Ibid., 35.

[38] Pullman. *The Amber Spyglass*, 200.

[39] Ibid., 200.

[40] Wood, "Dismembered Starlings and Neutered Minds," 21.

CHAPTER 8: THE TALES BEHIND
BEEDLE THE BARD

The Tales of Beedle the Bard first appears when Dumbledore bestows an original copy on Hermione in *Harry Potter and the Deathly Hallows*. Ron already knows the stories, which he describes as popular fairytales known to all wizarding world children (and thus, not Voldemort or Harry). It is described as an ancient-looking small book with its binding "stained and peeling in places," written in runes.[1] "The Tale of the Three Brothers" gives the trio important information about their true quest for the Deathly Hallows.

> It's interesting that Beedle wrote the stories in runes. Historically, runic alphabets were in use from 150-1000 AD, after which they were replaced by Latin alphabets. There has never been a 'runic' version of the English written language. In fact, already before Beedle's time, written English was becoming standardised and the vocabulary more rich, in the Wizarding as well as the Muggle world. We see evidence of this in other Harry Potter canon sources. For example, the famous Wizards' Council Decree from that time period banning Quidditch anywhere near a Muggle town or village was written in very colloquial English. Mumps' description of Quidditch was also written in English. The stories Beedle collected would certainly have been handed down orally in English. Yet Beedle clearly wrote the stories in runes, which suggests that he was trying to hide them, possibly to make them inaccessible to Muggles.[2]

After book seven, Rowling published *The Tales of Beedle the Bard* as a charity project. It contained five stories: one, "The Warlock's Hairy Heart," is not mentioned in *Harry Potter and the Deathly Hallows* and is emphasized as being too dark for many children's books; three others, "The Wizard and the Hopping Pot," "The Fountain of Fair Fortune," and "Babbitty Rabbitty and her Cackling Stump," get a quick mention, as Ron grew up with these but doesn't know Cinderella. "The Tale of the Three Brothers" is reproduced from *Deathly Hallows*, now, like the others, with Dumbledore's commentary.

Beedle the Bard came from Yorkshire in the fifteenth century, before the Grimm's Brothers, but after many of their stories had been created. His tales carry similar messages to those in classic folklore, though they add elements of the Wizarding World like Animagi and Horcruxes. Dumbledore writes in his introduction, "These stories share many themes with the Muggle stories, including the theme of goodness always prevailing and evil being punished. In the Muggle fairytales, we usually find magic is the root of all problems and trouble, however in Beedle's stories both heroes and villains are able to perform magic."

Dumbledore also offers a satire of the competing collection, Beatrix Bloxam's *Toadstool Tales* (a clear parody of Beatrix Potter's works). He writes:

> Mrs Bloxam believed that *The Tales of Beedle the Bard* were damaging to children because of what she called "their unhealthy preoccupation with the most horrid subjects, such as death, disease, bloodshed, wicked magic, unwholesome characters and bodily effusions and eruptions of the most disgusting kind." Mrs Bloxam took a variety of old stories, including several of Beedle's, and rewrote them according to her ideals, which she expressed as "filling the pure minds of our little angels with healthy, happy thoughts, keeping their sweet slumber free of wicked dreams and protecting the precious flower of their innocence."
>
> The final paragraph of Mrs Bloxam 's pure and precious reworking of "The Wizard and the Hopping Pot" reads:
> Then the little golden pot danced with delight – hoppitty hoppitty hop! – on its tiny rosy toes! Wee Willykins had cured all the dollies of their poorly tum-tums, and the little pot was so happy that it filled up with sweeties for Wee Willykins and the dollies!
>
> "But don't forget to brush your teethy-pegs!" cried the pot.
>
> And Wee Willykins kissed and huggled the hop-pitty pot and promised always to help the dollies and never to be an old grumpy-wumpkins again.
>
> Mrs Bloxam's tale has met the same response from generations of wizarding children: uncontrollable retching, followed by an immediate demand to have the book taken from them and mashed into pulp.[3]

"The Wizard and the Hopping Pot"

A wizard who always generously made cures for his Muggle neighbors dies and leaves his excellent cauldron to his son. After his father's death, the son finds the pot and a single slipper inside it together with a note from his father that reads, "In the fond hope, my son, that you will never need it." The selfish son turns away his neighbors: a man with warts, a laborer whose cart needs fixing, a woman with an ill baby. Each time he does so, the pot takes on the symptoms of the ones who ask for help, clattering around on its iron foot and bristling with warts and sobs all day and night.

> At last the wizard could bear it no more. "Bring me all your problems, all your troubles and your woes!" he screamed, fleeing into the night, with the pot hopping behind him along the road into the village. "Come! Let me cure you, mend you and comfort you! I have my father's cooking pot, and I shall make you well!"[4]

Upon his doing this, the pot's ailments vanish one by one and finally the soft slipper his father provided tumbles from the pot. He puts the slipper on the pot's foot to muffle its clanging and the two walk off into the sunset.

Certainly, there are many folktales about the object that won't stop working – not only the Sorcerer's Apprentice. There's a Grimm's tale of a magic mill that forever grinds until it's thrown into the sea, where it endlessly produces salt. Another similar Grimm's tale is "The Magic Porridge Pot," a magic tool that the villagers must eat their way to as a team so they can order it to stop. The Finnish epic the *Kalevala* features the magical *Sampo*, a mill that produces money, flour, and salt, but is callously locked away. Perhaps a better correlation are the many lessons appearing in magical books and among Wiccans that every act has an equal reaction and that one's talents are meant to be shared.

Many tales begin with the gift of a magic object, and most objects have a rule or prohibition. Invariably, the hero, even a good one, breaks the taboo somehow and must quest to make it right. In this story, the clatter of the hopping pot emphasizes the man's conscience and the townsfolk's need as a constant clattering that won't stop until he does his duty. "*Clang, clang, clang,* went the cooking pot's single brass foot upon the floor, but now its clamor was mixed with the brays of a donkey and human groans of hunger, echoing from the depths of the pot."[5] This reminds him of those suffering, whom he's refused to help. Even when the neighbors don't seek help, the pot keeps clamoring and growing ever-worse:

> Though no more villagers came to seek help at the wizard's cottage for the rest of the week, the pot kept him informed of their many ills. Within a few days, it was not only braying and groaning and slopping and hopping and sprouting warts, it was also choking and retching, crying like a baby, whining like a dog, and spewing out bad cheese and sour milk and a plague of hungry slugs.[6]

This is a graphic scene, but a valuable teaching tale for children. Ignoring problems won't make them go away, and being selfish with one's gifts just makes everything worse. Dumbledore adds in his notes: "A simple and heart-warming fable, one might think – in which case, one would reveal oneself to be an innocent nincompoop. A pro-Muggle story showing a Muggle-loving father as superior in magic to a Muggle-hating son? It is nothing short of amazing..." Thus he emphasizes the theme of the prejudiced wizard learning sympathy for those who have no magical gifts.

One English folktale with interesting connections here is "The Bogey-Beast":

> THERE was once a woman who was very, very cheerful, though she had little to make her so; for she was old, and poor, and lonely. She lived in a little bit of a cottage and earned a scant living by running errands for her neighbors, getting a bite here, a sup there, as reward for her services. So she made shift to get on, and always looked as spry and cheery as if she had not a want in the world.
> Now one summer evening, as she was trotting, full of smiles as ever, along the high road to her hovel, what should she see but a big black pot lying in the ditch!
> "Goodness me!" she cried, "that would be just the very thing for me if I only had something to put in it! But I haven't! Now who could have left it in the ditch?"
> And she looked about her expecting the owner would not be far off; but she could see nobody.
> "Maybe there is a hole in it," she went on, "and that's why it has been cast away. But it would do fine to put a flower in for my window; so I'll just take it home with me."

And with that she lifted the lid and looked inside. "Mercy me!" she cried, fair amazed. "If it isn't full of gold pieces. Here's luck!"

And so it was, brimful of great gold coins. Well, at first she simply stood stock-still, wondering if she was standing on her head or her heels. Then she began saying: "Lawks! But I *do* feel rich. I feel awful rich!"

After she had said this many times, she began to wonder how she was to get her treasure home. It was too heavy for her to carry, and she could see no better way than to tie the end of her shawl to it and drag it behind her like a go-cart.

"It will soon be dark," she said to herself as she trotted along. "So much the better! The neighbors will not see what I'm bringing home, and I shall have all the night to myself, and be able to think what I'll do! Mayhap I'll buy a grand house and just sit by the fire with a cup o' tea and do no work at all like a queen. Or maybe I'll bury it at the garden-foot and just keep a bit in the old china teapot on the chimney-piece. Or maybe— Goody! Goody! I feel that grand I don't know myself."

By this time she was a bit tired of dragging such a heavy weight, and, stopping to rest a while, turned to look at her treasure.

And lo! it wasn't a pot of gold at all! It was nothing but a lump of silver.

She stared at it and rubbed her eyes and stared at it again. "Well! I never," she said at last. "And me thinking it was a pot of gold! I must have been dreaming. But this is luck! Silver is far less trouble – easier to mind, and not so easy stolen. Them gold pieces would have been the death o' me, and with this great lump of silver—"

So she went off again planning what she would do, and feeling as rich as rich, until becoming a bit tired again she stopped to rest and gave a look round to see if her treasure was safe; and she saw nothing but a great lump of iron!

"Well! I never!" says she again. "And I mistaking it for silver! I must have been dreaming. But this is luck! It's real convenient. I can get penny pieces for old iron, and penny pieces are a deal handier for me than your gold and silver. Why! I should never have slept a wink for fear of being robbed. But a penny piece comes in useful, and I shall sell that iron for a lot and be real rich – rolling rich."

So on she trotted full of plans as to how she would spend her penny pieces, till once more she stopped to rest and looked round to see if her treasure was safe. And this time she saw nothing but a big stone.

"Well! I never!" she cried, full of smiles. "And to think I mistook it for iron. I must have been dreaming. But here's luck indeed, and me wanting a stone terrible bad to stick open the gate. Eh my! but it's a change for the better! It's a fine thing to have good luck."

So, all in a hurry to see how the stone would keep the gate open she trotted off down the hill till she came to her own cottage. She unlatched the gate and then turned to unfasten her shawl from the stone which lay on the path behind her. Aye! it was a stone sure enough. There was plenty light to see it lying there, sweet and peaceable as a stone should.

So she bent over it to unfasten the shawl end, when—

"Oh my!"

All of a sudden it gave a jump, a squeal, and in one moment was as big as a haystack. Then it let down four great lanky legs and threw out two long ears, flourished a great long tail and romped off, kicking and squealing and whinnying and laughing like a naughty mischievous boy!

The old woman stared after it till it was fairly out of sight, then she burst out laughing too.

"Well!" she chuckled, "I am in luck! Quite the luckiest body hereabouts. Fancy my seeing the Bogey-Beast all to myself; and making myself so free with it too! My goodness! I do feel that uplifted – that *GRAND!*"—

So she went into her cottage and spent the evening chuckling over her good luck.[7]

This woman is an eternal optimist, rather the opposite of the selfish young man in Rowling's tale. Still, for both, their luck gets worse and worse, thanks to the magical cauldron. When each gets the cauldron, he or she assumes it will be full of treasure, but is surprised to discover it has a mind of its own. The themes here are different, as the old woman should learn to beware of unexplained fortune, but some of the imagery is shared.

"The Fountain of Fair Fortune"

High on a hill in an enchanted garden, enclosed by tall walls and protected by strong magic, flowed the Fountain of Fair Fortune. Once a year, between the hours of sunrise and sunset on the longest day, a single unfortunate was given the chance to fight their way to the Fountain, bathe in its waters and receive Fair Fortune for evermore.[8]

In this tale, three witches all quest to reach the fountain. The first, Asha, suffers from an incurable disease. The second, Altheda, has been robbed and now feels poor and powerlessness. The third, Amata, has been abandoned by her beloved. The three agree decide to try to reach the fountain together. They are dragged inside, and a Muggle knight is taken in with them. He finds their claims to helplessness silly.

> Now, Sir Luckless, as the knight was known in the land outside the walls, observed that these were witches, and, having no magic, nor any great skill at jousting or duelling with swords, nor anything that distinguished the non-magical man, was sure that he had no hope of beating the three women to the Fountain. He therefore declared his intention of withdrawing outside the walls again.
>
> At this, Amata became angry too.
>
> "Faint heart!" she chided him. "Draw your sword, Knight, and help us reach our goal!"[9]

On their path to the fountain, they face three challenges. The first involves a giant worm that demands "proof of [their] pain." The second, a steep slope where they have to bring the "fruit of their labours." The third challenge, crossing a river, requires them to pay with "the treasure of [their] past." One witch conquers each with tears, sweat, and memories.

At the fountain, Asha collapses from exhaustion and Altheda saves her with an herbal potion. Asha is cured, and Altheda realizes she can cure others and thus make a new fortune. Amata, who gave up her memories, decides she no longer cares about her lover. All their problems solved, they invite Sir Luckless to bathe in the water, after which he flings himself at Amata's feet and asks for her hand in marriage. She happily agrees. "The three witches and the knight set off down the hill together, arm in arm, and all four led long and happy lives, and none of them ever knew or suspected that the Fountain's waters carried no enchantment at all."[10]

The fountain seems an exaggerated version of a wishing well, which originated in the sacred springs of Europe. These pools had associated gods and spirits, and people would bring offerings of food or money there. One famed one was Mímir's Well from Nordic myths, also known as the "Well of Wisdom," a Well that could grant infinite wisdom in return for a true sacrifice.

Healing fountains are common in folklore, and often kings and princesses who need the water commission a hero to fetch it. Interestingly, the three women who reach the fountain are questers themselves, and they make a pact to unite and win the water together, rather than settling into bickering or competition as three fairytale siblings generally do. Here they display some of the generosity of Harry and Cedric, who decide sharing a prize is certainly good enough. Like Harry and Cedric, they face three tests and generously help each other. Only their tears, sweat, and memories – real effort – will do for payment, not riches.

On the quest, they learn to solve their own problems, and thus the quest itself is the prize. A tale with a similar theme exists across cultures, often with a female hero. It's called "The Lion's Whisker" or "The Tiger's Whisker." The following version comes from Sudan.

There was once a second wife who married a wealthy man with one son already. The son was rude to her, kicking her and refusing to do a single task to help her, from picking up his clothes to bringing water for the crops. She had to do it all herself. Her husband ordered the boy to behave, and he seemed to obey, but in private, things only grew worse. In desperation, the young wife fled to the village elder. "My stepson hates me!" she cried. "When we're alone together, he calls me names, and flings rocks at my back when no one is looking. What am I to do?"

The elder considered. "What do you want to happen?"

"I want him to love me as part of the family. I want us to be friendly."

"This is powerful magic indeed," said the wiseman. "But it is possible. How much do you desire this?"

"Oh, I will do anything!" the woman vowed.

"Very well. Bring me the whisker of a living lion."

"What!"

"With it, I can construct a potion that will make your stepson love you. But it cannot be made without the whisker."

"Very well." Though her heart was beating like a drum, the young woman straightened proudly. "I will."

The next morning, she carried a huge piece of raw meat down to the river where lions drank. She hid behind a tree and waited. After many hours of nerves and patience, a lion ambled down to the river to drink. He sniffed at the raw meat she had laid there, and then finally gulped it down. He raised his mighty head. The young wife held her breath. Clearly, he knew that she was there, watching. At last, the mighty lion moved slowly back into the forest and disappeared.

For days and then weeks, the young woman repeated this pattern. Each day the lion came. Each day he ate the meat. Every few days, she moved the meat a hair closer to herself and watched and waited, unmoving. Finally, one day she sat beside the lion as he ate. He ignored her. The next day, willing her hand not to shake, she reached out and gently pulled a whisker from his face with a single light tug. She remained there, quite still, as he shook himself and walked away.

Face aglow, the young woman brought the whisker to the wiseman. "Now you can make the potion!"

He smiled proudly at her. "Ah, but a woman as brave and patient as you needs no potion to charm her stepson. You've already learned how to do it."

So the woman went home and coaxed her stepson with patience, with diligence, with strength to accept her small kindnesses, to talk to her, to share his concerns. And within a year, they had become a happy family, just as she had wished.[11]

"This folktale is also notable for its universality, appearing across Asia and other cultures. In some, the woman must coax a battle-weary husband back to his family and away from his brutal memories of war."[12] Like the three questing witches, she learns courage and self-reliance from the quest assigned to her. Afterwards, she's so pleased with the skills she's acquired that she doesn't mind the whisker's being fake.

Harry Potter scenes that share this epiphany include the Mirror of Erised and (sadly) Voldemort's locket in the sixth book. Finally, Dumbledore reveals in the final book that uniting the Deathly Hallows is not meant to be a quest of acquisition or power, but of understanding. Harry has solved the riddle, not by finding all three Hallows, but by realizing he doesn't need them to win. He has a similar insight about the Elder Wand in his final duel with Voldemort.

"The Warlock's Hairy Heart"

This story follows a haughty and handsome warlock who decides to never fall in love. However, when he hears servants whispering that no one will wed him, he decides to marry to gain everyone's resentment.

> He resolved at once to take a wife, and that she would be a wife superior to all others. She would possess astounding beauty, exciting envy and desire in every man who beheld her; she would spring from magical lineage, so that their offspring would inherit outstanding magical gifts; and she would have wealth at least equal to his own, so that his comfortable existence would be assured, in spite of additions to his household.[13]

He meets such a girl and invites her to a grand feast. When she criticizes his lack of a heart, he protests that he does indeed have one, and leads her down to the cellar, where he shows her his heart, long preserved in a box. She begs him to put it back where it belongs. "The warlock drew his wand, unlocked the crystal casket, sliced open his own breast and replaced the hairy heart in the empty cavity it had once occupied."[14] The maiden is thrilled and embraces him, certain this will mean his redemption.

> The touch of her soft white arms, the sound of her breath in his ear, the scent of her heavy gold hair: all pierced the newly awakened heart like spears. But it had grown strange during its long exile, blind and savage in the darkness to which it had been condemned, and its appetites had grown powerful and perverse.[15]

He craves her own innocent heart, and the visitors finally discover him in the cellar, having cut out the maiden's heart and trying to jam it into his own chest. Thus he and the maiden both die, with him holding both hearts in his hands.

Certainly, many fairytale kings plan for a perfect bride. While some plan "bride tests" like riddle-guessing, others are selfish and cruel. The king seeking a perfect wife becomes disturbing, with even traces of incest in "Tattercoats" stories, when his own daughter is the only one to fit the criteria. Themes shared with *Harry Potter* include marrying for love versus prestige, a choice Draco makes when he marries Astoria Greengrass rather than someone from the oldest families. His son Scorpius explains, "She said that Grandfather didn't like her very much – opposed the match – thought she was too Muggle-loving – too weak – but that you defied him for her. She said it was the bravest thing she'd ever seen."[16] Draco tells Harry later, "I said it didn't matter whether the Malfoy line died with me – whatever my father said. But Astoria – she didn't want a baby for the Malfoy name, for pureblood or glory, but for us."[17] Only after Hogwarts does he discover honest love instead of appearance.

The tale of the selfish, isolated prince who finds a perfect match and has a happy ending is "Beauty and the Beast." The dark inversion of this legend is "Bluebeard," in which the young lady arrives to find, not a gruff beast who's kind on the inside, but a charming-faced murderer. In the English tale of Mr. Fox or "The Robber Bridegroom," a young lady has many suitors.

> Now amongst them there was a certain Mr. Fox, handsome and young and rich; and though nobody quite knew who he was, he was so gallant and so gay that everyone liked him. And he wooed Lady Mary so well that at last she promised to marry him. But though he talked much of the beautiful home to which he would take her, and described the castle and all the wonderful things that furnished it, he never offered to show it to her, neither did he invite Lady Mary's brothers to see it.
> Now this seemed to her very strange indeed; and, being a lass of spirit, she made up her mind to see the castle if she could.[18]

There she discovers the dead bodies of his former wives in a scene of horror – afterwards, she accuses him publicly and her brothers tear him to pieces. This, like "The Warlock's Hairy Heart," is the dark, gory side of folklore – grisly stories from before the tales were softened for children. Dumbledore notes that, like the tale of Bluebeard, this one has been passed down largely unchanged.

"The young woman herself was both fascinated and repelled by the warlock's attentions. She sensed the coldness that lay behind the warmth of his flattery, and had never met a man so strange and remote," Rowling writes.[19] Similar language appears in Bluebeard tales, as something feels off, despite the man's charm. In this tale, she accuses him of having no heart, and he shows her where it's locked. "Bidding her follow, he led her from the feast, and down to the locked dungeon where he kept his greatest treasure. Here, in an enchanted crystal casket, was the warlock's beating heart."

This Horcrux-evoking image appears throughout folklore, as monsters keep their hearts locked away to keep themselves invulnerable. The hero invariably finds and destroys it. This brings out the unnaturalness of denying the lifecycle by creating Horcruxes or similar life-shattering magic. Dumbledore notes in his commentary for the story, "It speaks to the dark depths in all of us. It addresses one of the greatest, and least acknowledged, temptations of magic: the quest for invulnerability."[20] The monsters with their hearts stored away are always defeated, emphasizing that one cannot cheat the lifecycle forever.

The Russian monster Koshchei the Deathless carries off a princess, whose husband quests to find her. After Ivan arrives, she charms the monster, asking how it is he can't die. He boasts to her, "My death is far from here and hard to find, on the wide ocean. In that sea is an island, and on the island there grows a green oak, and beneath the oak is an iron chest, and in the chest is a small basket, and in the basket is a hare, and in the hare is a duck, and in the duck is an egg; and he who finds the egg and breaks it, kills me at the same time."[21] Ivan of course, takes the egg hostage and rescues his princess.

Variants on this tale exist the world over. In a tale from India, Ravana, the King of Ceylon, uses spells to take his soul out of his body and leave it in a box at home, while he goes to the wars. A hermit called Fire-eye is to keep it safe for him. However, an ally of the hero Rama magically transforms himself into the likeness of the king and requests his soul back from the hermit. The Navajo "Maiden that becomes a Bear" is a great warrior and quite invulnerable; for when she goes to war she removes her vital organs and hides them, and when the battle ends, she puts the organs back in their places again. In the Greek tale of Atalanta, the mother of Prince Meleager gets a message from the fates that her child will live as long as a branch remains unburnt. However, when she receives word that he plans to marry Atalanta, a wild woman from the mountains, she spitefully burns the branch herself.

In another modern Greek story the life of an enchanter is bound up with three doves which are in the belly of a wild boar. When the first dove is killed, the magician grows sick; when the second is killed, he grows very sick; and when the third is killed, he dies. In another Greek story of the same sort an ogre's strength is in three singing birds which are in a wild boar. The hero kills two of the birds, and then coming to the ogre's house finds him lying on the ground in great pain. He shows the third bird to the ogre, who begs that the hero will either let it fly away or give it to him to eat. But the hero wrings the bird's neck, and the ogre dies on the spot.[22]

In a Celtic tale, recorded in the West Highlands of Scotland, a giant is questioned by a captive queen as to where he keeps his soul. At last, after deceiving her several times, he confides to her the fatal secret: "There is a great flagstone under the threshold. There is a wether under the flag. There is a duck in the wether's belly, and an egg in the belly of the duck, and it is in the egg that my soul is."[23] In the story of Seyf el-Mulook in the *Arabian Nights* the genie tells the captive daughter of the King of India:

"When I was born, the astrologers declared that the destruction of my soul would be effected by the hand of one of the sons of the human kings. I therefore took my soul, and put it into the crop of a sparrow, and I imprisoned the sparrow in a little box, and put this into another small box, and this I put within seven other small boxes, and I put these within seven chests, and the chests I put into a coffer of marble within the verge of this circumambient ocean; for this part is remote from the countries of mankind, and none of mankind can gain access to it."[24]

But Seyf el-Mulook got possession of the sparrow and strangled it, and the genie fell upon the ground a heap of black ashes.

This German story shares some of the language of Rowling's tale, as a treacherous maiden betrays her father to run off with her lover:

An old warlock lived with a damsel all alone in the midst of a vast and gloomy wood. She feared that being old he may die and leave her alone in the forest. But he reassured her. "Dear child," he said, "I cannot die, and I have no heart in my breast." But she importuned him to tell her where his heart was. So he said, "Far, far from here in an unknown and lonesome land stands a great church. The church is well secured with iron doors, and round about it flows a broad deep moat. In the church flies a bird and in the bird is my heart. So long as the bird lives, I live. It cannot die of itself, and no one can catch it; therefore I cannot die, and you need have no anxiety."

However the young man, whose bride the damsel was to have been before the warlock spirited her away, contrived to reach the church and catch the bird. He brought it to the damsel, who stowed him and it away under the warlock's bed. Soon the old warlock came home. He was ailing, and said so. The girl wept and said, "Alas, daddy is dying; he has a heart in his breast after all."

"Child," replied the warlock, "hold your tongue. I *can't* die. It will soon pass over." At that the young man under the bed gave the bird a gentle squeeze; and as he did so, the old warlock felt very unwell and sat down. Then the young man gripped the bird tighter, and the warlock fell senseless from his chair.

"Now squeeze him dead," cried the damsel. Her lover obeyed, and when the bird was dead, the old warlock also lay dead on the floor. [25]

"Babbitty Rabbitty and her Cackling Stump"

This story begins with a greedy king who wants to keep all magic to himself, even though he's not a wizard. He creates a cruel "Brigade of Witch Hunters" and hires a charlatan to be his instructor in magic. Meanwhile, Babbitty, the king's washerwoman, laughs at the king's struggles, and the king demands the charlatan join him in a public demonstration of magic. The charlatan, realizing that Babbitty is a witch, insists she cast the spells on his behalf. However, when the king tries to resurrect a dead hound, Babbitty can do nothing – wizards cannot reverse death. The charlatan exposes Babbitty, insisting she's an evil witch who's blocking the spells. At once, Babbitty flees into a forest and disappears at the base of an old tree. There, the charlatan cuts down the tree, but then Babbitty takes her revenge and speaks from the stump, cackling all the while:

"By cutting a witch in half, you have unleashed a dreadful curse upon your kingdom!" it told the petrified King. "Henceforth, every stroke of harm that you inflict upon my fellow witches and wizards will feel like an axe stroke in your own side, until you will wish you could die of it!"[26]

The king relents, calls off his witch hunters, and builds a statue to Babbitty to be reminded of his foolishness.

When the grounds were deserted once more, there wriggled from a hole between the roots of the tree stump a stout and whiskery old rabbit with a wand clamped between her teeth. Babbitty hopped out of the grounds and far away, and ever after a golden statue of the washerwoman stood upon the tree stump, and no witch or wizard was ever persecuted in the kingdom again.[27]

There's more than a little of the Pied Piper, or the tailors of "The Emperor's New Clothes" in the charlatan. Certainly, audiences loved hearing the foolish, tyrannical king get outwitted into ridiculousness. Dumbledore comments, "The King in Beedle's story is a foolish Muggle who both covets and fears magic. He believes that he can become a wizard simply by learning incantations and waving a wand. He is completely ignorant of the true nature of magic and wizards, and therefore swallows the preposterous suggestions of both the charlatan and Babbitty."[28]

It's also nice seeing the old woman as empowered hero in the tale, something that hearkens back to older fireside tales before male retellers co-opted and edited the legends. Brer Rabbit, the trickster rabbit hero, may be readers' first thought. There are also several elderly female tricksters in world folklore, ones willing to even face down kings.

In an Armenian tale, a king had the presumption to laugh at a little old woman scurrying about. "She looks like a she-devil from the bottom of a well," he laughed.

She scowled at him up in his palace window. "We'll see which of us laughs last!" But the king kept laughing whenever he saw her.

The old woman had the power of transformation, so she changed herself into a young, pretty girl and got herself appointed as the queen's maid. But as soon as she set a brush to the queen's hair, the queen turned into a hideous old woman. When the queen saw herself in the mirror, she screamed and screamed.

With that, the old woman vanished.

Back in her own form, the woman went to see the king. "Clear off, you horrid old creature!" the guards laughed.

"Let her in," the king commanded.

"So, you've guessed that I transformed your wife," the old woman said.

"Please change her back! I'll give you anything!"

"Well, I feel sorry for her, if not for you." She changed the queen back into her old form, and never again did the king mock his subjects.

Here, the crone teaches the king a valuable lesson—don't discount little old ladies![29]

Women make excellent tricksters, as both are battlers of the tyrannical ruler with all the power. "Tricksters are marginalized figures, as are women, so the two combine well into the outsider, the one determined to wreck the status quo. While she need not overturn society permanently, she calls attention to its flaws, superficialities, and ego-driven powerful figures, asserting her own dominance."[30] Along with the feminism, this story reminds readers not to discount washer-women, or quieter hidden figures like Molly Weasley. The *Harry Potter* books emphasize this theme in characters like Kreacher and Dobby, who help bring down Lord Voldemort with their own unnoticed contributions.

"The Tale of the Three Brothers"

In this, the most important tale to the *Harry Potter* series, three brothers build a bridge, keeping themselves and future travelers safe from the roaring river. Angry at being cheated but pretending to admire them, Death offers them each a reward. The oldest brother asks for an unbeatable dueling wand, so Death makes him the Elder Wand from a nearby tree. The middle brother, who wants the ability to resurrect the dead and be Master of Death himself, gets the Resurrection Stone. The youngest brother asks to leave in safety, so Death reluctantly gives him his own Cloak of Invisibility. However, the first brother, bragging about his powerful wand, is murdered for it while he's asleep. The middle brother resurrects the woman he loves, only to find she's a shadow of herself whom he can never get back, so he kills himself to join her.

Only the clever youngest brother lives a long life of safety. "It was only when he had attained a great age that the youngest brother finally took off the Cloak of Invisibility and gave it to his son. And then he greeted Death as an old friend, and went with him gladly, and, equals, they departed this life."[31]

"The Tale of the Three Brothers" shapes the arc of *The Deathly Hallows*. Rowling has said it was inspired by Geoffrey Chaucer's "The Pardoner's Tale" from *The Canterbury Tales*.[32] In this story, three men quest to kill Death and search for him at an oak tree where he's been sighted. When the men arrive at the tree, they find a cache of buried gold coins and forget their quest. However, they all plot to kill one another – one goes off for food and laces it with rat poison, while the remaining two men conspire to stab him. They all carry out their plots and are killed – thus Death defeats them all. As the Pardoner, who's telling the tale, concludes, "Greed is the root of all evil." Dumbledore writes:

> The moral of "The Tale of the Three Brothers" could not be any clearer: human efforts to evade or overcome death are always doomed to disappointment. The third brother in the story ("the humblest and also the wisest") is the only one who understands that, having narrowly escaped Death once, the best he can hope for is to postpone their next meeting for as long as possible. This youngest brother knows that taunting Death – by engaging in violence, like the first brother, or by meddling in the shadowy art of necromancy, like the second brother – means pitting oneself against a wily enemy who cannot lose.[33]

Most human cultures have legends about a person seeking his lover in the realm of death. However, these generally follow the Orpheus pattern – death is final, and one cannot succeed in bringing their beloved back. In this tale, the dead lover "was silent and cold, separated from him as though by a veil. Though she had returned to the mortal world, she did not truly belong there and suffered."[34]

Man often struggles with Death himself and loses. The Grimm's story "Godfather Death" has Death in fact become a Godfather and give his protégé medicine that will save people from death…though only with his permission. Fairytale analyst Maria Tatar explains, "Death is chosen as the godfather precisely because of his exquisite sense of social justice. Unwilling to snuff out one life even for his godson, he points out just why he is unable to act on the physician's desire.[35] Death may be unrelenting, but he's also fair.

As always happens, the young man defies his master to try to save a lovely princess and pays the consequences with his life – medicine sometimes may cheat death, but not forever. Tatar notes that the tale "…reveals the complete powerlessness of the hero against death."[36]

Stories of an excellent weapon go better, as in Grimm's "The Table, the Donkey, and the Stick," in which the wielder of the all-powerful stick (usually the youngest of three brothers) reclaims the other two stolen treasures. The Harry Potter books, however, emphasize that weaponry is not the answer, but love and self-sacrifice. Thus the first brother is killed by ambitious competitors who also long to be the most powerful.

The third brother outwits and evades death through a clever choice of gift and through a lack of greed. This of course mirrors all the "three brothers" tales in Grimms and elsewhere, with the youngest being modest, humble, and clever. Historically, the oldest son got the money and property, while the younger ones had to find a way to fend for themselves, most often with cleverness and luck. Thus these stories rang especially true for listeners.

Outwitting Death or the Devil stories appear through folklore too. In the Northern European "The Smith Outwits the Devil," a blacksmith is given the skills of a master smith and in return will belong to the Devil after a certain time. Eventually St. Peter visits the smith and works miracles, which the smith can't copy, emphasizing the illusion of power he's been given – likewise, the Deathly Hallows will not bring true strength or wisdom. St. Peter offers the smith three wishes, and he chooses objects which give him power over the devil.

> "Well," said the smith, "first and foremost, I wish that any one whom I ask to climb up into the pear-tree that stands outside by the wall of my forge, is to stay sitting there till I ask him to come down again. The second wish I wish is, that any one whom I ask to sit down in my easy chair which stands inside the workshop yonder, has to stay sitting there till I ask him to get up. Last of all, I wish that any one whom I ask to creep into the steel purse which I have in my pocket, has to stay in it till I give him leave to creep out again."[37]

When the Devil comes, the smith makes him do all three, then hammers on the purse with the Devil inside until he agrees to leave in peace. Later, the smith travels down to hell on his own. "But when the devil heard who it was he charged the watch to go back and lock up all the nine locks on the gates of Hades." He protests that the smith will just "turn Hades topsy-turvy!"

> "Well!" said the smith to himself, when he saw them busy bolting up the gates, "there's no lodging to be got here, that's plain; so I may as well try my luck in the realm of lordship;" and with that he turned round and went back till he reached the cross-roads, and then he went along the path the tailor had taken. And now, as he was cross at having gone backwards and forwards so far for no good, he strode along with all his might, and reached the, gate of Poker just as St. Peter was opening it a very little, just

enough to let the half-starved tailor slip in. The smith was still six or seven strides off the gate, so he thought to himself, "Now there's no time to be lost;" and grasping his sledge-hammer, he hurled it into the opening of the door just as the tailor slunk in; and if the smith didn't get in then, when the door was ajar, why I don't know what has become of him.[38]

Thus he makes it to heaven and wins after all.

---

[1] J. K Rowling, *Harry Potter and the Deathly Hallows,* (USA: Scholastic, Inc, 2007).

[2] J.K. Rowling, "The Tales of Beedle the Bard," *HP Lexicon.* https://www.hp-lexicon.org/source/other-potter-books/tbb.

[3] J.K. Rowling, *The Tales of Beedle the Bard,* (USA: Scholastic, 2007), 18-19.

[4] Ibid., 8.

[5] Ibid., 5-6.

[6] Ibid., 7.

[7] Flora Annie Steel, "The Bogey-Beast," *English Fairy Tales, The Baldwin Project.* http://www.mainlesson.com/display.php?author=steel&book=english&story=bogey.

[8] Rowling, "Beedle the Bard" 20.

[9] Ibid., 24.

[10] Ibid., 33-34.

[11] Valerie Estelle Frankel, *From Girl to Goddess* (Jefferson, NC: McFarland and Co, 2010), 143-144.

[12] Ibid., 143-144.

[13] Rowling, "Beedle the Bard" 46-47.

[14] Ibid., 51.

[15] Ibid., 51.

[16] J.K. Rowling, Jack Thorne, and John Tiffany, *Harry Potter and the Cursed Child* (Crawfordsville, IN: Pottermore, 2016), 172.

[17] Ibid., 261.

[18] Flora Annie Steel, "Mr. Fox," *English Fairy Tales, The Baldwin Project.* http://www.mainlesson.com/display.php?author=steel&book=english&story=fox

[19] Rowling, "Beedle the Bard" 48.

[20] Ibid., 55-56.

[21] Sir James George Frazer, "The External Soul in Folk-Tales," *The Golden Bough.* 1922. Bartleby.com. http://www.bartleby.com/196/166.html.

[22] Ibid.

[23] Ibid.

[24] Ibid.

[25] Ibid.

[26] Rowling, "Beedle the Bard" 74-75

[27] Ibid., 76-77.

[28] Ibid., 82-83.

[29] Frankel, *From Girl to Goddess* 298-299.

[30] Ibid., 298-299.

[31] Rowling, "Beedle the Bard" 92-93.

[32] Rowling, J.K. "Webchat with J. K. Rowling." *Interview with The Leaky Cauldron. Accio Quote!.* 30 July 2007. http://www.accio-quote.org/articles/2007/0730-bloomsbury-chat.html

[33] Rowling, "Beedle the Bard" 94-95.

[34] Ibid., 92.

[35] Maria Tatar, *The Annotated Brothers Grimm* (New York: W. W. Norton, 2004), 200.

[36] Ibid., 196.

[37] "The Master Smith," *Norwegian Folktales.* http://oaks.nvg.org/ntales13.html

[38] Ibid.

VALERIE ESTELLE FRANKEL

PART III: MYTH, HISTORY AND CULTURAL COMMENTARY MEET

FANTASTIC BEASTS

CHAPTER 9: *FANTASTIC BEASTS*
AND THE 1920s TREND

Fantastic Beasts arrived in 2001 as a charity project; it was sold as Harry Potter's textbook, complete with his and his friends' scribbles. Newt Scamander, Magizoologist, is the author. As he begins it:

> I look back to the seven-year-old wizard who spent hours in his bedroom dismembering Horklumps [giant mushroomlike garden pests] and I envy him the journeys to come: from darkest jungle to brightest desert, from mountain peak to marshy bog, that grubby Horklump-encrusted boy would track, as he grew up, the beasts described in the following pages.[1]

He reports tracking animals "across five continents" and "in a hundred countries" pursuing his passion.[2] Presumably much of this has already transpired by the time of his film, as the book is published only a year later, and he already has a case of fantastic creatures.

For 2016, J.K. Rowling crafted her first screenplay. It's based on the book, though adding a story and with it, a new continent of magic. In it, Newt Scamander (Eddie Redmayne) journeys to America in 1926, carrying a briefcase filled with his beloved creatures. This suitcase that Newt has been "meaning to get fixed" has a special latch that makes it appear "Muggle Worthy" – he opens it to reveal ordinary British luggage with pajamas, magnifying glass, maps, handkerchief…and a Hufflepuff scarf.

"You're an interesting man, Mr. Scamander. Just like your suitcase, I think there's much more to you than meets the eye. Kicked out of Hogwarts for endangering human life with a beast. Yet one of your teachers argued strongly against your expulsion. I wonder, what makes Albus Dumbledore so fond of you?" With this comment, the Auror Percival Graves links this series to events back at Hogwarts (where young Dumbledore is teaching Transfiguration). The story has another Hogwarts link, as this backstory is basically what happened to

Hagrid. With Graves' first name, he seems doomed to misjudge the world and make bad choices, as Dumbledore, his father, and Percy Weasley all did.

When Newt accidentally swaps cases with a No-Maj (the American equivalent to the term Muggle), his beasts escape into New York City. This creates the story's plot as Newt insists, "We're going to recapture my creatures before they get hurt. They're currently in alien terrain, surrounded by the most vicious creatures on the planet: humans." There is a greater conflict as well, since Newt's screw-up comes at a terrible time, considering how politicians are stirring up anti magical feelings. Wizarding president Seraphina Picquery (Carmen Ejogo) warns him: "Magical beasts are terrorizing No-Majs. When No-Majs are afraid, they attack." He's joined by witch sisters Tina and Queenie Goldstein along with Jacob Kowalski, the first Muggle main character in Harry Potter's world.

Unlike the more contemporary *Harry Potter*, Newt's story takes place almost a century ago. 1926 was the jazz age, a time of hedonism and fun, as the world became modern. Early motorcars and electric lights filled the New York streets. This seems a sudden shift in Rowling's fantasy world, but it actually fits well into recent culture.

> Right now, a lot of our most popular stories are set in the 1920s, from *Downton Abbey* and *Boardwalk Empire* to the forthcoming Baz Luhrmann adaptation of *The Great Gatsby*. 1920s styling has worked its way into science fiction too, especially in the gleaming world of Andrew Niccol's *In Time*, Woody Allen's time-travel idyll *Midnight in Paris*, and the soaring *Metropolis*-like cities of the Dark Knight series and *Cloud Atlas*.[3]

Fantastic Beasts shares themes with all these series. *The Great Gatsby* emphasizes the public face of propriety with everyone's secret affairs and frustrations concealed underneath. Gatsby remakes himself with a fantastical backstory, presenting himself to high society as one of them, though he truly isn't. In much this way, the wizards lead double lives. Of course, Newt's friendship with a Muggle shows him letting a single person into his world, battling the constant pretense with a solitary friendship, much as Gatsby does with the protagonist Nick.

Boardwalk Empire (2009-2014) features temperance lecturers, silent movies, and all the trappings of a world long vanished. Central is the politician Enoch "Nucky" Thompson, who ruled Atlantic City during the Prohibition era. Like characters in *Downton Abbey*, Nucky interacts with famed historical characters like Al Capone and Andrew W. Mellon to delight fans. All the while, he introduces them to a world as festive as it is dangerous. *Salon's* Heather Havrilesk notes:

> One of the unexpected joys of "Boardwalk Empire," though, lies in the way the show revels in the oddities of its time, peeling back the layers of polite society to reveal a giddy shadow world of criminals and politicians collaborating to keep the liquor flowing. As the old system crumbles, it challenges the bonds between rivals and friends, and new alliances are formed as a more chaotic age dawns. Just as you think you understand a particular character or a situation, the ground shifts underneath you.[4]

The show focuses on the dual worlds – one of the respectable politician campaigning for votes from devout widows and one of gambling, bootlegging and murder. Everyone has two faces and follows two sets of laws – the police division determined to stop alcohol smuggling are dismissed as useless "dogcatchers" by the powerful mob. However, among their own, betrayal results in death. This parallels the Wizarding World, who maintain ordinary faces for the hapless Muggles, then sneak into goblin speakeasies. Wizards don't follow the Muggle rules, for, as J.K. Rowling wrote in her North American history of magic lessons:

> Unlike the No-Maj community of the 1920s, MACUSA allowed witches and wizards to drink alcohol. Many critics of this policy pointed out that it made witches and wizards rather conspicuous in cities full of sober No-Majs. However, in one of her rare light-hearted moments, President Picquery was heard to say that being a wizard in America was already hard enough. "The Gigglewater," as she famously told her Chief of Staff, "is non-negotiable."

Newt even smuggles forbidden goods into the US, though they're magical animals, not liquor. Underneath, of course, the wizards have their own far different legal system and must answer for real transgressions. True, the heroes are out of school, but between the haughty wizards of a time gone by and a foreign American world of gangsters and new money, there's a similar tension.

Harry Potter, of course, has "an exotic, theme-park quality" itself – especially now with the new theme parks. Like *Downton Abbey*, it's a far-off magical world with clearly-defined good and evil. Years ago, some critics were positing that this world of simpler times was part of Harry Potter's draw. Critic Abigail Grant explains:

> The *Harry Potter* series, books and movies, give popular culture a change of pace and a break from the technological advance of present day. It partially takes us back in time with ceremonial robes, candlelit rooms, writing on parchment, and a devout recognition of history of the magical demographic. However, it is also quite modern: there is electricity, there is an attention to modern fashion, and there is a sense of dramatic popular culture as demonstrated by the excited fandom surrounding both Victor Krum and Harry Potter. Technology does certainly play a role in the portrayal of the *Harry Potter* world, but it is quite limited in comparison to the technological advances of "real life."[5]

Likewise, the twenties blend modern and old-fashioned with an aesthetic far from our own society. The fabulous 1920s gowns and elegant hats are a draw for the new film, just as they are on *The Great Gatsby* or *Downton Abbey*. The film introduces the Magical Congress of the United States of America (MACUSA), the American counterpart to England's Ministry of Magic (Ah, how Americans love their acronyms!). MACUSA has an Art Deco style, dramatically setting it apart from the old world in favor of color and glitz. Gold and light are everywhere, with gilded phoenixes adding to the glamour. Eddie Redmayne says of his character, Newt:

> When he first arrives in New York, you see him walking down the street, and the way he's observing the city is the way that he would observe a natural habitat. He's kind of smelling it; it's as if he were in the jungle. It's totally alien to him to see somewhere that's filled with such vibrancy and people.[6]

It was a giddy time, in which everyone knew the rules didn't apply to them. Americans moved from farms to cities and the nation's total wealth more than doubled between 1920 and 1929, creating a strange new consumer society. Radios spread across America. At the same time, the 1920s marked a massive transformation – the time was bounded by World War I and the Great Depression, periods of some of the greatest horror in American history. The horrors of the war propelled society into a frantic search for distraction – anything to drown out the shock and despair. One reaction, as always occurs, was backlash. An anti-Communist "Red Scare" in 1919 and 1920 encouraged anti-immigrant hysteria. Fascism and totalitarianism were on the rise, socialism was gaining popularity. There's a hint of this in the film, as Seraphina Picquery worries, "This is related to Grindelwald's attacks in Europe. This could mean war." Already, like Hitler, Grindelwald is beginning his campaign by targeting the vulnerable. Charlie Bertsch, who teaches 1920s culture at the University of Arizona, explains:

> That decade marked the realization that old ways of life were dying out, even for the rich, and the concomitant fear that this passing of "tradition" would result in a complete social chaos. The backlash against this overwhelming impression that a new era had dawned, from middle-American insularism to the resurgence of the Klu Klux Klan and the rise of fascism in Europe, reflected a futile desire to turn back the clock.[7]

Family values, too, loudly protested the glitter and partying, leading to a successful ban on alcohol in the United States from 1920 to 1933. In *Boardwalk Empire,* temperance is framed as a religious and moral issue, with one character pressured to join the police through an appeal to his values and respectability. Many middle-class white Americans maintained the illusion that Prohibition allowed them to control the unruly immigrant masses. Continuing the hysteria and scapegoating, the National Origins Act of 1924 set immigration quotas on Eastern Europeans and Asians. As women got the vote and took secretary jobs, many others sought refuge in tradition – flappers emerged but so did Bible-thumpers. This contingent, upturning society under the guise of morality, can best be seen in the film's "Second Salemers."

Mary Lou Barebone (Samantha Morton), leader of The New Salem Philanthropic Society, is dedicated to eradicating people with magical abilities. She feeds the people's paranoia, warning, "Something is stalking our city! Wrecking destruction. And then disappearing without a trace. Witches....live among us!" Magic, as shown through the *Harry Potter* backlash, has always been feared by conservative religion, and the Second Salemers mirror this fear. In both eras, there's a general suspicion of magic and the harm it can inflict on family values.

Outside Shaw's political rally, her No-Majs shout "We want a second Salem" and hold signs saying "No witchcraft in America." In the *New York Ghost* (the wizarding version of the *New York Gazette*), the biggest headline is "Magical Disturbances Risk Wizarding Exposure," with a supporting article stating that President Picquery is to "address fearful American Wizarding Community." Other articles fuss about "Wizarding Exposure" and "Magical Exposure." As the public goes on what can only be called a witch-hunt, Newt and his friends are warned to keep all traces of magic under wraps. MACUSA's central memorial to the Salem Witch Trials thus contrasts with the sugary and unrealistic Fountain of Magical Brethren in the Ministry in England. Here, it's a statue to wizard persecution and the reasons to hide. The giant warning dial overhead likewise hints at the constant paranoia of their world.

The response to all this fear was actually escapism into the world of science fiction and fantasy, much like today.

> The 1920s were a time of social change and wild financial speculation, and the entire world seemed gripped with futurist fever. German auteur Fritz Lang's science fiction epic, *Metropolis*, was in theaters. Czech writer Karel Čapek invented the word "robot," and group of amateur fiction writers in the U.S. founded influential pulp magazine *Weird Tales*, which started publishing dark, bizarre stories of undersea aliens by a young man named H.P. Lovecraft. And in New York, the Harlem Renaissance was in full swing, bringing poetry, fiction and jazz from the African American community into the mainstream.[8]

As cinema, recorded music and radio gained popularity, an entertainment-driven disconnect appeared, much like the one today.

The shocking changes in the Roaring Twenties are dramatized in another show with a truly groundbreaking fandom. As critic Laura Miller describes it, *"Downton Abbey*, the object of almost as much fascination as the *Harry Potter* books before it" is set in Northern England in episodes stretching from 1912 to 1925. "The drama, which debuted in the US in 2011, was the highest rated cable or broadcast show when its third series finale aired in February this year, reaching 12.3 million viewers and becoming the most popular drama in the history of the Public Broadcasting Service."[9]

The characters' main conflict comes from the fall of social divides in England – after the war, one of the earl's daughters marries a chauffeur and the others consider businessmen over titled aristocrats. One manages the estate and her sister edits a newspaper. Their cousin becomes engaged to a Black man, then marries a Jewish one and moves to New York. With new kitchen gadgets and slip-on dresses, servants become redundant and look for other work as well. It's the end of centuries of aristocrats and tenant farmers, with modern city life taking over.

Why are these stories fitting our lives today so well? "I think most of the stories are about emotional situations that everyone can understand," Julian Fellowes, the series creator and writer, told the *New York Times*.[10] Of course, there was also the uncertainty of a new way of life, much like the new social rules of today's digital age. In this increasingly modern world, with new life-changing gadgets each generation, a great cultural divide is stretching, seen now with each generation of gadgets today.

> In the 1920s, we also witnessed the beginning of youth culture and college hijinks – you could say that young people in this era were the first to experience a stark generation gap with their parents. Kids who had grown up with technologies like telephones, movies, and electric lights were accustomed to a radically different world than people who grew up with horse-drawn carriages and gas lamps. And so those kids began to create their own culture.[11]

Steampunk, science fiction set in the Victorian era or thereabouts, has become a cultural phenomenon as well, suggesting a desire to return to simpler times yet reimagine them – a tool for understanding our own culture. Retro stories of the twenties also offers much of this:

> Both periods are marked by intense political crisis. In the 1920s, many people's lives had been destroyed by World War I and the global disruptions of 1919. Then, the decade ended with the Great Depression. The 2000s began with the 9/11 attacks and ended with financial crisis and mortgage meltdown. Now, in the teens, we are living in the aftermath of both events, trying to figure out what just happened. Revisiting the 1920s could be a way of thinking through the upheavals of the last decade. And then, of course, there's the wild popularity of the Hunger Games franchise, which are a callback to the hungry years of the 1930s.[12]

Desirina Boskovich, co-author of *The Steampunk User's Manual:*

An Illustrated Practical and Whimsical Guide to Creating Retro-futurist Dreams, notes that steampunk has gained massive popularity because of its fondness for mash-ups "in a culture obsessed with mixing and remixing, fanfic, memes, and 'shipping."

> Gotham. Sleepy Hollow. Bates Motel. Guardians of the Galaxy. Fifty Shades of Grey. Kindle Worlds. Lately, we really seem to be into creative takes on the old classics. And Steampunk is like the ultimate mash-up genre – both futuristic and retro. Plus, it's got room for anything and everything fandom's little heart can dream up: Aliens and AIs, zeppelins and zombies, pirates and corsets, goggles and gaslights, mad scientists and scullery maids. It's romance, horror, science fiction, fantasy, and adventure (and even occasionally a whodunit or a spaghetti western). Basically, it's the kind of structured yet flexible framework that allows for endless reinvention, and it rewards experimentation within the shared yet ever-evolving universe of the alternate past.[13]

Indeed, comic-cons have produced steampunk Marvel and DC superheroes, steampunk *Star Wars*, and more. The shows *Doctor Who* and the film *Through the Looking Glass* seem to be leaping onto the bandwagon, incorporating gleaming gears into their time travel plots. *Harry Potter* has a similar cultural impact, with mash-up costumes, vids, and more fanfic than for any other work. In these projects, unsurprisingly, Harry travels through time, space, and reality to meet just about every fictional character. A *Downton-Harry* mashup, as *Fantastic Beasts* appears, isn't very surprising.

The new film transplants many elements of the Potterverse like the magical newspapers, now reporting American politics, and the moving bricks, now concealing Prohibition-era alcohol smuggling tunnels. MACUSA is located in the Woolworth Building, while Queenie is a legilimens (meaning she can see into minds like Snape and Voldemort). Characters clamber onto the Squire Building and battle monsters in Times Square, blending history and the fantastical. Newt arrives on a boat, in a stereotypical shot of those arriving on Ellis Island at the time, clutching his briefcase of treasures…though they're more unusual than keepsakes the historical immigrants brought. He casts spells against the classic 1920s New York skyline, jazz playing in the background. Newt also climbs into the inner world of his suitcase, echoing Hermione's beaded bag and Mad-Eye Moody's trunk from *Goblet of Fire*. Adding to the mash-up, he has something of a *Doctor Who* look.

It's hard to ignore that all these eras had massive class distinctions. Boskovich adds that Steampunk too is class conscious as it takes place in the Victorian Era and the Gilded Age, just before the First World War. Lords and ladies spent millions, while hundreds of workers shoveled the coal. "Many Steampunk writers are drawing on this obvious metaphor to our current age and exploring pressing social issues." As she concludes: "We live in an era of massive inequality and an exponentially increasing gap between the rich and the poor. While some movements like Occupy address the inequality head on, science fiction and fantasy have always provided a means for writers and artists to critique their society indirectly." *The Hunger Games* too is critiquing such moments of history, with the severe disparity between the haves and have-nots. However, Americans don't seem to mind the stories of the entitled, judging by *Downton Abbey*'s success:

> Americans may have suffered class wounds of their own, but not at the hands of toffs, whether motheaten or freshly laundered. Most Americans don't even know what a toff is and the finer delineations of the British social hierarchy – the way a person's speech can immediately place him or her in a very precise slot, for example – are largely lost on us…Americans have always found British manners and formality amusing, especially from a distance, where it is a lot less intimidating. There are few distances more unassailable than a century. The geographic, historical and cultural gulf between modern America and Edwardian Britain gives the milieu of *Downton Abbey* an exotic, theme-park quality. Even if Americans might daydream about what it would be like to work as a housemaid at the abbey or swan around in Lady Grantham's spectacular dresses while being waited on hand and foot, neither scenario is even remotely an option for us.[14]

At the time, there was rampant racial discrimination, and also sexism and homophobia. These issues are addressed in the shows, and addressed or sometimes reimagined in Steampunk. Many were disappointed, however, to discover the heroes of *Fantastic Beasts* were a white hero with his male and female best friends, just like in the original series. A Black female MACUSA president is a nice gesture, demonstrating wizards' progressivism. (The first female US senator served in 1922, as a comparison. While two African-American senators served during the Reconstruction of the 1870s, another didn't appear until 1967.) However, like Kingsley Shaklebolt, President Picquery is more an image of tokenism than a central hero.

They're not very diverse, but the heroes are the underdogs. In *Fantastic Beasts*, Porpentina Goldstein, played by *Inherent Vice* star Katherine Waterston, is an employee of MACUSA who is in disgrace. Reportedly, she "stood up for the wrong person" and was demoted for trying to do what was right – a plot straight from the Potter books. Dan Fogler's Jacob Kowalski, as the first No-Maj main character, is more marginalized than any of the original trio. A factory worker, he's a reminder that it's not just a world of wizards and lords anymore. Likewise, Newt is rather fragile. Eddie Redmayne says of his character:

> Newt's been damaged by human beings, and at the beginning of the film, he's someone that's pretty content in his own company and the company of the beasts. He enjoys his solitude, and he's also spent a year out in the field. So he really hasn't had to deal with people.[15]

He has a dazzling magical world in his suitcase where he can retreat, and presumably he does when the real world grows too threatening.

Credence Barebone., played by Ezra Miller, is the adopted middle child of Mary Lou Barebone (Samantha Morton). As she crusades against magic, he "appears withdrawn, extremely shy and far more vulnerable than his two sisters. Credence is defenseless against the abuse that comes in response to the slightest infraction of Mary Lou's strict rules. But his loneliness also makes him susceptible to the manipulation of Percival Graves (Colin Farrell), who has taken a personal interest in Credence."[16] "We've lived in the shadows for too long," he insists, frustrated with the double life that characterizes the twenties. Graves concludes, "I refuse to bow down any longer." As a powerful Auror and the Director of Magical Security, he has the ability to change their world forever.

Like romance novels and other class-based period pieces, *Downton Abbey* resembles high school for Americans, at least according to critic Laura Miller:

> In place of the captain of the football team, the Regency romance has a duke, and instead of a shy bespectacled girl, the heroine is likely to be a young lady of ordinary looks and no

fortune whose inner merits the hero, alone of all others, readily perceives. Instead of a catty cheerleader as the heroine's romantic rival, there is a society beauty, complete with a mean-girl clique that might as well have been lifted right out of a John Hughes film. The sexual mores of the characters' social circle, instead of being founded in the Christian morality, male supremacism and class prejudices of 19th-century England, is merely a matter of prudish scandalmongering and mean-spirited, small-town gossip. The intricate, exclusionary subtlety of centuries of upper-class manners gets translated into the bratty snootiness of American adolescence.

Downton Abbey may not fit as exactly on to the familiar stock figures of the American high school but the rigid, claustrophobic social hierarchies of the high-school experience remain the easiest point of reference for US viewers. Lord Grantham resembles the highminded yet out-of-touch principal and his daughters the student body's most popular belles, girls whose social and romantic lives serve as universal topics of conversation. Matthew Crawley is the new transfer student, who turns out to be a catch despite his modest background. The conniving O'Brien and Thomas are recognisable as the bullies who afflict so many sensitive adolescents, Mr Carson and Mrs Hughes function as the wise and seasoned teachers who can be counted on to intervene before things get too bad, and Daisy, with her string of hopeless crushes, speaks to many a formerly dreamy mouse.

It's a class system, but one that's long vanished in America and leaves as the Americans depart high school. Miller concludes: "For Americans, high school is rife with cruelty and unfairness, with an elite that benefits from the arbitrary blessings of birth (money, good looks, athletic prowess), but it doesn't necessarily define you for life. High school is formative, but not conclusive."

Thus, the twenties culture presents a situation all can understand, blended with a great deal of nostalgia for simpler times, whether high school or the pre-technological past. Further, old fashioned is becoming cool again. Desirina Boskovich explains:

We're in the middle of a massive generational shift, originally led by a hipster vanguard but now becoming mainstream: what's old is new again. Gen X'ers and Millennials are raising urban chickens, dipping candles, planting vegetable gardens in their front yards, canning jam, keeping bees, sewing their own clothes, and rediscovering the joys of an old-fashioned shave.

183

Part of it is practicality; these are valuable skills to learn, practice, and pass on, based on the kind of folk knowledge that can get lost forever if it's not carefully preserved. Part of it is just the zany, passionate joy of developing an expertise, and making something practical and beautiful with your own hands.

To many, this is *Harry Potter*'s appeal, as much as *Downton Abbey*'s and Steampunk's – a return to a time before chattering cellphones and laptops, in the distant boarding school in a medieval castle. Now Newt Scamander can combine all these qualities in his own story, along with the glitz of the jazz age.

---

[1] Newt Scamander, *Fantastic Beasts and Where to Find Them* (New York: Scholastic, 2001), xvii.

[2] Ibid., xvii.

[3] Annalee Newitz, "Why Is Pop Culture So Obsessed with the 1920s?" *Io9*, 13 Feb 2013 http://io9.gizmodo.com/5983062/obsessing-over-the-1920s.

[4] Heather Havrilesky, "*Boardwalk Empire*: Gangsters Return Triumphantly to HBO." *Salon.com*, 11 Sept 2010. http://www.salon.com/2010/09/11/boardwalk_empire.

[5] Abigail Grant, "Harry Potter and a World of Words: Back to Basics in a Time of Advance" in *Harry Potter, Still Recruiting: An Inner Look at Harry Potter Fandom*, ed. Valerie Estelle Frankel (USA: Zossima Press, 2012), 5.

[6] James Hibberd, "*Fantastic Beasts*: Eddie Redmayne Answers our Burning Questions," *EW*, 9 Aug 2016. http://www.ew.com/article/2016/08/09/fantastic-beasts-eddie-redmayne-interview.

[7] Qtd. in Newitz.

[8] Newitz.

[9] Laura Miller, "Why do Americans Love Downton Abbey so Much?" *New Statesman*, 5 September 2013. http://www.newstatesman.com/tv-and-radio.013/09/why-do-americans-love-downton-abbey-so-much.

[10] Qtd. in Miller.

[11] Newitz.

[12] Ibid.

[13] Desirina Boskovich, "7 Reasons Why Steampunk Is Totally 'Now,'" *Huffington Post*, 27 Oct 2014. http://m.huffpost.com/us/entry/6053796.

[14] Miller.

[15] Hibberd, "*Fantastic Beasts*: Eddie Redmayne."

[16] James Hibberd, "*Fantastic Beasts*: First Look at Ezra Miller's Mysterious Character," *EW*, 10 Aug 2016. http://www.ew.com/article/2016/08/10/fantastic-beasts-ezra-miller.

Chapter 10: Harry Potter and the Rise of Nazism

In 2004, J. K. Rowling recounted visiting the Holocaust Museum in Washington D.C. She described her shock and disgust at realizing "that the Nazis used precisely the same warped logic as the Death Eaters" in identifying people who did not have pure "Aryan" blood (Johnston). Since then, the racism and corruption in *Harry Potter* have grown deeper and more unmistakable with each volume. In fact, the Harry Potter series recreates the climate leading to World War Two in its entirety, detailing the depression and corruption that can send a society into madness.

The Wizarding World of Harry Potter is rife with prejudice. Muggle-born wizards are denied status because of their "inferior blood." Centaurs are confined to ghettos and werewolves denied work, much like the marginalized Jews, Gypsies, and homosexuals in 1930's Germany. Toward the middle of the Harry Potter series, this world slides irrevocably into totalitarianism, with Minister Fudge fearfully snatching power by corrupting education, the media, and the justice system with help from his High Inquisitor, Dolores Umbridge. "We are poised on the brink," Headmaster Dumbledore warns, but it is a brink far viler than the Wizarding World anticipates. With the weakened government and Fudge's feeble policies of appeasement and denial, the evil Voldemort glides in, conquers the Wizarding World, and begins a regime unmistakable to students of history. "Muggle-borns are weakening us," he declaims. "We need a society of pure blood wizards ruling, for the good of the lesser races." With this, Muggle-borns are expelled from Hogwarts and must report to a "Muggle-born registration committee" where they sit quaking in lines as Dementors glide by. One man who protests is threatened with the Dementors' lethal kiss, like a single protestor overpowered by Nazi rifles.

Other allusions to the Second World War abound in the series, from Dumbledore's climactic battle in 1945 which ended World War Two in the Wizarding World to Nurmengard prison, where wizard supremacist Gellert Grindelwald spends his life with his motto of "For the Greater Good" tattooed above the door. Grindelwald hails from the German-named Durmstrang, which welcomes only the Wizard-born students and produces Death Eaters, torturers, and bigots. He plans "a new Wizarding Order" through racial superiority, a program that clearly echoes Hitler's agenda. The timeframes, locations, and dogma coincide: can we doubt that Grindelwald and Hitler worked together?

In the end, the greatest link between these two wars is their ideologies: a society where the pure-born race dominates the world under a dictator who preaches hypocrisy and violence to advance his power. Harry Potter defeats this world, proving that only vigilance can prevent Nazism's return.

Nazi Timeline	Voldemort's Timeline (Some events are out of order to show historic parallels).
World War I ended a generation before, in 1918.	War against Voldemort ended one generation before
1924 Hitler arrested and jailed. In jail, he solidifies his policies.	Voldemort is "a shadow of his former self." He schemes to regain power.
He writes *Mein Kampf,* an explanation of his racist policies.	Voldemort's diary appears, with a younger self who is heir to Slytherin and determined to kill the Muggle-borns of Hogwarts.
Depression 1929-1933	Literal depression in Wizarding and Muggle Worlds
1933 Nazis stage boycott of Jewish shops and businesses.	Muggle-baiting common
Feb 28, 1933 Law for the Protection of People and State: civil liberties suspended. Gleichschaltung, exertion of totalitarian control, begins.	Voldemort takes over the Ministry, newspapers, compulsory education, secret police, propaganda, and more in a new totalitarian regime.
Jul 6, 1933 At a gathering of high-ranking Nazi officials, Hitler	Voldemort summons the Death Eaters and announces his

declares the success of the revolution.	return. He intends to kill Harry Potter to commemorate this.
1936 Hitler remilitarizes the Rhineland, unopposed.	Voldemort returns to a body, but the Wizarding World doesn't unite against him.
1936-1939 Spanish Civil War— Hitler holds back, allowing the two sides to destroy each other.	Fudge and Dumbledore have conflicting agendas—Voldemort hides, allowing them to battle
1937 Jews are banned from many professional occupations including teaching Germans.	Muggles-borns fired from many jobs and their wands are confiscated.
1938 Nazis order Jews to register. Jewish pupils are expelled from all non-Jewish German schools.	Muggle Registration Act Muggle-borns expelled from Hogwarts
1938 Kristallnacht – the Night of Broken Glass.	Random murders of Muggles
Prime Minister Chamberlain attempts appeasement in 1938 since he can't face another world war.	Minister of Magic Fudge denies Voldemort's return since he can't face another wizarding war.
Sept 1, 1939 Hitler invades Poland, begins World War II	Voldemort kills Scrimgeour and begins open war.
1939 Political uncertainty, Churchill's defiant speech	Dumbledore's speech at the end of *Goblet of Fire:* "We are facing dark and difficult times but must stand together."
Weak Chamberlain replaced by stronger Churchill	Weak Fudge replaced by stronger Scrimgeour

Prejudice

Hitler believed in Nietzsche's superman philosophy – that some men or races were so great they needn't follow ordinary rules. Certainly, this applies even more strongly to the wizarding world. Voldemort has no respect for Muggles, or for many magical creatures. In *Deathly Hallows,* Dumbledore tells Harry:

That which Voldemort does not value, he takes no trouble to comprehend. Of house-elves and children's tales, of love,

> loyalty, and innocence, Voldemort knows and understands
> nothing. *Nothing.* That they all have a power beyond his own, a
> power beyond the reach of any magic is a truth he has never
> grasped.[1]

Prejudice against every possible minority group has characterized both the Wizarding World and Europe for centuries, plunging them into devaluation of key support groups. Hitler didn't create anti-Semitism in Europe – he only exploited the preexisting fears. Throughout Europe, Jews were different, with their own foods, laws, religion, language, and customs. As far back as the Middle Ages, as people groped for supernatural explanations, they blamed their Jewish neighbors for poisoning wells, spreading plagues, and killing children, all based on rumor and superstition. Venice was the first place to create the ghetto in the 1200s, where Jews were confined. Outside it, they had to wear special badges, with both practices paving the way for later Nazi regulations. Jews, forbidden many professions, turned to commerce and banking in later centuries; as some few became as rich as the Rothschilds, envy descended. Expulsion from Western European countries was common, while in the East, millions died in pogroms and massacres.[2]

The more modern and disturbing aspect of anti-Semitism (a word coined by a German in the 1870s) is its pseudo-biology.[3] Through Hitler's propaganda, Jews were labeled as genetically different from Aryans, with corrupted "blood":

> The Nazis believed that Jews were a different race than Aryan
> Germans, and that the economic, cultural, and political lives and
> values of Jews and Aryan Germans were determined by their
> very different and quite incompatible biological natures. In
> Hitler's eyes, Jews could never become Aryan Germans
> because each of the two races had different and opposed
> "blood," or what we might call genetic makeup.[4]

As early as February 24, 1920, a Nazi party program explained, "None but members of the nation may be citizens of the state. None but those of German blood, whatever their creed, may be members of the nation. No Jew therefore may be a member of the nation."[5] Even a converted Jew and his grandchildren were considered member of the "Jewish race" – a complete genetic fallacy. "Anthropologists who have classified human races deny the existence of a Semitic race" – there is only a family of Semitic languages including Arabic and Hebrew.[6] Many Israelis are light-skinned and blond, while many Germans are dark and fit Hitler's stereotypes. Hitler himself was short and dark. Thus Hitler's policies were as logically unsound as those of slave owners and Death Eaters—thin justifications for murder and degradation.

In Harry Potter's world, being pure blood makes all the difference. "The Wizarding World is divisible into three main classes by purity: pure-blood, half-blood, and Muggle-born… Blood purity fanatics regard half-bloods as an inferior kind of wizard, though they think of them as superior to Muggle-born wizards," Craig L. Foster explains in his essay, "Where Have All the Pure-Bloods Gone?" Salazar Slytherin, one of the four Hogwarts founders, wanted to deny entry to students of mixed blood, and centuries later, his ideas still linger. The first time Harry meets Draco, Draco asks about Harry's parentage and says, "I really don't think they should let the other sort in, do you? They're just not the same; they've never been brought up to know our ways…I think they should keep it in the old wizarding families."[7] All Slytherin characters begin with the assumption that pure-blood wizards have more talent, showing how far the stereotype has spread. Even the "good Slytherin" Horace Slughorn apes this attitude, as Harry considers him "much too surprised that a Muggle-born should make a good witch."[8] Thus, as John Granger, celebrated Potter scholar, notes, the prejudicial structure is already in place, simply awaiting Voldemort's exploitation:

> This blind spot in the consciousness of wizards, their exclusive hold of power and misuse of those they think of as "brethren" as well as their totally marginalized others, is the agony of the wizarding world and the cause of the Voldemort crisis. Lord Voldemort, the Nazi and totalitarian madman of these books, is anything but an incomprehensible and aberrational evil without beginning or cause. He is only the logical extension and symptom of the prejudice against all non-wizards held by all witches and wizards with few exceptions.[9]

Of course, Muggle-born Hermione is the best in her class, quickest to master most of the lessons. Meanwhile Neville Longbottom is pure-blood and, according to Ron Weasley, he can hardly stand a cauldron the right way up.[10] Clearly, the blood prejudice is a fallacy. It continues past pure-blood or Muggle-born status into half-blood and other such meaningless distinctions. As Ron explains, "Most wizards these days are half-blood anyway. If we hadn't married Muggles we'd've died out."[11] Even the "Toujours pur" Blacks have Muggles on the family tree, much as they try to hide them behind burn marks.

All the same, many pure-blood families devote themselves to eugenics, like the sallow and inbred Gaunts (Voldemort's mother's side), living in squalor, with nothing to brag about but their bloodline. While the male Gaunts are too insular to even leave home, Voldemort's obsession with world power is in part fueled by the opposite side of his ancestry: he longs to have wealth in Gringotts, respect from pure-bloods, and everything else he was denied as he suffered in a Muggle orphanage. In fact, we learn that Voldemort's father was a Muggle, much as he tries to hide this by discarding his original name of "Tom Riddle." As author Peg Kerr notes, "It is clear that Voldemort has been suppressing the truth about his heritage, as evidenced by Bellatrix Lestrange's rage at the very suggestion that Voldemort is a half-blood during the battle at the Ministry of Magic.[12] As he remakes himself into the purest dark wizard of them all, he covers his former identity in a blanket of prejudice and denial, though it still finds outlets: Voldemort attacks Harry Potter as a child because he considers Harry, the half-blood, a more powerful wizard than Neville. As Dumbledore explains, "He [Voldemort] chose, not the pureblood (which according to his creed is the only kind of wizard worth being or knowing) but the half-blood, like himself."[13] Even Voldemort himself doesn't believe his ideology. Family purity is false superiority, nothing more.

We see the Death Eaters aping this hypocrisy over and over: Umbridge, first a stooge for the corrupt Ministry and then a collaborator with Voldemort, is one of the worst offenders, replacing fact with her own pseudo-science. She repeatedly calls centaurs "half breeds," ignoring the fact that they are a separate race and not part-humans. In the final book, Umbridge tells the quaking Mrs. Cattermole that "Wands only choose witches or wizards. You are not a witch,"[14] all because her parents were greengrocers. Mrs. Cattermole has been taken in "for questioning" in a test of bloodline rather than magical ability, and despite Ministry attempts to prove otherwise, Muggle-borns can certainly do magic. This false science and dependence on genetic purity harkens back to the false scientific claims of many groups as they tried to prove genetics made their race "superior":

> Similarities between the turn-of-the-century southern states and, more particularly, Nazi Germany and the Wizarding World are hauntingly and disturbingly close. Muggle-born and halfblood witches and wizards are not only looked down upon by pure-blood fanatics who fear what they view as polluting and diluting pure-blood, but even pure-bloods who are sympathetic toward the others are hated and called blood traitors. And, Muggle-born witches and wizards are called Mudbloods, a derogatory term meaning their blood was dirty rather than pure.[15]

The mention of southern states here is eerily apt. For the Wizarding World does employ slaves treated far more cruelly than Muggle-borns: the house elves. Tiny Dobby describes his situation as "enslavement," forced by his own magic to punish himself for disobedience, and follow every command to the letter, even those against his own conscience.[16] Dobby gets death threats five times a day at the Malfoys, and a flogging for burning dinner. He calls his race "the lowly, the enslaved, us dregs of the magical world."[17] Slughorn, too, has a house-elf taste all his wine for poison in a brutally callous abuse of power.[18] Kreacher is likewise enslaved by masters he detests: Sirius Black calls him vicious names and manhandles him, while Harry forces him to spy on his beloved Malfoys. Kreacher's betrayal of Sirius, rather than an act of pure spite, is the only weapon the entrapped elf has to strike out with. As Dumbledore notes about the betrayal, "We wizards have mistreated and abused our fellows for too long, and we are now reaping our reward."[19]

The problem is the house elves' conditioning: they see it as their duty to love and protect their masters, and a betrayal to leave. House elves have powerful magic but "usually can't use it without their masters' permission."[20] They refer to themselves in third person (thus subordinating the self) and repeat that house elves should only try to please others, rather than be happy themselves. The Hogwarts kitchen elves, especially, are embarrassed by Dobby, the free elf they see as reaching above his station. One critic is deeply disturbed by these messages, "as Rowling reinscribes and normalizes the marginalized status" of these elves, and suggests "oppressed people can and should be satisfied with their lot."[21] The greatest problem is in fact psychological: even an elf like Dobby who longs for freedom and betrays his hated masters, the Malfoys, at each opportunity, passively waits for clothing in order to be freed. He feels he is bound, thus he cannot escape. As Karen A. Brown explains in *Prejudice in Harry Potter's World*:

> The very idea that he [Dobby] "needs to be freed" by his masters is a mitigated form of mental bondage: The slave has the ability to leave the master at any time, but the walls inside his mind (mostly fear) hinder him from making such an empowered decision.[22]

Dobby, despite his powerful magic, believes he is physically bound by the rules: even years after gaining his freedom, he still punishes himself for speaking ill of his former masters. Most wizards perpetuate this system, rejecting Dobby as a paid employee because "That's not the point of a house elf."[23] Clearly, the wizards don't understand that these powerfully magical creatures have not always been enslaved. After centuries of elf subordination, both masters and slaves believe this is the natural order, and perpetuate the unjust system.[24] Only Hermione, an unindoctrinated bystander, can see elf-life for the vicious exploitation it truly is, and she devotes her life to changing it. This will take time: The Hogwarts elves view her as "mad and dangerous"[25] and feel insulted by her gifts of clothes, showing how uncomfortable they feel outside their well-defined roles in the kitchen. Clearly, the damage that the wizards have caused for centuries won't disappear overnight.

Nazi Germany used slave labor within the work camps and ghettos, provided by groups the Nazis deemed sub-human. Like the wizards, the Nazis planned education and indoctrination, teaching subject races to take pride in serving their "betters" and providing necessary functions. In a memorandum to Hitler dated May 25, 1940, Heinrich Himmler explained what the Nazi control of Poland would mean for the subject peoples with their high Jewish and Slavic populations:

> For the non-German population of the East there must be no higher school than the four-grade elementary school. The sole goal of this school is to be simple arithmetic – [being able to count] up to five hundred at the most, – writing of one's name, – the doctrine that it is a divine law to obey the Germans and to be honest, industrious, and good. I don't think that reading is necessary. Apart from this school there are to be no schools at

all in the East....The population will, as a people of laborers without leaders, be at our disposal and will furnish Germany annually with migrant workers and with workers for special tasks (roads, quarries, buildings).[26]

This doctrine of brainwashing and directed education was intended to leave the Eastern countries slaves to Germany based on their alleged genetic inferiority, accepting abuse and degradation as their due. Thus, offered minimal education and indoctrination to German pre-eminence, the Polish people would become willing manual laborers, suited for nothing else and, over time, accepting their new position.

Worse off still are the races judged "evil" and "beastly," rather than useful to the current regime. One critic comments that veelas, giants, and werewolves, "although these are all human-like creatures...are portrayed as being substandard, like the elves."[27] Wizards regard giants as bloodthirsty savages, who have nearly killed one another into extinction through their own brutality. Yet, Hagrid, the most gentle adult in series, and the only one entrusted with baby Harry, is half-giant. In addition, this extinction is actually caused by wizards, who confined giants to a progressively smaller area. As Granger notes:

> The giants are perhaps Ms. Rowling's caricature of traditional people hounded onto reservations and into ghettos who have become only the monstrous shadow of their former greatness. The Dementors, too, are an excellent depiction of what a nightmare a magical creature can become when confined to the narrow existence of their worst traits by government policy – and the repercussions on society when released from their confinement by a greater evil.[28]

Fleur is not mistreated because of her Veela blood, but Lupin is discriminated against time and again, all within the law. He loses all possibility of employment thanks to Umbridge, and grows shabbier and shabbier. Though he's an excellent Defense Against the Dark Arts teacher, he's fired, as parents "wouldn't want" a werewolf teaching their students. He only attends Hogwarts in the first place on a condition of total secrecy to protect not only the students but also their sensibilities.

It's no wonder goblins, merfolk, and centaurs remain hostile. They have limited choices in the Wizarding World: brainwashed servitude like house elves or classification as dangerous monsters. The goblins have found in niche in the banking system where they work well, despite Bill's warnings that they shouldn't be trusted, thanks to all the bad blood and hostility between species. The merfolk and centaurs keep themselves apart, though they willingly help the kindly Dumbledore, who provides the exception to every racial rule. The greatest problem is the lack of governmental representation, allowing wizards unlimited exploitation:

> Don't look for representatives of even the centaurs, goblins, and house-elves in the Ministry of Magic. There may be a Committee for the Disposal of Dangerous Magical Creatures at the Ministry but the prejudice against nonwizards is universal enough that there are no Magical Brethren in the Ministry or liaisons to these groups.[29]

Thus, in both worlds, genetics are exploited to claim the pure-blooded master race is the most powerful, and all other races only suited to serve them. This is best exemplified by the Ministry of Magic statue fount called "The Fountain of Magical Brethren," with its false depictions and stereotypes:

> A group of golden statues, larger than lifesize, stood in the middle of a circular pool. Tallest of them all was a noble-looking wizard with his wand pointing straight up in the air. Grouped around him were a beautiful witch, a centaur, a goblin, and a house-elf. The last three were all looking adoringly up at the witch and wizard.[30]

Here the witch, centaur, goblin, and elf all regard the wizard admiringly and artificially, while other despised races such as giants and werewolves don't appear at all. Without an overwhelming change in perception, the false stereotypes and exploitation will continue indefinitely. Of course, Hermione works through her years at Hogwarts to protect the House-elves. As Rowling explains after the series concludes, "Hermione began her post-Hogwarts career at the Department for the Regulation and Control of Magical Creatures where she was instrumental in greatly improving life for house-elves and their ilk. She then moved (despite her jibe to Scrimgeour) to the Dept. of Magical Law Enforcement where she was a progressive voice who ensured the eradication of oppressive, pro-pureblood laws."[31] Rowling finishes:

The Potter books in general are a prolonged argument for tolerance, a prolonged plea for an end to bigotry, and I think it's one of the reasons that some people don't like the books, but I think that's it's a very healthy message to pass on to younger people that you should question authority and you should not assume that the establishment or the press tells you all of the truth.[32]

Totalitarianism

Totalitarianism throughout history involves control of every aspect of society, including suppression of the free press, appointment of fanatically devoted followers to key positions, deportation of malcontents, directed compulsory education, recruitment, propaganda, secret police with unlimited power, censorship, biased trials, scapegoating, and torture as a means of interrogation. "The perfectly primitive Nazi conception of the conduct of a state was that one had to annihilate or render harmless all adversaries or suspected adversaries," David Crew explains in *Hitler and the Nazis: A History in Documents*.[33] While Hitler employed all these methods, the Ministry of Magic, even before Voldemort, shows similar signs of ambition. First Minister of Magic Fudge takes a stranglehold on the government, aided by his willing follower, Dolores Umbridge. He then weakens and corrupts the government to the point where Voldemort can easily take over and recruit many of Fudge's disciples through prejudice and misinformation. From there, Voldemort can become the new dictator in a reign of corruption reminiscent of Nazism at its worst.

Historically, Hitler began his campaign during a heavy depression. In 1919, "All the assumptions of national life were denied by defeat, famine, disorder, the war-guilt accusation, the loss of the colonies," and much more.[34] One of the key provisions of the Versailles Treaty was Article 231, the so-called War Guilt Clause, which made Germany accept complete responsibility for starting World War I. That and the demand for financial reparations in Article 232 created incredible anger and frustration at the unjust punishment: Thanks to the ending of World War One, the Germans had humiliating, crushing reparations to repay at a time when their own country needed the funds.[35] Inflation skyrocketed, and there was a constant fear.[36] The winter of 1929 saw three million unemployed in Germany; the Weimar leaders were helpless to prevent the massive unemployment caused by the worldwide Great Depression.[37] The people were desperate for change, enabling Hitler to easily take power.

Hitler created the SA (Storm Troopers in English) to protect Nazi party meetings, but this quickly changed to smashing meetings of their political opponents. Hitler's Storm Troopers recruited "adolescents who in other times and countries have formed into fighting gangs,"[38] refining their anger into brutality. One ten-year-old in a Hitler Youth organization later recalled discipline and political indoctrination, as he added:

> At the induction ceremony, my spine tingled in the conviction that I now belonged to something both majestic and threatened by bitter enemies...I accepted the two basic tenets of the Nazi creed: belief in the innate superiority of the Germanic-Nordic race, and the conviction that total submission to Germany and to the *Fuhrer* was our first duty.[39]

Thus, unemployed, restless teens turned to devoted followers, a future army pledged to violence in the protection of their ideals. Nazism had begun.

The Wizarding World is in a more literal type of depression. Gray fog coats the land and Dementors wander freely, dispensing panic and despair. "They're the creatures that drain hope and happiness out of people,"[40] as Minister Fudge explains, and they're breeding in the misery shrouding the populace. Chilly mist in July is only one symptom: Wizards barricade themselves in their homes and expect thugs and murderers daily. The newspapers catalogue murders but few arrests. Worst of all, the Ministry and its regulations prove utterly useless against the threat.

The Ministry of Magic is, as celebrated Potter-critic John Granger puts it, "a gaggle of self-important airheads busying themselves with laughable trivia (cauldron bottom reports) or international bread-and-circus functions like the Quidditch World Cup, while neglecting to take care of even their own."[41] Too often, the Ministry folds before the rich and powerful, censuring Arthur Weasley for his fondness for Muggles and granting special favors to Lucius Malfoy, who can always be found where he doesn't belong. Justice is likewise corrupt:

> The Wizengamot as we have seen it in Dumbledore's Pensieve and in Harry's hearing in Order of the Phoenix is either celebrity

sham (Ludo Bagman standing in for OJ), Stalinist show trial with only the pretense of fairness, or an outright assault on the innocent in Harry's case to advance a government position.[42]

To appear proactive, the Ministry under Fudge sends the innocent Hagrid to Azkaban. Sirius Black later reveals his life sentence in Azkaban was just for the appearance of acting with strength: Both Fudge and his successor Scrimgeour want to be seen as in control of events, rather than events controlling them.

Likewise, Fudge recruits Dolores Umbridge, who would do absolutely anything for her beloved "Cornelius," including cast Unforgivable Curses. Umbridge, of course, is best known for "her furious desire to bring every aspect of life at Hogwarts under her personal control."[43] In fact she deprives Harry of "everything that made his life at Hogwarts worth living: his visits to Hagrid's house, letters from Sirius, his Firebolt, and Quidditch."[44] Mail is opened, owls are diverted and attacked, the Floo network is under surveillance. Umbridge's Educational Directives cancel clubs and forbid teachers to say anything outside their subjects. She uses these directives as tools to exert pressure, even hesitating over allowing the Gryffindors to play Quidditch in order to punish Harry for his rebellious outspokenness. Umbridge recruits the Inquisitorial Squad, school bullies from Slytherin who punish fellow students because "you're a Mudblood, Granger," "I don't like you, Potter,"[45] and other such violations of authority. Scarier still are the Dementors the Ministry employs in the third and fifth books, welcome to murder wizards they find unprotected. Their prison, Azkaban, is "a psychic concentration camp where few survive."[46] The Dementors torture those imprisoned there, sucking everything good and beautiful from their souls until only haggard, insane shells remain. All of these followers, from thugs to Dementors, crave violence and cruelty, making them perfect followers for corrupt regimes.

Of course, despite his stranglehold on power, Fudge's greatest mistake is underestimating Voldemort, just as Neville Chamberlain will be remembered throughout history for ceding Czechoslovakia to Hitler and discounting him as an enemy. As Churchill himself said, putting the most generous-possible spin on matters:

> It fell to Neville Chamberlain in one of the supreme crises of the world to be contradicted by events, to be disappointed in his hopes, and to be deceived and cheated by a wicked man. But

what were these hopes in which he was disappointed? What were these wishes in which he was frustrated? What was that faith that was abused? They were surely among the most noble and benevolent instincts of the human heart-the love of peace, the toil for peace, the strife for peace, the pursuit of peace, even at great peril, and certainly to the utter disdain of popularity or clamour.[47]

Chamberlain was tricked by Hitler while pursuing peace, but he allowed Hitler that foothold, even with his noble goal. Likewise, Fudge feels unequal to leading the war against Voldemort and clings stubbornly to appeasement and denial, speedily losing both popularity and credibility. As Dumbledore warns him, "Fail to act – and history will remember you as the man who stepped aside and allowed Voldemort a second chance to destroy the world we have tried to rebuild!"[48] Fudge's tool, the *Daily Prophet,* spends months discrediting Dumbledore and Harry Potter as outspoken whistle-blowers, and then, the instant Fudge relents, recants its position completely and "tells a story saying the complete opposite without a blush for the lies and distortions of the previous months."[49] These weak choices, like Chamberlain's, mark Fudge as a failed leader. He, like Chamber-lain, later assists the new stronger government in its fight against Voldemort, but that can't atone for the foothold he allows the enemy.

Both worlds then appoint stronger leaders (Churchill for the British and Scrimgeour for the wizards), but it's too late. The enemy has gained too much power, launching himself to the head of the strongest army of all: a totalitarian regime where questions are met by death and only one voice commands armies of true believers. Thus only one course remains: war.

While the SA were Hitler's chosen force, after he became chancellor in 1933, he also used official government agencies to illegally detain those he considered a threat. After a Dutch anarchist set fire to the German parliament building in February 1933, the Nazis rounded up Communists and Socialists in hastily-assembled concentration camps; politicians, doctors, lawyers, and other leading citizens were likewise imprisoned and killed, in a total and unheard-of suspension of civil rights. In his testimony at the postwar Nuremberg trials, Rudolf Diels, the first head of the Gestapo, described how these political prisoners were mistreated and sometimes murdered. Once in a concentration camp, no appeal was possible, no rights existed.[50] Torture and murder were commonplace, even before the advent of the death camps. Some homosexuals were castrated in return for a release from the camps (where most were dying of starvation and disease), while other prisoners later succumbed to gruesome medical experiments.[51]

From the Death Eaters' first robed and masked appearance at the Triwizard Tournament, these henchmen appear like the KKK or SA, determined to hide their identities. Many of Voldemort's Snatchers are "uneducated boys who suddenly find themselves with extraordinary amounts of power."[52] One Potter critic calls the Slytherin students "the pragmatists, the careerists, the manipulators, and the deceivers, the power-hungry, and the just plain nasty."[53] These words absolutely describe Hitler's thugs. Some Snatchers are clearly caught up in the euphoria of targeting minority groups, free to unleash violence on the less fortunate. Other lieutenants like Bellatrix Lestrange display the fanatical devotion Voldemort expects from his inner circle, as she eagerly volunteers to murder her niece and offers her family home, Gringotts locker and life for Voldemort's plans. Barty Crouch Jr. spends a year befriending Harry at Voldemort's wishes. Even terrified Wormtail slices off his own hand to aid the Dark Lord. In just this way, "'It is the Fuhrer's order' became the standard method of terminating opposition, for against that qualification there could be no appeal."[54]

These disciples eagerly resort to torture, as Bellatrix does when she uses the brutal Cruciatus curse on the Longbottoms and Hermione Granger. Under Voldemort's gaze, Dementors flourish, draining the populace of hope and killing indiscriminately. Umbridge, first a follower of Fudge and then later accomplice of Voldemort, forces Harry to carve "I must not tell lies" on the back of his hand and then indulges in Veritaserum as a means of interrogation, drugging Harry without his knowledge. She manhandles Marietta Edgecombe when the girl gives an answer she dislikes. Most frightening is her determination to use the Cruciatus curse on Harry, insisting that she's left with no alternative and that "what Cornelius doesn't know won't hurt him."[55] She displays her sickening pleasure at hurting others, "panting slightly as she pointed her wand at different parts of Harry's body in turn, apparently trying to decide what would hurt the most."[56] Her henchman, Filch, is likewise prepared to whip Fred and George Weasley for their pranks.[57] Afterward, Umbridge even keeps her position. Rowling adds:

> She has good contacts at the Ministry. She is one of those people, and they do exist in real life, who will always side with the established order. As far as she is concerned authority cannot be wrong so she doesn't question it, and I would go as far as to say that whatever happened and whoever took over at the Ministry, Umbridge would be there, she likes power. So she is going to side with the people who give her the authority.[58]

Only at the end of book seven does she find justice as "She was arrested, interrogated and imprisoned for crimes against Muggleborns."[59]

Under Voldemort's (and Umbridge's) regime, Hogwarts education becomes compulsory, as a recruitment center for pure-blood youth. "They don't want to spill too much pure blood," Neville explains, "so they'll torture us a bit if we're mouthy but they won't actually kill us."[60] Voldemort is even willing to give Neville, a pureblood from "noble stock" a second chance.[61] "Every drop of magical blood spilled is a loss and a waste," he insists.[62] Now all students learn the Dark Arts and the new Muggle studies. The latter covers "how Muggles are like animals, stupid and dirty, and how they drove wizards into hiding by being vicious to them, and how the natural order is being reestablished."[63] This echoes Nazi propaganda about the menace of "the threat from the east" and how the Aryan race deserved to dominate the world. Children in elementary schools studied from teachers who believed in Hitler's philosophies and texts filled with "Nazi and militaristic doctrine."[64] Hitler Youth filled the schools, as his government emphasized Aryan values and German strengths.

Another symptom of totalitarianism is a ruthless suppression of the free media, leaving news loyal only to the new regime. Hitler and Stalin purged literature and the arts to reflect their new societies, rejecting modernism for national superiority.[65] On the tenth of May, 1933, the Nazis ceremonially burned all the books they found by writers they distrusted.[66] Newspapers slanted facts and blasted propaganda, as when a seventeen-year-old Jew shot a German clerk in revenge for the deportation of his family, Reich propaganda minister Goebbels claimed in a newspaper article that this shooting was the work of a "World Jewish Conspiracy" planning to destroy Germany. This November 1938 incident and the accompanying media explosion precipitated Kristallnacht, the Night of Broken Glass, in which 7500 Jewish shop windows were smashed.

Newspapers proclaimed it a spontaneous eruption by the German people, but in reality, most of the violence was carried out by the SA and Nazi officials.[67]

Still, freedom fighters published small papers and underground radio stations, determined to spread messages of hope and resistance. The Wizarding World has its counterparts: Many secretly listen to *Potterwatch*, which is, as Ron puts it, "the only one [radio station] that tells the truth about what's going on! Nearly all the programs are following You-Know-Who's line, all except *Potterwatch*."[68] Though the Death Eaters pay them "a number of house calls,"[69] *Potterwatch* stays under the radar and keeps broadcasting messages of hope and support.

The *Daily Prophet* is far from a free newspaper, as proved as early as book four, as reporter Rita Skeeter writes unflattering pieces, some of which she makes up. The *Daily Prophet* "intentionally creates or fosters prejudice against individuals and groups in toadying service to the government," casting blame on Stan Shupike, Sirius Black and other innocents to cover its blunders.[70] This abuse of the media intensifies in book five when it reports Harry insane and denies Voldemort's return. Only *The Quibbler* protests, printing the true story and standing firmly behind Harry. The repercussions for this appear in the final book, as Lovegood's daughter is kidnapped to threaten him into ceasing publication. The *Quibbler*s he publishes under duress list Harry as Undesirable Number One. "They took my Luna," he explains. "Because of what I've been writing."[71] The trio forgives him, understanding he has no choice.

Pictures of Hitler himself appeared on stamps, billboards, postcards, and far more, in order to create a "Hitler myth" of unheard-of popularity. After 1933, the Nazis monopolized the images produced in Germany, and spread this process to other countries after 1939. Posters and paintings of the Third Reich flourished, showing smiling Germans caring for local citizens and children (millions of whom they in fact murdered).[72] Nazis publicized that the inflation and depression of the 1920's and '30s had been caused by "aliens from the East," the accepted euphemism for foreign Jews. Everything from communism to World War One's defeat was blamed on an "International Jewish Conspiracy." Nazis filled airwaves with the "seduction of young German girls by 'alien' doctors, stage producers and film directors."[73] Similarly, Umbridge's followers print pamphlets titled "Mudbloods and the danger they pose to a peaceful society." The cover shows a rose "being strangled by a green weed with fangs and a scowl."[74]

Together, all this propaganda, violence, and abandonment of civil rights help the government to control the population and direct its thoughts. Reeducation and scapegoating ensure loyalty, as the younger, more vicious teens find an outlet for violence, all encouraged and legalized by the totalitarian regime. Once these impressionable soldiers have pledged absolute loyalty to their leader and abandoned all judgment and responsibility, the violence truly begins.

Nazism and the Occult

The seventh book follows Voldemort's quest for the most powerful weapon of all, and his obsession with mystic symbols that will cement his power. He has split his soul and placed the parts in objects owned by the Hogwarts founders, objects with "a certain grandeur."[75] Dumbledore explains, "His pride, his belief in his own superiority, his determination to carve for himself a startling place in magical history, these things suggest to me that Voldemort would have chosen his Horcruxes with some care, favoring objects worthy of the honor."[76] Hitler had a similar quest, to collect the mystic objects that might increase his might and tie him to the mythic heroes of the past.

In Trevor Ravenscroft's book, *The Spear of Destiny: The Occult Power Behind the Spear Which Pierced the Side of Christ*, he describes the mythic spear and the fascination Hitler had for it. While there's speculation involved, he also interviewed and read many first person sources to track Hitler's fascination with ancient myth. While still young, Hitler beheld the Vienna Lance, a spear long-believed to be the Spear of Destiny, in the Hofburg Museum:

> Phineas, the ancient Prophet, had caused this Spear to be forged to symbolise the magical powers inherent in the blood of God's Chosen People. Already old as a talisman of power, it had been raised in the hand of Joshua when he signaled his soldiers to shout the great shout which crumbled the walls of Jericho. The very same Spear was hurled at the young David by King Saul in a fit of jealousy.
>
> Herod The Great had held this insignia of power over life and death when he ordered the massacre of the innocent babes throughout Judea in his attempt to slay the Christ child who

would grow up to be called the "King of the Jews". Now the Spear was carried on behalf of the son of Herod The Great, as a symbol of authority to break the bones of Jesus Christ.[77]

Much in the way Voldemort grew intrigued by tales of the Elder Wand, Hitler was drawn in by the purported power of the Spear, and other artifacts as well. He read many other epics of myth: *Rig-Veda*, the *Upanishads*, the *Gita*, *Zend-Avesta*, Egyptian *Book of the Dead*, and others.[78] Professor Alan Bullock, a historian, writes: "His intellectual interests seemed to follow the same pattern. He spent much time in the public libraries, but his reading was indiscriminate and unsystematic – *Ancient Rome, the Eastern Religions, Yoga, Occultism, Hypnotism, Astrology...!*"[79] He studied Nordic and Teutonic mythology and was fascinated by the operatic spectacles Wagner wrote, all dramatizing the Norse gods and heroes through their divine struggles.

> Richard Wagner, an artist of staggering talent and almost miraculous powers of imagination, attempted "to combine the verse of a Shakespeare with the music of a Beethoven". He saw himself as a prophet with a life destiny to awaken the Germans to the grandeur of their ancestry and the superiority of the blood of their race. He compared the greed for gold in his Götterdämmerung to the "tragedy of modern capitalism and the spirit of yiddish usury" which he claimed was threatening to destroy the German people.
>
> By tradition the sleep which followed the Götterdämmerung was not an eternal sleep. It was prophesied that the Horn of Heimdall, guardian of the threshold between Gods and men, would one day sound its eerie call once more to herald the awakening of the Germanic Race from its deathlike slumbers. And Adolf Hitler was excited to find that the prediction of such an awakening out of an intellectual and materialistic darkness was confirmed by the religious texts, myths and legends of almost every ancient civilisation. Innumerable sources pointed to the twentieth century as the dawn of the great spiritual awakening of mankind.[80]

Hitler took the Spear from its case in the Hofburg Museum on the day of his entry to Vienna, absorbing Austria into Greater Germany. Through his campaign, Hitler appropriated Christian symbolism, such as the Spear of Destiny, for his own purposes. He also famously reversed the swastika from the Hindu/Sanskrit symbol for the Sun and made it his own.

Richard Wagner's Opera *Parsival*, which was inspired by the mysteries of the Holy Grail, also influenced him. It focused on the struggle between the Grail Knights and their adversaries over the possession of the Spear of Longinus. To Sir Parsival, who served the Archangel of the Grail, the Spear reflected God's sacrifice and was a sacred talisman of healing and redemption.

Of course, book seven sees Voldemort questing for the Elder Wand – the greatest weapon of the Wizarding World and one he's convinced will make him undefeatable. He travels the world tracking ancient legends, determined to master the wand's long-rumored power. For this he needs many experts, and even kidnaps Ollivander the wand maker.

While studying the Grail legend for its deep significance, Hitler made the acquaintance of Ernst Pretzsche, a bookseller who had made an extensive study and practice of the art of Black Magic along with medieval occultism, alchemy and astrology.

> His father, Wilhelm Pretzsche, ran an Apothecary's business and spent his leisure hours in an extensive study of the customs and ritual magic of the ancient Aztecs, an interest which the son took up as soon as he was old enough to do so. Returning to his homeland in 1892, Ernst Pretzsche became inflamed by the current Wagnerian Pan-Germanic movement and very soon took an active part in circulating anti-Semitic literature throughout Vienna. Through the medium of his bookshop dealing in occultism and kindred subjects, he became known to an extensive circle of adepts, who regarded highly his expert knowledge of ritual magic. It was in this manner too that Pretzsche came to meet Guido von List, the Alcister Crowley-like figure whose Blood Lodge and black magic rituals shocked the German speaking world in 1909.[81]

Continuing to study Grail lore, "Hitler was able to identify the drug-induced imagery of his previous incarnation." He was a new incarnation of the historical figure behind Richard Wagner's Klingsor, Landulf of Capua, who ruled from Naples to Sicily. "Instead of some resplendent Germanic hero he had discovered himself to be the physical re-embodiment of the most dreaded personality in the whole history of Christendom. The chalice for the Spirit of the Anti-Christ."[82]

The publishing house COTUM (Catalog of the Universal Mind)

released an English-language edition of *Magic: History/Theory /Practice* in 2009, the first English translation of a book written by Dr. Ernst Schertel in 1923. Schertel sent a dedicated copy to Hitler, which was discovered as part of Hitler's library – complete with his extensive annotations. *Magic: History/Theory/Practice* covers a range of esoteric territory, with an emphasis on the demonic. Schertel says near the end of the book: "The first and only important thing is communion with the demon." The passages Hitler highlighted include "False images are necessary for the recognition of truth" and "He who does not have the demonic seed within himself will never give birth to a magical world." As he marked "Satan is the beginning…" he certainly may have seen himself as a dark figure of prophecy, echoing Voldemort.[83]

As Hitler came to power, he kept the mythic obsession in place. One strange story has astrologer Erik Jan Hanussen telling him to get a mandrake root from his hometown and keep it with him always. This protective charm has the suggestion of the Horcruxes about it, as mandrakes are human-shaped roots that represent the person. Hanussen promised a sudden rise to power, and, shockingly, the Reichstag fire occurred on the very day he had predicted, allowing recently appointed Chancellor of Germany Adolf Hitler to seize absolute power in 1933.[84]

Heinrich Himmler was the true force of occultism in Hitler's regime. He decorated his SS headquarters at Wewelsburg, a Renaissance castle, with a black, jagged-armed sun from an "old Aryan emblem." It was meant to mimic the Round table of Arthurian legend with each spoke of the sun wheel representing one "knight" or officer of the "inner" SS.[85] The Black Sun symbol united the three most important symbols of Nazi ideology – the sun wheel, the swastika and the stylized victory rune and represented the twelve SS Knights of The Order of the Death's Head and their three retainers.[86] Voldemort brings in Slytherin's symbolism, from the snake Nagini to the Horcruxes he creates. He builds a teenage base in the Chamber of Secrets, appropriating the ancient magic for his own.

Himmler's *Ahnenerbe* ("ancestral-inheritance") was a Nazi institute claiming to research the archaeological and cultural history of the so-called Aryan race. It was founded on July 1, 1935, by Heinrich Himmler, Herman Wirth, and Richard Walther Darré, and conducted experiments and expeditions in an attempt to prove that mythological Nordic populations had once ruled the world. Due to Himmler's obsession with mysticism, it quickly began using pseudoscience. He sent expeditions to document soothsayers and examine petroglyphs, discovering some Nordic runes but little evidence of working magic. There were also massive lootings of captured museums.

Nazi occult-hunters appear in much of pop culture – likely the most famous is the *Indiana Jones* films. In these, a Nazi society based on the *Ahnenerbe* seeks ancient artifacts of power like the Holy Grail. As one of the characters in *Raiders of the Lost Ark* says, Hitler is "obsessed with the occult." *Captain America: The First Avenger* likewise deals with the Nazi "deep-science division," Hydra, who power their machines with occult magic. Cap and Hydra had frequent run-ins in the comics for decades. *Constantine* features the Holy Spear as a main plot point – it is found buried in Mexico, wrapped in a Nazi flag.

Likewise, in the Marvel Comics series, "Fear Itself," the Red Skull leads the Thule Society and uses them to summon and protect the mythic Hammer of Skadi. The historic Thule Society included many of Hitler's top staff. It was a German occultist group in Munich, named after a mythical northern country said to be the Aryan ancestral home. The Society sponsored the Deutsche Arbeiterpartei (DAP; German Workers' Party), which was later reorganized by Hitler into the Nazi Party. This known connection between the occult and Hitler's friends spawned other adaptations. On *Supernatural*, a ledger is discovered recording the group's experiments in necromancy. In the film *Hellboy*, the main character comes to earth through the Thule Society's portal. Professor Bruttenholm refers to Adolf Hitler having joined in 1937, describing them as "a group of German aristocrats obsessed with the occult." Thus Hitler and Himmler believed their own propaganda, that destiny and dark mysticism were aiding their rise to power. Voldemort feels much the same.

World War II Direct Allusions

While totalitarianism and bigotry (and even belief in dark magic) have appeared throughout many eras of history, the Harry Potter series also offers direct allusions to World War Two. When asked about them, Rowling responds:

> I think most of us if you were asked to name a very evil regime we would think Nazi Germany. There were parallels in the ideology. I wanted Harry to leave our world and find exactly the

same problems in the wizarding world. So you have the intent to impose a hierarchy, you have bigotry, and this notion of purity, which is this great fallacy, but it crops up all over the world. People like to think themselves superior and that if they can pride themselves in nothing else they can pride themselves on perceived purity. So yeah that follows a parallel. [87]

The most significant of these parallels is what several important characters (Voldemort, Dumbledore, and Grindelwald) were doing from 1939-1945, according to the official dates provided.

Tom Riddle began advocating the beliefs of Salazar Slytherin, that only purebloods should attend Hogwarts, in 1942 [Y-38], with the first opening of the Chamber of Secrets.[88] Thus, as young Voldemort was a developing student, he was mimicking Nazi ideologies from the great war being fought on his very doorstep.

The philosophy of Voldemort, which preaches that might makes right and that power goes beyond ideals of good and evil, is not very far away from the political conduct of Adolf Hitler. It can easily be argued that a young man like Riddle would admire that conduct, and see in Hitler's madness a man casting away his boundaries and attempting to bring about his own personal ideals. [89]

As a child at the London orphanage, young Riddle would have known extreme poverty and possibly borderline starvation through the Great Depression. During his summers home from Hogwarts, he would have seen violence and despair as all of London succumbed to aerial bombardment.[90] As the bombs fell on London, Riddle surely cursed the Muggles so violent and brutal, so quick to starve children and raze the city around him. Moreover, he witnessed a world where Hitler took what he wished, citing racial superiority as a motive for controlling the "lesser races." Surely Riddle observed this and began to ponder: if Muggles could preach genetic perfection, how much more so did pureblood wizards deserve to rule the world?

Still, World War Two was not fought solely in the Muggle World. Rowling stated in an interview, "It amuses me to make allusions to things that [are] happening in the Muggle world so my feeling would be that while there's a global Muggle war going on, there's also a global wizarding war going on."[91] Indeed there was, particularly in the 1940's.

From German Durmstrang comes famed dark wizard Gellert

Grindelwald, who subverts the Deathly Hallows symbol, just as Hitler adapted the swastika. Grindelwald preaches Wizarding Rule through racial superiority, a program that clearly echoes Hitler's agenda. The same time, the same country, the same ideology, the same defeat in 1945: can we doubt they were partners? Dumbledore describes "Muggles forced into subservience" and a revolution "all for the greater good."[92] Grindelwald dreams of an army of Inferi, undead zombies that kill without remorse. He plans "a new Wizarding Order" with a vast following.[93] Then Dumbledore's sister dies, and young Dumbledore accepts that Grindelwald's plans are too violent, too blind to the suffering of innocents. Grindelwald flees.

Still, his home ground of Durmstrang, quite a contrast from the genteel and light-hearted Hogwarts, remains significant. Critic David Colbert comments, "Durmstrang is a more severe place [than Hogwarts], breeding wizards who can't be trusted—just as Eastern Europe has long been viewed by outsiders."[94] The students wear deep blood red and learn the Dark Arts, not just defense from them. Further, it does not admit Muggle-born students.[95] Thus the school seems less enlightened than the British families where the pure-bloods are dying out and the majority of wizards welcome Muggle-borns. Durmstrang is a breeding ground for dark wizardry, as several Hogwarts teachers note: The students immediately sit at the Slytherin table. Though Krum plays Quidditch for Bulgaria, the school seems a blend of German and Slavic influences, as Dumbledore calls them simply "our friends from the North." Headmaster Igor Karkaroff, dressed in furs, suggests a Russian origin, harkening to the Hitler-Stalin pact of the thirties. Whatever his nationality, Karkaroff is a known Death Eater, and as head of the school, he, like Dumbledore, has a heavy influence over his students. His prize student, Victor Krum performs the Cruciatus curse on Harry, and as we later learn, "you have to mean them." Is Victor Krum a darker character than we had previously realized?

The name Durmstrang itself comes from the German phrase "Sturm und Drang," which translates to "Storm and Stress," a tradition in German literature. The foremost writer in this movement, Goethe, was most famed for *Faust*, his tale of a pact with the devil, reminiscent of Karkaroff's pact with Voldemort. Sturm und Drang composer Richard Wagner also wrote many operas about a wizard with an invisibility cloak, an interesting similarity given Grindelwald's obsession with the Deathly Hallows.[96] "The artists of the *Sturm und*

Drang movement, and Wagner in particular, were favorites of the Nazi government in Germany just before and during the second World War."[97] Durmstrang, thus, makes an ideal supremacist breeding ground.

Looking back over the century, Dumbledore tells Harry the tale of Grindelwald, describing the dark wizard's "plans for seizing power and his schemes for Muggle torture."[98] Grindelwald raises an army and finds a weapon of immense power, as dark rumors begin to circulate. At last, Dumbledore defeats Grindelwald in 1945. This significant date indicates that Grindelwald's defeat clearly ended the war in the Wizarding World. The war that ended in the Muggle World coincides, as critic Faisal M. Ahmad notes:

> Grindelwald, being a great Dark wizard in 1945, could only quite possibly belong to the darkest of nations of that time period, Nazi Germany. Whether he fulfilled a position as the Nazi-equivalent of the Minister of Magic, or something entirely different cannot be known. I would imagine that Hitler's suicide towards the end of April would have coincided somewhat with the death of his Minister (if that is indeed what Grindelwald was).

With the defeat of Grindelwald and with Britain's triumph over Nazism, the Dark Wizards found themselves a reviled minority, muttering about racial purity but curtailed or imprisoned. While Grindelwald rotted away in Nurmengard, (a clear allusion to Nuremburg, prison and site of the famed Nazi war trials) dark wizards like Lucius Malfoy would hide their proclivities and fume behind a false mask of celebration. In this atmosphere lives a young Voldemort, creating Horcruxes to preserve his life, surrounded by British wizards working to repair the damage Grindelwald and his allies caused, while cursing those dark wizards who murdered in the name of racial purity. Just as Hitler smoldered at the reparations and humiliating surrender of the Germans from World War One, wouldn't young Tom Riddle burn with the knowledge that his pure-blood elitists were defeated and slandered at every turn, only for killing the Muggles he deemed worthless? Bitter and dissatisfied, Voldemort took on his dark name, growing in power and recruiting those pure-blood allies who would support his cause. The dark wizards were not defeated, he would boast: they were betrayed by the Muggle-born and blood traitors among them, who weakened the battle and made those born to lead fail at the critical moment. And thus, fifty years later, the cycle begins again.

The racism and racial supremacy of World War Two had lingered for hundreds of years, and in some ways, linger today, as do the rationalizations that can lead to discrimination. In this world, dictators of all sorts can gain power. Only the "constant vigilance" espoused in the Harry Potter series can stop the darkest leaders of our past from claiming yet another foothold on our futures.

---

[1] J. K Rowling, *Harry Potter and the Deathly Hallows,* (USA: Scholastic, Inc, 2007), 709.

[2] Yisrael Gutman, "Why the Jew? Modern Antisemitism," in *Critical Issues of the Holocaust,* ed. Alex Groman and Daniel Landes, (Rossel Books: New York, 1983), 97-98.

[3] Ibid., 96.

[4] David F. Crew, *Hitler and the Nazis: A History in Documents* (Oxford: Oxford University Press, 2005), 65.

[5] Ibid., 42.

[6] Gutman 96.

[7] J. K Rowling, *Harry Potter and the Philosopher's Stone* (London: Bloomsbury Publishing Plc, 1997), 61.

[8] J. K Rowling, *Harry Potter and the Half-Blood Prince,* (USA: Scholastic, Inc, 2005), 74.

[9] Granger, John. "Disney Does Derrida: Joanne Rowling as a Writer of Our Times," in *Lumos 2006: A Harry Potter Symposium*, 2006 [CD-ROM] OmniPress, 5.

[10] Rowling, *Chamber* 89.

[11] Ibid., 89.

[12] Kerr, Peg. "A Shining Silver Thread: Memory and Identity in the Harry Potter Novels," in *Lumos 2006: A Harry Potter Symposium*, 2006 [CD-ROM] OmniPress, 6.

[13] Rowling, *Order* 842.

[14] Rowling, *Deathly Hallows* 261.

[15] Craig L. Foster, "Where Have All the Pure-Bloods Gone? A Look at Family and Lineage in the World of *Harry Potter.*" in *Lumos 2006: A Harry Potter Symposium*, 2006 [CD-ROM] OmniPress,

[16] Rowling, *Chamber* 133.

[17] Ibid., 133.

[18] Rowling, *Half Blood* 485.

[19] J. K Rowling, *Harry Potter and the Order of the Phoenix,* (USA: Scholastic, Inc, 2003), 833-834.

[20] Rowling, *Chamber* 27.

[21] Elizabeth E. Heilman and Anne E. Gregory, "Images of the

Privileged Insider and Outcast Outsider," in *Harry Potter's World: Multidisciplinary Critical Perspectives,* ed. Elizabeth E. Heilman (New York: Rutledge Falmer, 2003), 245.

[22] Karen A. Brown, *Prejudice in Harry Potter's World* (USA: Virtual Book Worm Publishing, Inc, 2008), 111.

[23] Rowling, *Goblet of Fire* 330.

[24] Brown 113.

[25] Rowling, *Goblet of Fire* 539.

[26] Crew 101.

[27] Heilman and Gregory 251.

[28] Granger, "Disney Does Derrida" 5.

[29] Ibid., 4-5.

[30] Rowling, *Order of the Phoenix* 127.

[31] Rowling, J.K. "J.K. Rowling and the Live Chat," *Bloomsbury.com, Accio Quote!* 30 July 2007. http://www.accio-quote.org/articles/2007/0730-bloomsbury-chat.html.

[32] "J. K. Rowling at Carnegie Hall Reveals Dumbledore is Gay; Neville Marries Hannah Abbott, and Much More," *The Leaky Cauldron,* 20 Oct 2007. http://www.the-leaky-cauldron.org/2007/10/20/j-k-rowling-at-carnegie-hall-reveals-dumbledore-is-gay-neville-marries-hannah-abbott-and-scores-more

[33] Crew 54.

[34] Elizabeth Wiskemann, *Europe of the Dictators: 1919-1945* (New York: Harper and Row, 1966), 36.

[35] Crew 24.

[36] Ibid., 19.

[37] Wiskemann 83.

[38] Ibid., 87.

[39] Crew 89-90.

[40] Rowling, *Half Blood* 14.

[41] John Granger, *Looking for God in Harry Potter* (USA: Saltriver House Publishers, 2004), 54.

[42] Granger, "Disney Does Derrida" 9.

[43] Rowling, *Order* 551.

[44] Ibid., 553.

[45] Ibid., 626.

[46] Granger, *Looking for God* 54.

[47] Churchill, Winston S. *Winston S. Churchill: His Complete Speeches 1897-1963.* Vol. 6. Ed. Robert Rhodes James. (New York: Bowker, 1974), 87.

[48] Rowling, *Order* 708.

[49] Granger, *Looking for God* 53.

[50] Crew 53-55.

[51] Ibid., 155.

211

[52] Brown 84.

[53] Peter Appelbaum, "Harry Potter's World: Magic, Technoculture, and Becoming Human." in *Harry Potter's World: Multidisciplinary Critical Perspectives*, ed. Elizabeth E. Heilman (New York: Rutledge Falmer, 2003), 49.

[54] James Lucas, *World War Two through German Eyes* (Great Britain: DAG Publications ltd, 1987), 15.

[55] Rowling, *Order* 746.

[56] Ibid., 746-747.

[57] Ibid., 674.

[58] "Edinburgh 'Cub Reporter' Press Conference," ITV, July 16, 2005. http://www.accio-quote.org/articles/2005/0705-edinburgh-ITVcubreporters.htm

[59] J.K. Rowling, "J.K. Rowling and the Live Chat," *Bloomsbury.com*, *Accio Quote!* 30 July 2007. http://www.accio-quote.org/articles/2007/0730-bloomsbury-chat.html.

[60] Rowling, *Deathly Hallows* 574.

[61] Ibid., 731.

[62] Ibid., 659.

[63] Ibid., 574.

[64] Crew 147.

[65] Wiskemann 128.

[66] Ibid., 98.

[67] Crew 79-80.

[68] Rowling, *Deathly Hallows* 437.

[69] Ibid., 438.

[70] Granger, *Looking for God* 53.

[71] Rowling, *Deathly Hallows* 419.

[72] Crew 59.

[73] Lucas 10.

[74] Rowling, *Deathly Hallows* 249.

[75] Rowling, *Half-Blood Prince* 505.

[76] Ibid., 504.

[77] Trevor Ravenscroft, *The Spear of Destiny: The Occult Power Behind the Spear Which Pierced the Side of Christ* (USA: Samuel Weiser, Inc., 1982), EnkiLibrary, Prologue.

[78] Ibid., chap. 3.

[79] Ibid., chap. 3.

[80] Ibid., chap. 3.

[81] Ibid., chap. 5.

[82] Ibid., chap. 5.

[83] J.H. Kelley, "New Translation of German Book Links Hitler to Satanism," *PRLog*, 17 May 2009, https://www.prlog.org/10238075-new-translation-of-german-book-links-hitler-to-satanism.html.

[84] *Hitler and the Occult,* produced by Bram Roos and Phyllis Cannon (USA: A&E Home Video, 2000).

[85] Ibid.

[86] Ibid.

[87] "J. K. Rowling at Carnegie Hall Reveals Dumbledore is Gay; Neville Marries Hannah Abbott, and Much More," *The Leaky Cauldron,* 20 Oct 2007, http://www.the-leaky-cauldron.org/2007/10/20/j-k-rowling-at-carnegie-hall-reveals-dumbledore-is-gay-neville-marries-hannah-abbott-and-scores-more

[88] Faisal M. Ahmad, "The Early Life of Tom Riddle and the Second World War," *The Harry Potter Lexicon,* 2004. http://www.hplex.info/essays/essay-voldemort-childhood.html.

[89] Ibid.

[90] Ibid.

[91] "Bloomsbury Live Chat with J.K. Rowling." Webchat. 30 July 2007. http://www.bloomsbury.com/jkrevent.

[92] Rowling, *Deathly Hallows* 716.

[93] Ibid., 566.

[94] David Colbert, *The Magical Worlds of Harry Potter* (Toronto: McArthur and Co., 2001), 75.

[95] Rowling, *Goblet of Fire* 165.

[96] Colbert 73.

[97] Ibid., 74.

[98] Rowling, *Deathly Hallows* 717.

WORKS CITED

Ahmad, Faisal M. "The Early Life of Tom Riddle and the Second World War." *The Harry Potter Lexicon.* 2004. 10 December 2008. http://www.hplex.info/essays/essay-voldemort-childhood.html.

Apollodorus. *The Library of Greek Mythology.* Trans. Keith Aldrich. Lawrence, Kansas: Coronado Press, 1975. http://www.theoi.com/Text/Apollodorus1.html.

Appelbaum, Peter. "Harry Potter's World: Magic, Technoculture, and Becoming Human." In *Harry Potter's World: Multidisciplinary Critical Perspectives,* edited by Elizabeth Heilman, 25-52. New York: Rutledge Falmer, 2003.

Baum, L. Frank. *The Wonderful Wizard of Oz.* US: Signet Classics, 2006.

"Bloomsbury Live Chat with J.K. Rowling." Webchat. July 30, 2007. 29 March 2008. http://www.bloomsbury.com/jkrevent.

Bosanquet, Theo. "Review: *Harry Potter and the Cursed Child* Works Serious Magic on the West End Stage." *Time.Com* (July 26, 2016): 1. Business Source Elite, EBSCOhost.

Boskovich, Desirina. "7 Reasons Why Steampunk Is Totally 'Now.'" *Huffington Post,* 27 Oct 2014. http://m.huffpost.com/us/entry/6053796.

Brown, Karen A. *Prejudice in Harry Potter's World.* USA: Virtual Book Worm Publishing, Inc, 2008.

Catholic.org. "Saints and Angels." *Catholic.org,* http://www.catholic.org/saints.

Churchill, Winston S. *Winston S. Churchill: His Complete Speeches 1897-1963.* Vol. 6. Ed. Robert Rhodes James. New York: Bowker, 1974.

Cirlot, J.E. *A Dictionary of Symbols.* New York: Routledge, 1971.

Colbert, David. *The Magical Worlds of Harry Potter.* Toronto: McArthur and Co., 2001.

Crew, David F. *Hitler and the Nazis: A History in Documents.* Oxford:

Oxford University Press, 2005.

Danielson, Catherine. "Harry's Loves, Harry's Hates: A New Key to Their Mysteries, or, The Dumbledore Code." In *Lumos 2006: A Harry Potter Symposium*, 2006 [CD-ROM] OmniPress.

Dolgin, Kim. "Coming of Age in Svalbard, and Beyond." In *Navigating The Golden Compass*, edited by Glenn Yeffeth, 71-79. USA: BenBella Books, 2004.

"Edinburgh 'Cub Reporter' Press Conference." *ITV*, 16 July 2005. http://www.accio-quote.org/articles/2005/0705-edinburgh-ITVcubreporters.htm

Estés, Clarissa Pinkola. *Women Who Run with the Wolves*. New York: Ballantine, 1992.

Foster, Craig L. "Where Have All the Pure-Bloods Gone? A Look at Family and Lineage in the World of *Harry Potter*." In *Lumos 2006: A Harry Potter Symposium*, 2006 [CD-ROM] OmniPress.

Frankel, Valerie Estelle. *Buffy and the Heroine's Journey*. Jefferson, NC: McFarland and Co, 2012.

—. *From Girl to Goddess*. Jefferson, NC: McFarland and Co, 2010.

Granger, John. "Disney Does Derrida: Joanne Rowling as a Writer of Our Times." *Lumos 2006*.

—. *Harry Potter's Bookshelf: The Great Books behind the Hogwarts Adventures*. California, Berkeley Trade, 2009.

—. *Looking for God in Harry Potter*. USA: Saltriver House Publishers, 2004.

Grant, Abigail. "Harry Potter and a World of Words: Back to Basics in a Time of Advance." In *Harry Potter, Still Recruiting: An Inner Look at Harry Potter Fandom*, edited by Valerie Estelle Frankel, 4-11. USA: Zossima Press, 2012.

Green, Miranda. *Animals in Celtic Life and Myth*. USA: Routledge, 1992.

Gresh, Lois. *Exploring Philip Pullman's His Dark Materials*. USA: St. Martin's Griffin, 2007.

Gutman, Yisrael. "Why the Jew? Modern Antisemitism." In *Critical Issues of the Holocaust*, edited by Alex Groman and Daniel Landes. Rossel Books: New York, 1983.

Harry Potter and the Half-Blood Prince. Directed by David Yates. USA: Warner Bros. Pictures, 2009. DVD.

"Harry Potter Author Reveals Books' Christian Allegory, her Struggling Faith." *Christian Today*, 19 Oct 2007. http://www.christiantoday.com/article/harry.potter.author.reveals.books.christian.allegory.her.struggling.faith/14052.htm.

Havrilesky, Heather. "*Boardwalk Empire*: Gangsters Return Triumphantly to HBO." *Salon.com*, 11 Sept 2010. http://www.salon.com/2010/09/11/boardwalk_empire.

Heilman, Elizabeth E. and Anne E. Gregory. "Images of the Privileged Insider and Outcast Outsider." In *Harry Potter's World: Multidisciplinary Critical Perspectives*, edited by Elizabeth Heilman, 241-259. New York: Rutledge Falmer, 2003.

Hibberd, James. "*Fantastic Beasts*: Eddie Redmayne Answers our Burning Questions." *EW*, 9 Aug 2016. http://www.ew.com/article/2016/08/09/fantastic-beasts-eddie-redmayne-interview.

——. "*Fantastic Beasts*: First Look at Ezra Miller's Mysterious Character." *EW*, 10 Aug 2016. http://www.ew.com/article/2016/08/10/fantastic-beasts-ezra-miller.

Hitler and the Occult. Produced by Bram Roos and Phyllis Cannon. USA: A&E Home Video, 2000.

Hyginus. *The Myths of Hyginus*. Trans. M. Lawrence Grant. Kansas: University of Kansas Publications. http://www.theoi.com/Text/HyginusFabulae1.html.

"J. K. Rowling at Carnegie Hall Reveals Dumbledore is Gay; Neville Marries Hannah Abbott, and Much More." *The Leaky Cauldron*, 20 Oct 2007. http://www.the-leaky-cauldron.org/2007/10/20/j-k-rowling-at-carnegie-hall-reveals-dumbledore-is-gay-neville-marries-hannah-abbott-and-scores-more.

"J.K. Rowling Goes Beyond the Epilogue." *Beyond Hogwarts*, 2007, http://www.beyondhogwarts.com/harry-potter/articles/jk-rowling-goes-beyond-the-epilogue.html.

J.K. Rowling, interview by author, "Bloomsbury Live Chat with J.K. Rowling," July 30, 2007, Webchat, http://www.bloomsbury.com/jkrevent.

Jensen, Jeff. "Fire Storm." *Entertainment Weekly*, 7 September 2000. *Quick Quotes Quill*. 30 May 2006. http://www.quick-quote-quill.org/articles/2000/0900-ew-jensen.htm.

Johnston, Ian. "Author 'Chilled' to Learn Harry's Half-Blood Status has Nazi Parallels." *The Scotsman*. 8A: 28 July 2004.

Jung, Carl. *The Archetypes and the Collective Unconscious*. Trans. RFC Hull. New York: Princeton University Press, 1969.

Kelley, JH. "New Translation of German Book Links Hitler to

Satanism." *PRLog,* 17 May 2009.
https://www.prlog.org/10238075-new-translation-of-german-book-links-hitler-to-satanism.html.

Kerr, Peg. "A Shining Silver Thread: Memory and Identity in the Harry Potter Novels." In *Lumos 2006: A Harry Potter Symposium,* 2006 [CD-ROM] OmniPress.

L' Engle, Madeline. *A Wrinkle in Time.* USA: Random House, 2005.

Lambarski, Tim. "Ginny Weasley: A Gryffindor and a Match for Harry." *The Harry Potter Lexicon,* http://www.hp-lexicon.org/essays/essay-ginny-weasley.html.

Lee-Allen, Nancee. "Understanding Prejudice Utilizing the *Harry Potter* Series." In *Phoenix Rising: Collected Papers on Harry Potter,* edited by Sharon K. Goetz. USA: Narrate Conferences, Inc., 2008.

Lewis, Helen. "Pottering About." *New Statesman* 145, no. 5325 (July 29, 2016): 87. MasterFILE Premier, EBSCOhost.

Lockwood, William Burley. *Oxford Book of British Bird Names.* Oxford: Oxford University Press, 1984.

Lokrien. "What Are Runes." *Internet Book of Shadows,* 1999. *The Sacred Texts Archive.* http://www.sacred-texts.com/bos/bos064.htm

Lucas, James. *World War Two through German Eyes.* Great Britain: DAG Publications ltd, 1987.

Masson, Sophie. "Lord Asriel: Dad from Hell or Heroic Rebel?" In *The World of the Golden Compass: The Otherworldly Ride Continues,* edited by Scott Westerfeld, 31-41. USA: Borders Group Inc, 2007.

Mendlesohn, Farah. *Rhetorics of Fantasy.* USA: Wesleyan, 2008.

Miller, Laura. "Why do Americans Love *Downton Abbey* so Much?" *New Statesman,* 5 September 2013. http://www.newstatesman.com/tv-and-radio.013/09/why-do-americans-love-downton-abbey-so-much.

Murdock, Maureen. *The Heroine's Journey.* Boston: Shambhala, 1990.

Newitz, Annalee. "Why Is Pop Culture So Obsessed with the 1920s?" *Io9,* 13 Feb 2013. http://io9.gizmodo.com/5983062/obsessing-over-the-1920s.

Pullman, Phillip. *The Amber Spyglass.* USA: Dell Laurel-Leaf, 2000.

Ravenscroft, Trevor. *The Spear of Destiny: The Occult Power Behind the Spear Which Pierced the Side of Christ.* USA: Samuel Weiser, Inc., 1982. EnkiLibrary.

Rhiannon, Alexis. "J.K. Rowling's Response to Whether There Were

LGBT Kids at Hogwarts Will Melt your Heart." *Crushable,* 18 Dec 2014. http://www.crushable.com/2014/12/18/entertainment/lgbt-jewish-kids-at-hogwarts-j-k-rowling-confirms-harry-potter.

Ritter, Gretchen. *Goldbugs and Greenbacks: The Anti-Monopoly Tradition and the Politics of Finance in America.* NY: Cambridge University Press, 1997.

Roach, Emily E. "Epilogue? What Epilogue? Re-Visioning the Canon with Fanon." In *Harry Potter, Still Recruiting: An Inner Look at Harry Potter Fandom,* edited by Valerie Estelle Frankel, 61-73. USA: Zossima Press, 2012.

Rowling, "Colours." *Pottermore,* https://www.reddit.com/r/PottermoreWritings/comments/3li7r0/colours.

—. "Draco Malfoy," *Pottermore.* https://www.reddit.com/r/PottermoreWritings/comments/3l9s25/draco_malfoy_part_2_of_2.

—. *Harry Potter and the Chamber of Secrets.* London: Bloomsbury, 1998.

—. *Harry Potter and the Deathly Hallows.* USA: Scholastic, Inc, 2007.

—. *Harry Potter and the Goblet of Fire.* USA: Scholastic, Inc, 2000.

—. *Harry Potter and the Half-Blood Prince.* USA: Scholastic, Inc, 2005.

—. *Harry Potter and the Order of the Phoenix.* USA: Scholastic, Inc, 2003.

—. *Harry Potter and the Philosopher's Stone.* London: Bloomsbury, 1997.

—. *Hogwarts: An Incomplete and Unreliable Guide.* USA: Pottermore, 2016. Kindle Edition.

—. "J.K. Rowling and the Live Chat." *Accio Quote! Bloomsbury.com,* 30 July 2007. http://www.accio-quote.org/articles/2007/0730-bloomsbury-chat.html.

—. "Ilvermorny School of Witchcraft and Wizardry." *Pottermore,* https://www.pottermore.com/writing-by-jk-rowling/ilvermorny.

—. *Short Stories from Hogwarts of Heroism, Hardship and Dangerous Hobbies.* USA: Pottermore, 2016. Kindle Edition.

—. "Swooping Evil." *Pottermore.com.* https://www.pottermore.com/explore-the-story/swooping-evil.

—. *The Tales of Beedle the Bard.* USA: Scholastic, 2007.

Rowling, J.K., Jack Thorne, and John Tiffany, *Harry Potter and the Cursed Child.* Crawfordsville, IN: Pottermore, 2016.

Sales, Leila. "The Ol' Dead Dad Syndrome." *Publishers Weekly,* 20 Sept 2010. http://www.publishersweekly.com/pw/by-topic/columns-

and-blogs/soapbox/article/44502-the-ol-dead-dad-syndrome.html.

Scamander, Newt. *Fantastic Beasts and Where to Find Them*. New York: Scholastic, 2001.

Skeeter, Rita. "Dumbledore's Army Reunites at Quidditch World Cup Final." *Pottermore*, 8 July 2014.

Srafopedia, "Pantalaimon," *Srafopedia: The "His Dark Materials" Encyclopedia*, http://www.hisdarkmaterials.org/srafopedia/index.php/Pantalaimon.

Sturluson, Snorri. *The Prose Edda*. Trans. Arthur Gilchrist Brodeur, Ph.D. New York: The American-Scandinavian Foundation, 1916. http://www.sacred-texts.com/neu/pre/pre00.htm

Tatar, Maria. *The Annotated Brothers Grimm*. New York: W. W. Norton, 2004.

Vieira, Meredith. "JK Rowling One-On-One: Part One." *The Today Show*, 26 July 2007.

Vincent, Sally. "Driven by Daemons." *Guardian*, 10 Nov. 2001.

Walker, Barbara G. *The Woman's Dictionary of Symbols and Sacred Objects*. San Francisco: Harper, 1988.

Watkins, Tony. *Dark Matter: Shedding Light on Phillip Pullman's Trilogy "His Dark Materials."* USA: InterVarsity Press, 2004.

Weber, Ryan P. "Harry Potter's Quest: The Hero's Journey and the Shadow." *Headline Muse*. Issue #23: 2002. www.headlinemuse.com.

Wilkinson, Carole. "Pants on Fire." In *The World of the Golden Compass: The Otherworldly Ride Continues*, edited by Scott Westerfeld, 5-14. USA: Borders Group Inc, 2007.

Wiskemann, Elizabeth. *Europe of the Dictators: 1919-1945*. New York: Harper and Row, 1966.

The Wizard of Oz. Produced by King Vidor, Mervyn LeRoy, Richard Thorpe, and Victor Fleming. 1939. US: MGM, 1999. DVD.

Young, Ella. *Celtic Wonder Tales*. USA: Sacred Texts, 1910. http://www.sacred-texts.com/neu/celt/cwt/cwt08.htm

INDEX

221

VALERIE ESTELLE FRANKEL

ABOUT THE AUTHOR

Valerie Estelle Frankel is the author of 50 books on pop culture, including *Doctor Who – The What, Where, and How, Sherlock: Every Canon Reference You May Have Missed in BBC's Series 1-3*, and *How Game of Thrones Will End*. Many of her books focus on women's roles in fiction, from her heroine's journey guides *From Girl to Goddess* and *Buffy and the Heroine's Journey* to books like *Women in Game of Thrones* and *The Many Faces of Katniss Everdeen*. She's also written the award-winning *Henry Potty* parody series. Once a lecturer at San Jose State University, she's now teaching at Mission College. Come explore her research at www.vefrankel.com.

Made in the USA
Monee, IL
03 February 2020